Advance Praise for
Money

"In this fascinating book, Steve Forbes makes the case for sound money and shows why a money system based on free trade—a system that allows the entrepreneurial dream to flourish—is not just good business; it also makes for a good society. *Money* is a rock-solid argument for the virtues of capitalism."

—JOHN MACKEY, Co-Founder and Co-CEO,
Whole Foods Market; coauthor of the
New York Times bestseller *Conscious Capitalism*

"*Money* clearly illustrates that sound money is an essential foundation for a free and prosperous society and that the Federal Reserve's current policies are a greater threat to the economic future of the United States than government deficit spending. This is an important book well worth reading."

—JOHN A. ALLISON, President and CEO, Cato Institute;
author of the *New York Times* bestseller
The Financial Crisis and the Free Market Cure

"Economic and monetary policies can be difficult to master for even the savviest politicians. *Money* effectively communicates these complexities into a cohesive argument for economic recovery and preventing a new financial crisis. Steve Forbes and Elizabeth Ames deliver a gripping read and an intriguing viewpoint on how to get our economy back on track."

—GRETA VAN SUSTEREN, Host of *On the Record*, Fox News Channel

"*Money* is a rare treasure—it looks at the economy through eyes focused on common sense and logical solutions. Unlike most books of this genre, the authors look at historical events and apply the lessons learned to practical solutions going forward. This is a valuable contribution for economists and ordinary citizens alike."

—Benjamin S. Carson Sr., MD, President and CEO, American Business Collaborative; Emeritus Professor, Johns Hopkins School of Medicine

"In *Money*, Steve Forbes and Elizabeth Ames brilliantly explore the powerful implications that derive from a simple truth: the essence of money is to communicate value. The world economy would thrive if people had access to sound, trustworthy money: confidence would boom, trade would flourish, and political tensions would diminish. *Money* underscores the universal appeal of a golden anchor not as a throwback to an earlier era of monetary order but rather as a profoundly liberating and socially inclusive approach to global opportunity and greater future prosperity."

—Judy Shelton, PhD, Co-Director of the Sound Money Project at the Atlas Economic Research Foundation

"Few topics today are as misunderstood as the subject of money. Steve Forbes understands money better than most heads of state do, and in this provocative book he shares his vast knowledge and gives us sensible and time-tested recommendations for stopping future financial meltdowns."

—Lawrence Kudlow, CNBC Senior Contributor

"No one knows this topic better or from more perspectives than Steve Forbes, and he and Elizabeth Ames deliver what's promised in this book. Without the financial rudder of the pre-1972 gold standard, the global economy of the past 40 years has been battered from pillar to post at the fanciful whim of politics. *Money* is a compelling and well-informed argument for a twenty-first century gold standard and a sound dollar, which will be the foundation for a new era of global prosperity."

—ARTHUR B. LAFFER, PhD, Founder and Chairman,
Laffer Associates; member of President
Ronald Reagan's Economic Policy Advisory Board

"The purpose of science is to be predictive, but modern economics is no longer predictive. Things that should cause a crisis don't. Things we don't expect to cause a crisis do. Steve Forbes makes a significant contribution to understanding the failure of modern economic theory by showing how money is intrinsically part of broader social processes and that, without properly understanding money, the 'science' of economics can never predict anything. Forbes reveals the defects in how we think about our currency and also provides a valuable alternative. This book taught me a lot."

—GEORGE FRIEDMAN, Chairman, Stratfor;
author of the *New York Times* bestsellers
The Next 100 Years and *The Next Decade*

"Steve Forbes is one of the smartest people in the money world, with a keen sense of global financial trends. In *Money*, he provides a convincing argument that a stable dollar—until recently, China has kept its currency relatively stable, for example—can lead to worldwide economic prosperity."

—JUNHENG LI, Founder and Head of Research,
JL Warren Capital; author of
Tiger Woman on Wall Street

Money

*How the Destruction of the Dollar
Threatens the Global Economy—and
What We Can Do About It*

Steve Forbes
Elizabeth Ames

NEW YORK   CHICAGO   SAN FRANCISCO   ATHENS

LONDON   MADRID   MEXICO CITY   MILAN

NEW DELHI   SINGAPORE   SYDNEY   TORONTO

1 2 3 4 5 6 7 8 9 0   QFR/QFR   1 2 0 9 8 7 6 5 4

ISBN 978-0-07-182370-8
MHID   0-07-182370-0

e-ISBN 978-0-07-182371-5
e-MHID   0-07-182371-9

This publication is designed to provide accurate and authoritative information in regard to the subject matter covered. It is sold with the understanding that neither the author nor the publisher is engaged in rendering legal, accounting, securities trading, or other professional services. If legal advice or other expert assistance is required, the services of a competent professional person should be sought.

—*From a Declaration of Principles Jointly Adopted by a Committee of the American Bar Association and a Committee of Publishers and Associations*

McGraw-Hill Education books are available at special quantity discounts to use as premiums and sales promotions or for use in corporate training programs. To contact a representative, please visit the Contact Us pages at www.mhprofessional.com.

In remembrance of Alexander Hamilton,
our first Secretary of the Treasury,
who established a financial system that propelled
generations of entrepreneurs and made America
the most creative country on earth.
Like few others before or since, he showed that money,
properly understood, is the root of all good.

Contents

Acknowledgments

Many people played a role in making this book possible. Our agent, Jim Hornfischer, was critical in turning our idea into a reality. Tom Miller at McGraw-Hill was an excellent editor, not only with the copy but also in dealing with all the nitty-gritty details that go into a book's publication.

We also thank McGraw-Hill editing manager Jane Palmieri for her infinite patience and precision and for making this book happen on a tight production deadline. And we are extremely grateful to Lydia Rinaldi, Stacey Ashton, Mary Glenn, Christopher Brown, and Dannalie Diaz of McGraw-Hill; and to Mia Carbonell, Coates Bateman, Lauren Lee, Christina Vega, and Jessica Feintisch at Forbes for their enthusiasm and hard work on marketing and promotion.

We are especially grateful to researchers Nichole Hungerford, Lamont Wood, Mitch Baxter, Brett Shisler, Elizabeth Gravitt, and Sue Radlauer for their thoroughness and their commitment to this project.

We were inspired over the years by the astute writings on the subject of money by a number of outstanding experts, among them Lew Lehrman, Art Laffer, Larry Kudlow, Jeff Bell,

Mark Skousen, Judy Shelton, Chuck Kadlec, Ralph Benko, Louis Woodhill, David Malpass, Steve Hanke, Seth Lipsky, Alan Reynolds, Jim Grant, Larry White, and Paul Craig Roberts. This book also owes a debt to the groundbreaking work of two great economic thinkers no longer with us, Jude Wanniski and Peter Drucker.

We were greatly influenced by Nathan Lewis's two excellent books, *Gold: The Once and Future Money* and *Gold: The Monetary Polaris*, as well as by his advice and encouragement. John Tamny, who understands this subject as do few others, was also an inspiration.

We must give special acknowledgment to George Gilder, whose understanding of economics is unique and profound. We are also grateful for the constant encouragement of Amity Shlaes, whose histories of the 1920s and 1930s were pathbreakers, to see this project through. Needless to say, none of these individuals bears any responsibility for what we actually wrote in this book. Others made contributions that are also reflected in these pages. We thank Deroy Murdock, Heather Mac Donald, Bret Swanson, and Allison Ames for their comments and suggestions.

Thanks too go to Steve's associates Jackie DeMaria, Maureen Murray, and Merrill Vaughn, without whom he could not function, and to Bill Dal Col, who always provides ever-helpful insights and guidance. Elizabeth wishes to thank her mother, Dorothy Ames, for her understanding as well as for long-valued life lessons in the importance of persistence.

A book requires immense time and effort, and we are deeply grateful to our families for their understanding and, most hearteningly, their encouragement.

Preface

The Crisis of Modern Economics—and Money

Many of the ideas in this book may strike readers reared on traditional Keynesian and monetarist principles as being "too simple." But money *is* fundamentally simple: it is, as we repeatedly point out in these pages, an instrument of measurement. All perceptions, strategies, and government policies pertaining to money should proceed from this truth.

Why then is so much writing on the subject of money so needlessly complicated, with dense, impenetrable language and equations that make sense to only a handful of academicians? And why do so many people insist that bad ideas about monetary policy, like "inflation is needed to increase employment," are as settled and unassailable as scientific principles?

In this book we discuss the influence of centuries-old mercantilism—economic nationalism—in shaping the conviction that controlling the supply of money is the way to create wealth and a strong economy. The larger question is why this misguided idea has hung on for so many centuries. Why has it been championed by thinkers who are otherwise ideological adversaries?

The answer has to do with longstanding assumptions about the economy shared by Marxists, Keynesians, monetarists, classical economists, and even a number of supply-siders who all believe that the economy is a self-contained entity, a closed system—and that money is a calibrator of this machine.

Central to this thinking is the concept of equilibrium, the assumption that an economy has an ideal resting state that may be attained if all works as it should. Prices should be stable. There should be full employment, however one defines that. Supply should match demand. In the fusty world of economics, equilibrium is the equivalent of nirvana. There may be outside events including wars, droughts, hurricanes, earthquakes, the occasional financial crisis, or disruptions caused by transformative innovations like the steam engine, railroads, or the Internet. But when the dust clears, the economy is supposed to return to "normal."

Classical economists thought the economy was most likely to achieve equilibrium through low taxes, prudent levels of government spending, free trade, and sound money. Keynesians, who consider free markets inherently unstable, insist that a smooth-humming equilibrium must be engineered using tools such as spending, taxes, interest rates, and regulations. Monetarism, an offshoot of Keynesianism, believes that government should rely only on the central bank controlling the money supply to achieve smooth, perpetual growth.

Market swings, meanwhile, are seen by just about everyone as undesirable, an inconvenience that should be reduced or even eliminated. Textbooks routinely talk about the causes and cures of the business cycle.

Fundamental to this world view is the notion that there is such a thing as economic stability. There isn't. To paraphrase the brilliant technologist George Gilder, no one can reliably predict events in our daily lives, such as our future earning power, illness, or automobile accidents. So how are economists so confident that they can predict the future?

They can't. For centuries, the profession has suffered from science envy. It pains us to say this, but the great genius Isaac Newton is partly responsible. We most often remember Newton for his extraordinary contributions to physics, but he also played a pivotal role in the history of economics. At the end of the seventeenth century, the scientist, along with the philosopher John Locke, led the charge against a devaluation of the pound. Later, as Master of the Royal Mint, Newton fixed the value of the pound to gold at £3 17s 10½d or £3.89 an ounce in 1717, a ratio that held for more than 200 years.

Newton did great things for the world's understanding of money. His scientific genius, however, had less salutary effects on the broader discipline of economics. In 1687 he published one of the most important books ever written, *Philosophiae Naturalis Principia Mathematica* (*Mathematical Principles of Natural Philosophy*), which changed how people viewed the world, ushering in the Age of Science and acting as the spark for the Enlightenment. After the publication of this vastly influential tome, the world came to be seen as something resembling a great machine—a grand, immensely complicated clock governed by immutable laws.

After Newton, almost every area of nontheological study wanted the prestigious mantle of science attached to it. The study of politics to this day is often labeled political science. Economics, formerly called political economy, embraced the language and trappings of scientific inquiry with particular fervor.

In this book we will discuss how Adam Smith and his disciples demolished the monetary and economic pretenses of mercantilism, an ideology that rose up in the 1500s and exerted a viselike grip on European rulers for over 200 years. Smith and his fellow classical economists rightfully recognized how money functioned in the economy and how trade generated wealth. But Adam Smith's contemporaries, especially David Ricardo, also fell prey to science envy.

Ricardo, a disciple of Smith in the early 1800s, most famously explained how both rich and poor countries met their respective needs by trading with each other—his theory of comparative advantage. He also demonstrated how a state could have a gold standard without owning the precious metal itself through the buying and selling of bonds. This insight is the basis for what could become a new, modern gold standard for the United States, something we will discuss in Chapter 6.

Ricardo's obsession with numbers and mathematics, however, especially when he dealt with wages and profits, infects economics to this day. At one point, Ricardo posited that profits could only rise at the expense of lower wages for workers. Marx later took up this theme with a vengeance; indeed, some leftists before the rise of Marxism identified themselves as Ricardian socialists.

It is easy to understand the allure of science, with the authority it confers on academicians. Not surprisingly, the emphasis on mathematics and equations continued to grow, culminating in John Maynard Keynes's 1936 opus, *The General Theory of Employment, Interest, and Money*.

Like the classicists, Keynes presented a Newtonian-induced view of the economy as a closed system with the potential for an equilibrium in which demand and supply were in balance. But within this mechanistic framework, he made a radical change.

Traditional economists regarded the production of products and services as the real economy and money and credit as the "symbol economy," the tools of commerce.

Keynes defiantly reversed this pecking order: money and credit were the real drivers of the economy, upon which production was dependent. In this universe, government, which supposedly could control the flow of money and credit through bureaucratic fiat, was far more important in determining where an economy went than mere individuals, entrepreneurs, and companies. This was a radical departure from classical economics.

Keynes's pseudoscientific paradigm—what some have called neo-mercantilism—triumphed to become the new orthodoxy because of two catastrophes, the First World War and the Great Depression. Before World War I, it was a given that governments had to exercise careful restraint in how they treated their economies. The Great War blasted away these economic inhibitions. Governments learned they could mobilize a society's financial wealth through taxation, inflation, and borrowing on a scale previously unimagined. Later, the Great Depression, which was largely the calamitous consequence of a global trade war triggered by the U.S. Smoot-Hawley Tariff, encouraged the perception of unstable markets needing intervention. By reshaping traditional views of government and markets, both events provided the perfect historical opportunity for Keynesianism to become the reigning orthodoxy.

Its misguided precepts have been responsible for countless policies that over decades have done untold damage and provided the impetus for writing this book. One such occult idea that we discuss later is the Phillips curve, the graph purporting to show that creating inflation reduces unemployment and reducing inflation boosts joblessness—correlations that have never been true.

All of the graphs, technical-sounding lingo, and equations of Keynesians and monetarists—and the air of authority they engender—have created an effective smoke screen. It has prevented recognition that so many of their economic prescriptions and forecasts have turned out to be wrong.

This has been true from the start. In the late eighteenth and early nineteenth centuries, Reverend Thomas Robert Malthus, like a good scientist, gathered an impressive array of data to find out how large a population agriculture could support. His predictions of mass famine were totally erroneous and so grim that they caused economics to become known, more than a little facetiously, as the "dismal science."

Unfortunately, not only Malthus but also Ricardo overlooked a critical variable that few, if any, traditional economic models ever take into account when assessing economic conditions: the role of human creativity and problem solving in expanding resources and propelling economic growth.

Human ingenuity is the reason why, instead of the mass famine Malthus predicted, food is many times more abundant now than it ever was in the eighteenth century. Innovations in food production, in addition to technologies like refrigeration, have made it possible to bring more food to more people around the world. Starvation today has become an exceptional event produced by natural disasters or extreme dictatorial regimes.

Innovation is also why the energy shortage predicted in the 1970s has failed to materialize. Instead, the expectation today is for the United States to become a global energy powerhouse because of new technologies like hydraulic fracturing.

Yet only a handful in the economics profession have appreciated the central role of the entrepreneur and the fact that an economy is constantly changing. Most notable was Joseph Schumpeter, who regarded the classical model of equilibrium as nonsense. He famously identified the process of "creative destruction" that takes place in an ever-evolving economy. He explained that the economy, far from being a closed system, is more like a dynamic, living ecosystem with billions of people engaged in an incomprehensibly complex array of activities and transactions. Change and turbulence are the norm. Entrepreneurs and their innovations are not exogenous but are at the heart of the economy, part and parcel of growth and progress.

* * *

Fortunately, people both in and out of the economics profession are waking up to the fallacies of traditional thinking. Schumpeter's ideas about creative destruction are today considered mainstream. And there is a growing awareness that we are on the wrong track about money. Serious attention has recently focused on the possibility of a return to a gold standard.

Another indicator of a shift away from Keynesian orthodoxy: the emergence of new methods of economic measurement. The key statistic has long been gross domestic product (GDP), which posits that consumption is 70% of the economy, government is 20%, and investment the rest. In addition to GDP numbers, the Bureau of Economic Analysis of the Commerce Department will in 2014 also unveil a new statistic called gross output. Measuring intermediate steps needed to produce products and services, this provides a fuller picture of economic activity. Consumption goes from 70% to 40% of the economy. The importance of investment surges; the importance of government spending is sharply reduced.

The once dismal science is seeing a new wave of work breaking away from the Newton-influenced model of the economy as a mechanical entity and highlighting the importance of entrepreneurial creativity in bringing about growth. A critical breakthrough came in 2013 with the publication of George Gilder's book *Knowledge and Power*. Gilder makes the seemingly obvious point that the real source of wealth is the human mind. The catalyst for economic growth is the acquisition of new knowledge—information that comes from trial and error. The economy expands as a result of the constant, unending efforts of Schumpeter's entrepreneurs to do new things and create new products or whole new industries, to see what works—and what doesn't—and to learn from both failure and success.

Gilder asks: What is the difference between our age and the Stone Age? Answer: we know more. The cave dwellers of thousands of years ago had "the same set of physical appetites and natural resources that we have today. The difference between our lives and the lives of Stone Age penury is the growth of knowledge."

Gilder's observation is powerfully illustrated by the miraculous recovery of Western Europe and Japan from the devastation of the Second World War. Despite the tremendous loss of life and resources, nations were able to rebound because knowledge was not destroyed. Thanks to extraordinarily creative U.S. diplomacy that formed a sound monetary system based on gold (which was gratuitously wrecked years later), systematic reductions in trade barriers, and military security, these devastated lands surpassed their prewar levels of output in less than a decade after the cessation of hostilities.

The importance of knowledge to wealth creation is why societies that thrive economically are those that don't overprotect against risk and permit people to fail. Failure can be a source of new knowledge. Henry Ford went through two bankruptcies before his success producing automobiles.

When one grasps the truth that the mind is the source of all wealth, then one can see that all the concerns—about sustainable growth, about running out of natural resources, about population expanding faster than our ability to grow food, about fatal shortages of water—are groundless.

Gilder also cites the story of Israel: "Since the state was founded in 1948, its population has grown tenfold, its arable land threefold, its agricultural output sixteenfold, and its industrial output fiftyfold, yet its net water usage has *dropped* an astonishing ten percent. This unique achievement is the result not of sanctimonious laws or disruptive environmental litigation but of combining information with enterprise."

Information combined with trade and enterprise: that says everything one really needs to know about economics. Money—sound, trustworthy money—is the crucial facilitator that brings it all together.

INTRODUCTION

Few topics are as misunderstood today as the subject of money.
Since the United States abandoned a gold-linked dollar over
four decades ago, its policy establishment has slid into a dangerous ignorance of the fundamental monetary principles that
guided it for most of its history. The bureaucrats and officials
who set policy today know less about money than their predecessors did 100 years ago when the First World War erupted.
Americans and the rest of the world are now paying the price.

Today's system of fluctuating "fiat money"—whereby government manipulates the value of the dollar—has been behind
the biggest economic failures of recent decades, including the
financial crisis experienced by emerging countries in 2013 and
2014. Weak, unstable money was also responsible for the 2008–
2009 financial panic and the subsequent Great Recession, from
whose effects we continue to suffer.

The U.S. economy, as a consequence, has shifted from
wealth creation to wealth destruction. No wonder tens of millions of people feel that their real incomes are declining and
their financial situations are coming under more pressure.

These vastly misguided monetary policies are now setting the stage for a new economic and social catastrophe—one that could rival the financial crisis and the horrors of the 1930s. Something needs to be done. But for too long the pervasive misconceptions about money, and the mystique that surrounds the Fed and its "wise men," have inhibited scrutiny and public debate.

In order for the United States to stop repeating the same mistakes that led it into past crises—and which are certain to create new ones—we must develop a renewed appreciation of the monetary principles that guided America for most of its history. A plainspoken discussion intended to promote such understanding, this book demystifies the critical subject of money.

When you peel away the jargon of bureaucrats and economists, the classic monetary principles boil down to common sense.

Chapter 1, "How We Got Here," explores today's growing fears about the U.S. dollar and how its destruction over more than four decades affects the lives and the future of every person in the world.

Chapter 2, "What Is Money?," explains why money, in order to properly fulfill its role in the economy, must be stable, like any other unit of measurement. That's why both raising and lowering the value of money—which is what the Fed does when it strengthens or weakens the dollar—inevitably has destructive consequences.

Stability trumps just about everything else when it comes to money. Because they don't grasp this simple fact, bureaucrats rarely get it right when they tighten or loosen. The key to successful monetary policy is maintaining a stable monetary value.

Chapter 3, "Money and Trade: A Deficit in Understanding," points out the absurdity of our policy makers' obsession with monetary and trade policies aimed at avoiding a balance of payments deficit. Just as mercantilists in the sixteenth through the eighteenth centuries believed imports drained the strength of a nation by sending money overseas, today's neo-mercantilist policy makers believe it is necessary to weaken the value of a currency to encourage exports and discourage imports.

For reasons we explain in Chapter 3, the very idea of a trade or balance of payments deficit is a fallacy. Yet these policies over the years have resulted in needless protectionist measures that have damaged the United States and the global economy, in addition to inflaming tensions between nations. As we explain, it is a waste of time to tangle with nations over currency values. Commerce is not ultimately driven by the worth of currencies but rather by the real-world needs of people and companies. And whether it takes place between individuals, companies, or nations, trade always benefits both sides. Foreign investment in the United States each year more than offsets the so-called trade deficit.

Chapter 4, "Money Versus Wealth: Why Inflation Is Not a Good Thing," explains why arbitrarily increasing the supply of money most often backfires and hobbles wealth creation. Money is not only a measure of value but, as many wise people have pointed out, is also a system of communication that provides critical information to producers and consumers.

Artificially manipulating currency damages markets by producing false signals. We end up with supply and price distortions that produce shortages and inflation. This can take place even when there is supposedly minor inflation. The housing bubble of the early 2000s is a textbook example.

Chapter 5, "Money and Morality: How Debasing Money Debases Society," explores the phenomenon of currency manipulation leading to societal ills. Inflation resulting from the excessive printing of money, for example, helped give us communist dictatorships in Russia and China, and it laid the groundwork in Germany for the Nazis' rise to power. Such disastrous scenarios may seem remote, but the artificial manipulation of currency values recently produced adverse social consequences during the 2008 financial crisis and its aftermath.

Money is the foundation of trust and cooperation in a market and in all society. When money becomes unstable, trust unravels. Throughout history, inflation and loose money have been associated with higher rates of crime, corruption, political polarization, and unrest. We are seeing this today. The global monetary expansion of the last decade has been the catalyst for political unrest around the world—from the Arab Spring in the Middle East to the Occupy Wall Street protests in the United States. Alas, policy makers and most others rarely connect the dots.

Chapter 6, "The Gold Standard: How to Rescue the Twenty-First Century Global Economy," looks at what has always been the best way to achieve monetary stability: linking the dollar or any currency to gold. The refusal of many in the policy establishment to entertain the idea of a return to a gold standard is based on an astounding ignorance about just what a gold standard would mean and how it would work. In fact, there have been several different gold standards throughout history and several proposals have been put forward for a new gold standard.

Chapter 6 explores the history and the myths about gold and presents our own proposal for a gold standard for the twenty-first century. Contrary to the fears of critics, a return to gold would not mean a rigidly fixed money supply. Gold is far more flexible than most people generally acknowledge. Because the function of gold is to provide an anchor of value, a nation can actually have a working gold standard without possessing gold at all.

We believe that eventually a gold standard will be adopted, though it's impossible to tell when or under what precise circumstances that will occur. In the meantime, the destruction of the dollar will continue, with only intermittent pauses. Chapter 7, "Surviving in the Meantime: Protecting Your Assets from Unstable Money," offers some commonsense tips on what to do right now to safeguard your personal wealth.

Chapter 8, "Looking Ahead," explores what all of us can expect to take place in the world economy if it continues its present dangerous course—and what will happen when we finally rediscover the wisdom of the Founding Fathers and America's first treasury secretary, Alexander Hamilton, and adopt a gold standard.

The return to sound money will usher in the kind of long-term growth that turned the United States from a sparsely populated agricultural nation into the innovative industrial powerhouse that has been the envy of the world. Both America and the entire global economy will benefit.

Without an economy based on stable money, we will face ever bigger government, stagnation, and ever more severe political troubles. Not only is sound money the foundation of cooperation and progress, but it is also the way to a prosperous and moral society.

CHAPTER 1

How We Got Here

In the fall of 2008, the U.S. suffered its worst
financial crisis since the Great Depression. . . . Five
years on . . . the country's economy is still sick.
Unemployed middle-aged men look in the mirror
and see someone who may never work again. Young
married couples who should be on the way up are
living in their parents' basement.

—DANIEL HENNINGER, *Wall Street Journal*

THE WORLD HAS SUFFERED THROUGH A TURBULENT DE-
cade. The last 10 years have seen a financial panic
in the United States that nearly brought down the
global financial system. It was followed by the worst recession
in more than 30 years; solvency crises that imperiled governments in the United States and Europe; a financial meltdown
in Iceland; attacks on a succession of currencies, including the
rupee and the euro; and hyperinflation in Zimbabwe and civil
war–torn Syria.

By 2014, the Great Recession had passed. Yet while the fe-
ver may have spiked, unease lingers. Recovery in the United
States and around the world has been feeble. Polls show that
people are more politically polarized than they have been in

decades. From the Middle East to Latin America, countries have been rocked by street demonstrations and social unrest. Monetary crises have roiled emerging nations such as Russia, Brazil, India, Turkey, Indonesia, and South Africa. In January 2014 the Dow Jones Industrial Average plummeted more than 318 points, or 2%, in a single day.

In the words of one observer, a "1929 feeling" is back on Wall Street. Among many there is the fear that the market's gains could quickly evaporate and that a new global crisis lurks just around the corner. There is also growing anxiety about the future of the dollar. We have seen this in the rush to invest in gold; the emergence of alternative currencies like the bitcoin and the now-prohibited Liberty Dollar; and the proliferation of books forecasting doomsday scenarios like the total collapse of the dollar and currency wars. Many people are wondering: Could such predictions possibly be true?

Politicians and pundits worldwide have all sorts of explanations for the crises and malaise: greed, reckless speculation in dangerous currency markets, excess debt, inequality, and American capitalism itself. But the true cause is the ignorance of policy makers, whose ideas about money have been handed down from the mercantilists of the Middle Ages. These officials have been unable or unwilling to grasp a simple truth: *money is not wealth*. It is like a scale or a ruler—a measure of value.

Few people would see any advantage in constantly changing the number of inches in a foot or the number of minutes in an hour. Imagine the disruption that would cause. Nor does anyone think that each of America's 50 states should have its own currency or that each one should fluctuate against all the others. Think of how hard it would be for Americans in different states to buy and sell to each other. How hard would it be to travel if you weren't sure what your Wisconsin dollars would be worth in Florida? Most people would consider such a system uselessly complicated and chaotic. Yet this is what happens daily between nations as a result of our global monetary system of fluctuating exchange rates.

The End of the Gold Standard
Ushers in Currency Chaos

Astonishingly, bureaucrats and officials understand less about money today than they did a century ago. This basic ignorance has given us not only the disasters of the last decade but also the Great Depression and the Great Inflation of the 1970s. More than 40 years ago, it led to the end of the gold standard and the destruction of the U.S. dollar as a vital anchor of value for the world's currencies and the global economy.

The dollar had been linked to gold since George Washington was president. Near the end of World War II, with much of the global economy and monetary infrastructure in ruins as a result of that conflict and the Great Depression, Allied nations met in Bretton Woods, New Hampshire. Their objective: to devise a new international monetary system. It was agreed that the dollar would remain linked directly to gold at $35 an ounce. Other nations would fix their currencies to the dollar.

The Bretton Woods gold standard lasted from 1944 to 1971. Then, for reasons we will discuss, Richard Nixon abandoned it. Ever since, the value of the dollar and the rest of the world's currencies have been at the mercy of the U.S. Federal Reserve (the Fed) and other central banks, whose policies reflect the political whims of governments.

This ever-fluctuating system of "fiat money," with its gradual weakening of the dollar, has produced four decades of slow-motion wealth destruction. Since 1971 the dollar's purchasing power has declined by more than 80%. Much of that slide has been recent: since the year 2000, according to the consumer price index (CPI), the dollar's value has declined by about 26%.

This has major implications for the world economy. The dollar is the leading global currency. Commodities such as oil, copper, and wheat are priced in dollars. Other nations transact much of their business using the U.S. dollar or denominating contracts in dollars. The policy decisions of the U.S. Federal Reserve therefore are critical to the worldwide flow of capital and set the monetary agenda for other nations.

Studies show that since the 1971 end of the Bretton Woods gold standard system, the world has experienced more frequent crises and downturns. Fiat money is behind the many market eruptions erroneously viewed as an inevitable feature of free-market capitalism—the financial equivalents of hurricanes or monsoons.

We saw the toxic, disruptive effects of unstable money in 2013 when the Fed announced that it would begin "the taper," the scaling back of its gargantuan quantitative easing. The yield on 10-year Treasuries increased to almost 3%, about twice their 1.6% low during the period of quantitative easing (QE). These newly attractive interest rates caused global capital to flow back into the United States, causing a drop in demand and a sell-off of the bonds and currencies of the emerging nations known as the "Fragile Five" (Indonesia, South Africa, Brazil, India, and Turkey), whose currency values dramatically weakened on the global markets.

This is only one example of the chaos wrought by the fluctuations of the fiat dollar. Unfortunately it is among way too many.

More and More of the Same Bad Medicine

The correlation between unstable money and an unstable global economy would seem obvious. But it has been largely lost on our policy makers. The failure to understand money is shared by all nations, and this failure transcends politics and parties. The destructive monetary expansion undertaken during the Democratic administration of Barack Obama by then Federal Reserve chairman Ben Bernanke began in a Republican administration under Bernanke's predecessor, Alan Greenspan. Republican Richard Nixon's historic ending of the gold standard was a response to forces set in motion by the weak dollar policy of Democrat Lyndon Johnson.

For more than 40 years, one policy mistake has followed the next. Each one has made things worse. We will later detail how the Fed's loose money policies of the early 2000s led to the momentous worldwide panic and global recession that began in 2008. The remedy for that disaster? Quantitative easing—the largest monetary expansion in history.

Quantitative easing did not just fail as a stimulus. It *prevented* recovery by causing a destructive misallocation of credit. Perhaps even worse, it caused, in its early stages, spikes in the prices of commodities that raised the cost of food and fuel, inflaming political divisions and unrest in many developing nations.

Most of the supposed stimulus money never made it into the economy. One of the reasons was a distortionary bond-buying strategy that was part of QE known as "Operation Twist." The Fed traditionally expands the monetary base by buying short-term Treasuries from financial institutions. Banks then turn around and make short-term loans to those businesses that are the economy's main job creators. But QE's Operation Twist focused on buying *long*-term Treasuries and mortgage-backed securities. This meant that instead of going to the entrepreneurial job creators, loans went primarily to large corporations and to the government itself. It was a form of credit allocation.

Supporters insisted that Operation Twist's lowering of long-term rates would stimulate the economy by encouraging people to buy homes and make business investments. In reality this credit allocating is cronyism, an all-too-frequent consequence of fiat money. Fed-created inflation results in undeserved windfalls to some while others struggle.

Because of the widespread misconceptions about money, policy makers and economists have largely failed to perceive these and other failures. In fact there are movements afoot to give the Fed and central banks in other nations even more power.

Unstable Money: Odorless and Colorless

Unstable money is a little bit like carbon monoxide: it's odorless and colorless. Most people don't realize the damage it's doing until it's very nearly too late. A fundamental principle is that when money is weakened, people seek to preserve their wealth by investing in commodities and hard assets. Prices of things like housing, food, and fuel start to rise, and we are often slow to realize what's happening.

For example, few connected the housing bubble of the mid-2000s with the Fed's weak dollar. All they knew was that loans were cheap. Many rushed to buy homes in a housing market in which it seemed prices could only go up. When the Fed finally raised rates, the market collapsed.

The weak dollar was not the only factor, but there would have been no bubble without the Fed's flooding of the subprime mortgage market with cheap dollars. Yet to this day the housing meltdown and the events that followed are misconstrued as the products of regulatory failure and of greed. Or they are blamed on affordable housing laws and the role of the government-created mortgage enterprises Fannie Mae and Freddie Mac. The latter two factors definitely played a role. Yet the push for affordable housing existed in the 1990s, and we didn't get such a housing mania. Why did it happen in the 2000s and not in the previous decade?

The answer is that the 1990s was not a period of loose money. The housing bubble inflated after Alan Greenspan lowered interest rates to stimulate the economy after the 2001–2002 recession. Greenspan kept rates too low for too long.

The bursting of the subprime bubble put in motion a collapse of dominoes that started with the U.S. financial sector and European banks and led to the sovereign debt crisis in Europe, the Greek bankruptcy crisis, and the banking disasters in Iceland and Cyprus.

Other Problems Caused by the Weak Dollar

Many may not realize it, but the weakening of the dollar is at the heart of many other problems today:

High Food and Fuel Prices

As with the subprime bubble, the oil price rises of the mid-2000s (as well as the 1970s) were widely blamed on greed. Yet here too no one bothers to ask why oil companies suddenly became greedier starting in the 2000s. Oil prices averaged a little over $21 a barrel from the mid-1980s until the early part of the last decade when there was a stronger dollar, compared with around $95 a barrel these days.

Rising commodity prices spurred by the declining dollar have also driven up the cost of food. Many shoppers have noticed that the prices of beef and chicken have reached record highs. This is especially devastating to developing countries where food takes up a greater portion of people's incomes.

Since the Fed and other central banks began their monetary expansion in the mid-2000s, high food prices wrongly blamed on climate shocks and rising demand have caused riots in countries from Haiti to Bangladesh to Egypt.

Declining Mobility, Greater Inequality, and the Destruction of Personal Wealth

The destruction of the dollar is the reason that two incomes are now necessary for a middle-class family that lived on one income in the 1950s and 1960s. To see why, one need only look at the numbers from the U.S. Bureau of Labor Statistics. What a dollar could buy in 1971 costs $5.78 in 2014. In other words, you need *almost six times more money today than you did 40 years ago* to buy the equivalent goods and services. Say you had a 2014 dollar and traveled back in time to 1971. That dollar would be worth, according to the CPI calculator, a mere *17 cents*.

What has this meant for salaries? According to statistics from the U.S. Census Bureau, a man in his thirties or forties who earned $54,163 in 1972 today earns around $45,224 in inflation adjusted dollars—a 17% cut in pay. Women have entered the workforce in much larger numbers since then, and women's incomes have made up the difference for families. As Mark Gimein of Bloomberg.com points out, "The bottom line is that as two-income families have replaced single-earner ones, the median family has barely moved forward. And the single-earner family has fallen behind."

This drop in real incomes is a key reason why people feel they can't get ahead, creating fertile soil for resentment against the rich. Of course there are other contributing causes responsible for the increasing pressure on the middle class, the foremost being taxes. But the weak dollar has been the primary cause.

Increased Volatility and Currency Crises

The 2014 currency turmoil in emerging countries is just the latest in a succession of needless crises that have occurred over the past several decades as a consequence of unstable money. Today's huge and often-violent global markets, in which a nation's currency can come under attack, did not exist before the dollar was taken off the gold standard. They are a direct response to the risks created by floating exchange rates. The crises for most of the Bretton Woods era were mild and infrequent. It was the refusal of the United States to abide by the restrictions of the system that brought it down.

The weak dollar has also been the cause of banking crises that have been blamed on the U.S. system of fractional reserve banking. Traditionally, banks have made their money by lending out deposits while keeping reserves to cover normal withdrawals and loan losses. The rule of thumb is that banks have $1 of reserves for every $10 of deposits. In the past, fractional reserve banking has been criticized for making these institutions unnecessarily fragile and jeopardizing the entire economy. Indeed, history is replete with examples of banks that made bad loans and went bust.

Historically, the real problems have been bad banking regulations. In the post–Bretton Woods era, however, the cause has most often been unstable money. Misdirected lending is characteristic of the asset bubbles that result when prices are distorted by inflation. This has been true of past booms in oil, housing, agriculture, and other traditional havens for weak money.

The Weak Recovery

This bears repeating: the Federal Reserve's quantitative easing, the biggest monetary stimulus ever, has produced the weakest recovery from a major downturn in American history. The monetary expansion of the European Central Bank (ECB) produced even more feeble results in the euro zone, whose economy has long been impeded by suffocatingly high taxes and regulatory obstacles. The region is finally beginning to grow again, but barely.

QE's Operation Twist has not been the only constraint on loans to small and new businesses. Regulators have also compounded the problem by pressuring banks to reduce lending to riskier customers, which by definition are smaller enterprises. In 2014 the *Wall Street Journal* reported that this credit drought had caused many small businesses, from restaurants to nail salons, to turn in desperation to nonbank lenders—from short-term capital firms to hedge funds—that provide loans at breathtakingly high rates of interest. Interest rates for short-term loans can exceed 50%. Little wonder there are still so many empty storefronts during this period of supposed recovery.

Monetary instability encourages a vicious cycle of stagnation: the damage it causes is usually blamed on financial sector greed. The scapegoating and finger-pointing bring regulatory constraints that strangle growth and capital creation. That has long been the case in countries with chronic monetary instability, such as Argentina. Increased regulation is now hobbling capital creation in the United States as well as in Europe, where there is growing regulatory emphasis on preventing "systemic risk."

Regulators, the *Wall Street Journal* noted, "are increasingly telling banks which lines of business they can operate in and cautioning them to steer clear of certain areas or face potential supervisory or enforcement action."

In Europe, this disturbing trend toward "macroprudential regulation" is turning central banks into financial regulators with sweeping arbitrary powers. The problem is that entrepreneurial success stories like Apple, Google, and Home Depot—fast-growing companies that provide the lion's share of growth and job creation—all began as "risky" investments.

Not surprisingly, we're now seeing growing public discomfort with this increasing control by central banks. A 2013 Rasmussen poll found that an astounding 74% of American adults are in favor of auditing the Federal Reserve, and a substantial number think the chairman of the Fed has too much power.

Slower Long-Term Growth and Higher Unemployment

Even taking into account the economic boom during the relatively stable money years of the mid-1980s to late 1990s, overall the U.S. economy has grown more slowly during the last 40 years than in previous decades. From the end of World War II to the late 1960s, when the U.S. dollar had a fixed standard of value, the economy grew at an average annual rate of nearly 4%. Since that time it has grown at an average rate of around 3%. Forbes.com contributor Louis Woodhill explains that this 1% drop means a lot. Had the economy continued to grow at pre-1971 levels, gross domestic product (GDP) in the late 2000s would have been 56% higher than it actually was. What does that mean? Woodhill writes: "Our economy would have been more than three times as big as China's, rather than just over twice as large. And, at the same level of spending, the federal government would have run a $0.5 trillion budget surplus, instead of a $1.3 trillion deficit."

And what if the United States had *never* had a stable dollar? If America had grown for all of its history at the lower post–Bretton Woods rate, its economy would be about one-quarter of the size of China's. The United States would have ended up much smaller, less affluent, and less powerful.

Unemployment has also been higher as a consequence of the declining dollar. During the World War II gold standard era, from 1947 to 1970, unemployment averaged less than 5%. Even with the economy's ups and downs, it never rose above 7%. Since Nixon gave us the fiat dollar it has averaged over 6%: it averaged 8.5% in 1975, almost 10% in 1982, and around 8% since 2008. The rate would have been higher had millions not left the workforce.

The rest of the world has also suffered from slower growth, in addition to higher inflation, since the end of the Bretton Woods system. After the 1970s, world economic growth has been a full percentage point lower; inflation, 1.5% higher.

Larger Government with Higher Debt

By enabling endless monetary expansion, the post–Bretton Woods system of fiat money has helped propel the unchecked growth of government. In 1971 the total U.S. federal debt stood at $436 billion. Today it is more than $17 *trillion*. It's no coincidence that the federal debt has doubled since 2008, the same year that the Fed started implementing QE.

In 2011, three years after the Fed started quantitative easing, the United States' credit rating was downgraded by Standard & Poor's to below AAA. The picture is even worse in the euro zone, where the ECB has also been easing and which underwent a sovereign debt crisis, with nine nations receiving downgrades on their bonds.

In 1970, under Bretton Woods, European governments had balanced budgets. By the end of the decade they were all running deficits.

Pre-Copernican Monetary Policy in the Twenty-First Century

The Keynesian and monetarist bureaucrats who today set the monetary policies of the Fed and other central banks are like pre-Copernican astronomers who subscribed to the notion that the sun revolved around the earth. They are convinced that government can successfully direct the economy by raising and lowering the value of money.

After Janet Yellen, the new Federal Reserve chair, made some statements shortly after she took office, more than one news outlet wrote with characteristic awe that the Fed's newest mandarin "signaled" that she would continue the taper, the scaling back of QE that began in the final days under Ben Bernanke. She left open the option of changing course if the economy did not continue to improve, telling the House Financial Services Committee, "Too many people are unemployed."

This declaration reflects the prevailing Keynesian belief in the Phillips curve, a graph that purports to show that higher inflation increases employment. But, as we discuss later in Chapter 4 on inflation, this idea was long ago discredited by a succession of economists. Yet like so many other Keynesian assumptions, it is rarely if ever questioned.

The notion that a healthy economy requires a positive "balance of trade"—exports that bring in money from overseas—is absurd. And perhaps the most senseless and paradoxical idea is that the way to increase wealth creation is through policies that lower the value of people's money.

These dangerous beliefs have done global economies immense harm. When you think about them, they make little intuitive sense. There is no way that monetary bureaucrats all over the world can possibly guide the activities of billions of people who engage in tens of billions of transactions every week.

The great periods of job creation and growth throughout history were not responses to changes in currency values. They were the work of entrepreneurs responding to real-world needs by coming up with innovations, from the invention of the steam engine to the creation of the personal computer. Indeed, as we will discuss later, one of the most creative periods of technological innovation, the late nineteenth century, occurred during a rare interlude of stable money and unimpeded capital creation, the era of the classical gold standard.

There has not been one instance in history where active monetary management has advanced an economy. The only time central bank intervention has produced truly positive benefits is when it cleaned up a mess created by its own policies. The outstanding example is when the Federal Reserve under then chair Paul Volcker tightened money in the early 1980s to break the back of the 1970s' inflation, which the Fed's prior policies had created in the first place.

Four Decades of Money Mismanagement

Since the decimation of the Bretton Woods system, the dollar has been on a four-decade downward slide, with only periodic interruptions.

One interlude of relative stability was "the great moderation" during the Reagan administration under Paul Volcker. Successor Alan Greenspan's strengthening of the dollar in the late 1990s produced mild deflation, but the Fed then reverted to form: the weak dollar policy that led to the crisis of 2008–2009.

Greenspan was followed by Bernanke and his policy of quantitative easing. At its height, the Fed was expanding the monetary base by buying about $85 billion in bonds a month. To put that in perspective, in 1971 the entire monetary base was $85 billion. Today it is well past *$4 trillion* and climbing.

Over the last decade the United States has led the way in what has been a global monetary expansion. The European Central Bank increased its balance sheet to record levels in 2012, though not as much as the Fed. Even Japan, which has traditionally gone in the opposite direction with monetary policies based on tight money, has lately talked about weakening the yen.

The overall global expansion has slowed and the economy has improved somewhat thanks to the taper. But, given past history, the scaling back of QE is more likely to be a short-lived pause than a turn toward saner policy—unless the public awakens to the need for stable money.

The 1970s Redux?

There were such pauses in the inflationary 1970s after Richard Nixon ended the gold standard system. Keen observers like Nathan Lewis and others have pointed out that the malaise that began in the middle part of the last decade looks a lot like the 1970s, another period of global monetary expansion and instability.

There are some differences: unlike the 1970s, the past 10 years have not seen an enormous rise in consumer prices. Both periods, however, have experienced ferocious market swings, soaring energy and commodity prices, unrest in the Middle East, and high unemployment. As with the 1970s, gold prices soared, peaking at $1,896.50 in 2011. GDP growth, which as of 2014 is around 2%, is not much better than the average rate of growth from 1968 to 1982.

All of this should be no surprise. Today's disasters are the products of the same Keynesian thinking that gave us the stagflation of the 1970s. Those ideas were wrong then. They are wrong now.

Lifting the Veil off the Fed's Mystique

All of this raises the question: Why has there been so little discussion of these policy failures and of money? One explanation is that for many people, including those in the media, conversations about monetary policy can seem dry and somewhat forbidding—a surefire way to discourage unwanted conversations on airplanes. The mystique that surrounds the Federal Reserve is sufficient to have inspired William Greider to title his classic book about the Fed *Secrets of the Temple*.

The dense, bureaucratic lingo of central bankers has long elicited eye-rolling among journalists who have dubbed it "Fedspeak." Its most famous practitioner, former Federal Reserve chairman Alan Greenspan, famously quipped, "Since I've become a central banker, I've learned to mumble with great incoherence. If I seem unduly clear to you, you must have misunderstood what I said." As one former official put it, Fedspeak is "a language in which it is possible to speak without ever saying anything." Insiders insist that Fedspeak is needed to avoid strong statements that can jar markets. But the opaque jargon also discourages scrutiny.

Further inhibiting debate are the Keynesians and monetarists who dominate the media and policy establishment. Keynesians believe in the welfare state and fear that a return to fixed exchange rates will mean less spending and smaller government. That isn't true. The Germans under Otto von Bismarck invented the welfare state in the 1880s, and they were better able to afford it because they maintained sound money. Stable money, as well as continuous tax cutting, allowed the German economy after World War II not only to recover but actually to surpass the rest of Europe and Great Britain.

The misguided Keynesian perceptions about money have produced one disaster after the next. A better awareness of the origins and fallacies of today's thinking are crucial for turning things around.

More people must recognize that the seemingly dry pronouncements of monetary bureaucrats have serious and often destructive consequences. As this book will show, they play out not only on the financial pages but also in the lives of each and every individual in the world.

THE NUGGET

An unstable currency means an unstable economy and less prosperity.

CHAPTER 2

What Is Money?

Money is the foundation stone in the political
framework of a civilized community. . . . But stable
community requires a stable currency.

—LEWIS E. LEHRMAN, *Money, Gold, and History*

WHAT IS MONEY?
Millions of words have been written attempting to answer this question. Most of them have
decreased, rather than increased, understanding. The answer is
simple. Money has three roles in an economy:

1. It is a measure of value.

2. It is an instrument of trust that permits transactions to
   take place between strangers.

3. It provides a system of communication throughout a
   society.

Measurement. Trust. Communication. In order to function
in these roles, money, above all, must be stable. When it isn't,
it becomes impaired and an economy suffers. In the worst in-
stances, when money stops working altogether, a society can be
destroyed.

Money is a tool that *facilitates* transactions. It does not create them. And money, in and of itself, is not wealth—nor does increasing the supply of money by the whims of central bankers mean that wealth will be created. In fact, the opposite is the case.

This chapter discusses how money functions as a standard of measurement, a facilitator of trust, and a system of communication. Disasters wrought by bad monetary policy have all occurred because of a failure to grasp these three fundamental principles.

Money Is a Unit of Measurement

Money is a standard of measurement, like a ruler or a clock, but instead of measuring inches or time, it measures what something is worth.

Imagine what the world would be like if the number of minutes in an hour changed each day or if the number of inches in a foot kept changing. Life would become infinitely more difficult. How could a music teacher know what to charge for an hour-long music lesson if one hour was composed of 60 minutes one week and 70 minutes the next? How could an architect design a house if a foot consisted of 12 inches on a given day but a short time later it was 15 inches? Imagine how tricky it would be to bake a cake if the recipe called for 45 minutes in the oven, and you had to figure out if those were nominal minutes or *inflation-adjusted* minutes.

Just as we need to be sure of the number of inches in a foot or the minutes in an hour, people in the economy must be certain that their money is an accurate measure of worth. When the value of money fluctuates, as it so often does today, it produces uncertainty in addition to unnatural and often destructive marketplace behavior—artificial booms and busts that breed malignant economic and social consequences. Graphic examples include Germany after World War I and the United States during the 1970s, as well as in the past decade.

People, Not Government, Invented Money

People accustomed to Uncle Sam's ubiquitous dollar and other national currencies rarely recognize that government did not invent money. Money originated in the marketplace as a solution to a problem. It arose spontaneously, like the spoon or the personal computer, in response to a need. In this case, the need was for a stable unit of value to facilitate trade.

The earliest coins were invented in ancient times in response to the challenges of barter. In order for a successful exchange to take place, there had to be what economists have called a "double coincidence of wants." Each side had to want the precise item offered.

For example, if *Forbes* magazine had sold an advertisement before the advent of money, we might have been paid with a herd of goats. For the sake of illustration, let's say iPads existed in those days and we wanted to buy them for our writers. We'd take our herd of goats to an Apple Store. But the proprietor informs us that he wants sheep instead of goats. So now we have to figure out how to swap goats for sheep. In the process we would have to hire a shepherd to make sure wolves didn't eat the sheep. The shepherd wants to be paid in wine. We have red wine, but he wants white wine. You can readily see how utterly inefficient and cumbersome barter is for getting things done.

In economics class we all learn that money is a medium of exchange, that it has certain physical characteristics. It should be fungible. One unit, like a gold bar or coin, should be interchangeable with another, and it should be portable and easy to store for use later. (That's why, as some have observed, chocolate coins in gold wrappers would not work as money, especially in hot weather.)

First and foremost, money must be stable.

The Virtues of Stable Money

Stability is best achieved by a link to a commodity. Over the centuries, precious metals, such as silver and especially gold, most often have served this purpose. But other commodities, such as seashells, fur, fish, corn, rice, and tobacco, have also worked as currencies. Tobacco notes were used as money during colonial times. Prisoners of war used cigarettes as money during World War II, as did the Germans for several years after the war.

Milton Friedman's classic book *Money Mischief* tells the famous story of South Pacific Islanders who traded with giant stone coins known as *fei*. Because the islanders believed this money had great intrinsic value, the fei was extremely reliable as an indicator of worth. But the currency failed miserably when it came to portability. According to an eyewitness, it "[consisted] of large, solid, thick, stone wheels, ranging in diameter from a foot to twelve feet." Islanders had to insert a pole in the center of one of these giant coins to roll it around.

One couldn't ask for a less convenient currency. But the giant stones worked as currency because the islanders believed that they were a reliable measure of value. The Pacific Islanders did not fear that their tribal council would suddenly decree that there should be twice the number of fei—and their money would be worth less.

When Money Doesn't Work

Having a track record for soundness also helps fortify a currency. That's one reason why money has generally little value in communist nations racked by shortages of consumer goods. How can you know that your money is an accurate measure of worth if there's very little to buy? The Cuban government, for example, knows the Cuban peso is nearly worthless. That's why it demands that tourists buy pesos with dollars at a grossly inflated price far above black market rates.

In the Soviet Union, consumers were always hungering for decent meats, fruits, and vegetables. But even if you had a fistful of rubles, your money usually couldn't buy these scarce staples unless you were politically connected and had access to special stores used by the party elites.

All the East German ostmarks in the world could not have bought a Trabant, the government-manufactured automobile. The infamous clunker was harder to get than a BMW, not because it was desirable but because the Trabant was virtually the only vehicle East Germans were allowed to get, and Trabants were strictly rationed.

Little wonder that both the ostmark and the ruble were perceived as nearly worthless. Communist currencies all sold in black markets at a fraction of their official exchange rates. The country's communist governments may have maintained the charade of a sound and stable currency, but the reality of the marketplace said something different: you never knew the purchasing power of your money because you couldn't be sure what goods would be available from day to day.

In the Soviet Union, the situation was summed up by the commonly heard expression "we pretend to work, and they pretend to pay us." Not surprising that productivity and the quality of products was notoriously poor.

The communist currencies and the fei also illustrate the second critical characteristic of money: it's about trust.

In Money We Trust—or Not

Money facilitates trade by creating trust between both sides in a transaction. In the days of barter if you exchanged, say, eggs for a loaf of bread, you could not be certain whether you would be getting fresh bread or day-old bread. But if you exchanged your eggs for money, you could trust in the value of what you were getting.

The media like to portray money as a fomenter of conflict. In fact, throughout history, money has promoted cooperation, bringing together buyers and sellers who are total strangers but who agree upon a standard measure of value. The historian Jack Weatherford and others have described how money has transformed society by making traditional kinship and social relationships less important. For this reason money creates a meritocracy, empowering smaller players to challenge the established order.

The power of money to create meritocracy was why Alexander Hamilton, the first secretary of the treasury under George Washington, proposed a new U.S. Mint that would produce coins as small as copper cents and half-cent pieces in order to make possible prices that were affordable for the poor. Born in the West Indies to a single mother, Hamilton had a unique appreciation of the ability of money to promote a culture of opportunity that enabled outsiders to rise. In the words of biographer Forrest McDonald, Hamilton keenly understood that "money is oblivious to class, status, color and inherited social position; money is the ultimate, neutral, impersonal arbiter." Hamilton built a financial system based on money and markets because he wanted America to be, in McDonald's words, a "society fluid and open to merit."

Money must be trusted for an economy, and also a society, to function. The value of money has less to do with whether it is made of metal or paper and more to do with *perceptions*.

People can lose faith in money as a result of a cataclysmic event—for example, a war. But more often this loss of faith happens when governments, for whatever reason—such as building bloated welfare states or financing costly military conflicts—print too much money or seem likely to do so in the future.

A profound and far-reaching loss of faith can produce a disastrous, self-fulfilling scenario: a massive sell-off of a currency on the foreign exchange market. At its worst, this kind of attack can bring on a death spiral and collapse in monetary value. This can accelerate inflation at home and cause a government to sharply raise interest rates, throwing an economy into severe recession. It can set off a panic that can spread to other nations.

In 2013 when the Federal Reserve indicated that its promiscuous bond buying would taper off and thereby lead to higher U.S. interest rates, emerging countries such as Brazil, India, Turkey, and Indonesia saw the value of their currencies weaken in anticipation that banks and companies would pull money out of those nations to take advantage of rising interest rates in the United States.

Foreign exchange markets were ready to attack their currencies because they had little faith that the governments of these countries would do what was necessary to maintain currency stability. This could have easily been accomplished had these nations used the dollars held in reserve by their central banks to buy their own currencies and shore up their value. But such relatively simple steps are rarely taken or executed correctly because most nations today don't understand the importance of having stable money.

A similar loss of trust brought on the devastating Asian currency crisis in 1997. That disaster was precipitated by Thailand's easy domestic money policy as well as by the U.S. dollar, which had been strengthening as a result of growth-inducing tax cuts and the inadvertent tight money of the Federal Reserve.

A strong U.S. economy was causing investors to dump the baht and other currencies in favor of the dollar. Observers felt too many bahts were being created to keep it pegged to the greenback at a fixed exchange rate. Like most other monetary bureaucrats, Thailand's central bankers didn't know how to defend the baht, which would have meant temporarily reducing its supply. In its advice to other nations, the International Monetary Fund (IMF) was just as ignorant. In fact, it recommended devaluations.

Foreign exchange traders soon realized policy makers in Thailand didn't perceive the importance of maintaining a stable currency. Their loss of faith in the integrity of the baht led to a collapse.

Trustworthy Money: The Bedrock of Prosperity

When a country has stable, trustworthy money, the opposite scenario unfolds: people want to hold their currencies. Capital and investment flow into countries with stable money. That's why stable money is the bedrock of prosperity.

The classic example is Great Britain. The British pound was tied to gold at a fixed rate for over 200 years and holds the record for stability. After Great Britain formally established the ratio for the pound to gold in 1717, lenders could rest assured they would be paid back in money that wouldn't lose its value. Capital creation and investment in the country exploded. The strength of Great Britain's currency helped create capital markets that turned that island from a second-tier nation to the mightiest industrial power in the world.

Propelled by its stable money and capital markets, Great Britain gave us the steam engine, railroads, and countless other advances that marked the beginning of the modern era. Its spectacular success led the United States and other countries to follow its example. The late nineteenth century saw the era of the classical gold standard. The United States, most of Europe, and eventually Japan pegged their currencies to gold. More wealth was created by far in the 1800s than all the previous centuries put together.

In the twenty-first century, there is no such thing as stable money. But countries that manage to keep their currencies relatively sound tend to be better economic performers; examples are Switzerland, Singapore, and China. It's easier for them to have a vibrant economy because transactions are made easier.

In this era of unstable money, nations that have relatively sound currencies can occasionally suffer from too much of a good thing. During the sovereign debt crisis of 2011, which imperiled the euro, many sought refuge in Swiss francs. The value of the Swiss franc shot up so high relative to the euro that it hurt Swiss exporters. The Swiss government eventually had to place a cap on the franc's value vis-à-vis the euro.

The Importance of Monetary Demand

When you have desirable money you have global demand. The importance of demand in determining the value and supply of money is widely unappreciated.

Demand for money is created by a strong and growing economy. Proportionately there is a greater supply of U.S. than Canadian or Australian dollars because there are more uses for the U.S. dollar globally. The U.S. dollar is more desired around the world than those other currencies because our economy is bigger and our capital markets are deeper.

How can a government increase demand for its money? To quote Austin Powers: *behave*. Signal to markets that a future devaluation is unlikely by implementing economy-boosting, pro-market initiatives and by showing fiscal restraint.

After the United States cut tax rates and did not pass costly national healthcare reform in the late 1990s, money flowed into the States, strengthening the greenback. People wanted to invest in America, and they wanted more dollars.

Keynesians and monetarists focus too much on supply of money rather than demand. If demand is not there, an attempt to create money sets up what in the 1930s was called "pushing on a string." The economy doesn't move.

Economic Torpor and a Crisis of Faith in the Dollar

Stagnation has essentially been the story since the financial crisis of 2008–2009. The last several years have seen an explosion of the Fed's balance sheet, enormous stimulus spending, the historic expansion of government—most notably the thousands of pages of regulations coming from Dodd-Frank financial reform and the Affordable Care Act—along with record levels of government debt. These misguided policies have suppressed both the economy and monetary demand, undermining long-term faith in U.S. currency.

The price of gold, you may remember, shot up to a breathtaking high of $1,900 an ounce in 2011. And as we noted, the rating agency Standard & Poor's downgraded U.S. credit in 2011. China, our largest foreign creditor, and many others have worried that a U.S. default on bond payments could set off a worldwide financial meltdown many times worse than the 2008 financial crisis; that would cause the dollar to collapse. Even absent such a dire scenario, they worry that the dollar faces a long-term decline.

The Chinese see the U.S. economy as stalled and U.S. leadership as floundering. They see a government paralyzed by political disarray, seemingly unable to govern itself. During the 2013 partial government shutdown, an angry commentary by the Chinese government's Xinhua News Agency slammed "the cyclical stagnation in Washington for a viable bipartisan solution over a federal budget and an approval for raising debt ceiling [that] has again left many nations' tremendous dollar assets in jeopardy and the international community highly agonized." The editorial renewed calls for a "de-Americanized world" with a new reserve currency "to replace the dominant U.S. dollar, so that the international community could permanently stay away from the spillover of the intensifying domestic political turmoil in the United States."

Default was averted when Congress and the president eventually agreed to end the government shutdown. But this has not stemmed concerns about the dollar. To the contrary: Republicans agreed to let the Obama administration raise the debt ceiling and borrow even more. The move had some observers wondering whether the dollar's collapse was not a matter of if, but when.

The Bitcoin and Other Alternative Currencies

When people lose trust in a currency, alternatives start springing up. That is happening today as the result of faltering confidence in the dollar. In 2012 thirteen states were considering laws that would allow people to use gold and silver currency in place of the dollar. Other recent alternatives include the now-banned Liberty Dollar and the more recent and highly controversial digital currency known as the bitcoin.

These initiatives are not as radical as they sound. People today forget that for a good part of U.S. history, Americans used more than one currency. From the mid-1830s to the mid-1850s, it was legal in the United States to use gold and silver coins from different countries along with the U.S. dollar, as well as coins from U.S. mints. The Spanish silver dollar was used heavily in colonial America and as late as the mid-1800s.

Utah governor Gary Herbert may have had this history in mind when he signed a bill into law that allowed gold and silver coins from the U.S. Mint—American Gold and Silver Eagles—to be used in that state as money.

Then there's the bitcoin. The digital currency was designed as a stateless alternative to traditional money. A fixed number were created that could be purchased and used in online transactions beyond the reach of government or banks, in addition to being traded. Offering the advantage of freedom from government fiat and surveillance, the bitcoin initially created excitement and attracted a passionate following.

The euphoria came to an end when the digital money drew legal scrutiny. Its promise of anonymity made it a perfect cover for illegal transactions, including drug dealing. In 2013 the FBI arrested the drug kingpin known as Dread Pirate Roberts, a.k.a. Ross William Ulbricht, who used bitcoins for drug deals in the online black market known as Silk Road, which he allegedly created. The 29-year-old former grad student was collared inside a San Francisco public library, and his site was shut down by the Feds.

In 2014, Tokyo-based Mt. Gox, the world's largest bitcoin trading exchange, shut down abruptly when it was revealed that hundreds of thousands of bitcoins had been stolen. The massive sell-off that followed caused the currency to virtually collapse.

Critics attributed the failure of the bitcoin to the fact that it is unregulated and anonymous. The real reason was that it isn't really money. The high-tech bitcoin may have captured the imaginations of those seeking alternatives to the dollar, but with its wild fluctuations it is not a stable measure of value. For that reason, it can't function as an instrument of trust.

Forbes.com writer Kashmir Hill set out to live on bitcoins for a week. She invested $600 in bitcoins at $126.69 each. When she finally received the digital money, online trading had sent the value of her bitcoins up to $142 each.

Unfortunately, their value could also plummet just as fast—as much as 61% in a single day. To put that in perspective, the Dow crashed about 13% on Black Monday of 1929 and about 23% on Black Monday of 1987.

Little wonder that long before the crash of the bitcoin, Hill found few places willing to accept them.

The story of the bitcoin shows how money attempts to rise up when there is a need. But even if people were able to develop a viable alternative money, it would probably not last long in today's unstable environment because of a principle known as Gresham's law: *bad money drives out good*. History has shown that when money is debased, people tend to hoard the "good," accurately valued money while dumping the "bad," overvalued money in the marketplace. Gresham's law was why the printing of paper money by the colonial governments of New England drove out the silver coins that were also in circulation, pushing monetary values down further.

There's no refuge from the destruction caused by the debasement of money.

Money Communicates

Trust is not the only reason that we need currency stability. Stability is essential if money is to fulfill its role as an instrument of communication in the marketplace. The economist Friedrich Hayek explained that money facilitates communication in the market, and in society, through the mechanism of prices.

The price system is why products and services in a free economy seem to spring from out of nowhere without a bureaucrat ordering them to appear. Hayek observed: "The most significant fact about this system is the economy of knowledge with which it operates, or how little the individual participants need to know in order to be able to take the right action."

Prices don't simply inform buyers and sellers in a particular transaction; they also provide information that producers and consumers throughout an economy use to make decisions. Rising prices, for instance, indicate *increasing demand* for a product or service. Conversely, when the price of a product drops, rendering it less profitable, that's a signal people no longer want what is being offered.

One example is portable cassette players. Thirty years ago Sony created a sensation when it came out with the Walkman. You could listen to music with great fidelity on a pair of light headphones from a small device that you could keep in your pocket. The price of the very first Walkman sold in Japan was $1,000. It debuted in the United States at around $200 in 1979 dollars. Sales and profits went through the roof—overnight, everyone was making them.

Then a new technology appeared: the portable compact disc player. Demand for cassette players dropped—and so did prices and profits. Producers turned their attention to CD players. Then came the iPod and downloadable digital audio content. Portable disk players too became history. There are still portable cassette and CD players, but there's far less demand for them; you can now get one of those devices for as little as $20.

Prices also convey advances in productivity. Thirty years ago, a cell phone that was as big as a shoebox cost $3,995. Cell phones are now many times smaller and more powerful and they cost a fraction of that—and they're free with some calling plans.

Another example, out of many: flat-screen TVs. Prices are less than a tenth of what they were a decade ago, and they incorporate far more sophisticated technology.

That's why advocates of the need for price stability are of-ten off base. They can mistake price changes resulting from shifts in productivity and supply for inflation or deflation. In a vibrant, innovative, and productive economy, prices as a whole should decline as producers find ways to make products more cheaply. A dozen years ago the memory device in the iPad would have cost $10,000. Today, it costs a mere $50.

The prices and profits facilitated by money are what allow a market economy to provide for the needs of society. When money is made artificially unstable by government, the infor-mation it provides ends up being corrupted. Both producers and consumers respond to distorted market signals. The end re-sults are gluts, shortages, or market bubbles.

Money Is Not Wealth

As a standard of measurement, an instrument of communica-tion, and a promoter of trust, money facilitates the creation of wealth in a society. But money itself is not wealth. Money is simply a tool.

Adam Smith was among the first to recognize this truth. Smith defined money as "an instrument of commerce and a measure of value." Artificially increasing the amount of money in the economy, he wrote, was as futile as increasing the num-ber of cooking pots when there was no demand for them. In his influential masterwork *The Wealth of Nations*, he offered the brilliant observation that money, like other tools, appeared spontaneously when there was a need:

> If the quantity of victuals were to increase, the num-ber of pots and pans would readily increase along with it, a part of the increased quantity of victuals being employed in purchasing them, or in maintaining an

additional number of workmen whose business it was
to make them.

Just as buying too many unneeded cooking utensils would
impoverish a family, Smith wrote, government attempts to ac-
quire vast amounts of gold or silver "necessarily diminish[es]
the wealth which feeds, clothes, and lodges, which maintains
and employs the people."

Unlike others of his time—and, indeed, these days—Smith
recognized how money advanced society by facilitating profit-
making. Giving the example of the manufacturing of pins, he
explained how the increase in productivity brought about by the
division of labor means that "every workman has a great quantity
of his own work to dispose of beyond what he himself has occasion for." The surplus goods and services, he explained, are then
used as capital to create more wealth and "a general plenty dif-
fuses itself through all the different ranks of the society."

The *Wealth of Nations* was published in 1776, the year the
Declaration of Independence was signed. Smith's ideas about
free trade and sound money—and his rejection of mercantilism,
with its state controls—enormously influenced the Founding
Fathers, including, most notably, Alexander Hamilton.

Hamilton faced the challenge of restoring the economy of
the young republic that had been devastated by the Revolution-
ary War and the relentless money printing of "Continentals."
Like Smith, he knew history. The key to recovery, he wrote, was
"introducing order into our finances." In order to remain independent and not fall back into the clutches of Great Britain, the
new nation needed a banking system with expertise in the uses
of credit:

Banks were the happiest engines that ever were invented for advancing trade. Venice, Genoa, Hamburg,

Holland, and England are examples of their utility. They owe their riches, commerce, and the figure they have made . . . to this source. Great Britain is indebted for the immense efforts she has been able to make in so many illustrious and successful wars essentially to that vast fabric of credit raised on this foundation. 'Tis by this alone she now menaces our independence.

Following the example of Great Britain, Alexander Hamilton established the First Bank of the United States, as well as a mint with a dollar fixed by law to a specific weight in gold. Hamilton's system of banking and stable money quickly attracted and generated capital. It turned the American economy into the leading industrial power in the world.

THE NUGGET

Money measures wealth, but it does not create it.

CHAPTER 3

Money and Trade
A Deficit in Understanding

International transactions are always in balance, by
definition . . . for every buyer there is a seller. But
different items in the great circle carry different
labels. . . . The mystery is why we even collect these
figures; if we kept similar statistics for Manhattan
Island, Park Avenue would lie awake at night
worrying about its trade deficit.
                        —ROBERT BARTLEY, *The Seven Fat Years*

THE BUREAUCRATS WHO SET OUR MODERN MONETARY
policies are in many ways a throwback to the mercan-
tile era of the sixteenth to the eighteenth centuries.
Back then, currency consisted of precious metal—gold and silver bullion, or "specie." Money was synonymous with wealth.
Because nations were frequently at war, wealth was often ac-
quired through conquest.

Jean-Baptiste Colbert, Louis XIV's Machiavellian finance
minister and über-mercantilist, wrote in his *Mémoire*: "Commerce causes a perpetual combat in peace and war." To Colbert
and mercantilists throughout Europe, trade between nations
was a battle for supremacy, with money its foremost weapon.

Like many of his peers, Colbert looked with envy at Spain, whose New World mines flooded its coffers with gold and silver.

France and other nations did not have mines brimming with precious metal; instead, Colbert believed, they could generate such riches through trade. He declared, "Fashion is to France what the gold mines of Peru are to Spain." And just as Spain's vast mineral riches helped finance that nation's military, Colbert and his fellow mercantilists saw the riches generated by commerce as benefiting the cause of economic nationalism. Colbert wrote in his "Memorandum on Trade" that French goods would "bring us returns in money—and that, in one word, is the only aim of trade and the sole means of increasing the greatness and power of this State."

Colbert and mercantilist leaders throughout Europe did everything in their power to increase exports that would bring in ever-greater quantities of bullion. They limited or banned imports thought to deplete their economies of the money they saw as equating wealth and strength. Their regulatory regime also included capital controls, which in those days meant prohibitions on the export of gold or silver intended to bolster the domestic money supply.

Colbert's brand of mercantilism took this to an extreme, combining protectionism with a suffocating system of central planning and taxation intended to boost exports by increasing domestic production. *Colbertisme*'s staggering regulations and harsh enforcement tactics have been compared to communism and fascism.

Mercantilism, in many respects, reflected the fortress mentality inherited from the feudal era, when people lived behind castle walls and strength was equated with self-sufficiency. Colbert's draconian policies may have succeeded in financing the splendor of Louis XIV, the Sun King. But by the end of Louis's reign, France was suffering from a crushing burden of debt.

Mercantilism's monetary policies and its adversarial vision of trade were eventually discredited by Adam Smith and the philosophers of the Enlightenment. They pointed out that, whether it takes place within a country or across national borders, trade is the very opposite of war: it is a reciprocal exchange through which everyone benefits.

The veracity of Smith's perceptions has been borne out by the explosion of prosperity that has accompanied the loosening of trade barriers after World War II. According to one widely cited study published in 2006, overseas trade has added between $800 billion and $1.4 trillion in annual income to the U.S. economy—a total gain in products, goods, and services of about $7,000 to $13,000 per household. Global trade in the modern era is why, despite two world wars, there has been a long-term decline in military conflict since the feudal period.

Like their mercantilist forebears, our Keynesian policy makers persist in seeing trade as war, with monetary policy as the primary weapon. This thinking is as fallacious today as it was in Colbert's time. Worst of all, it has created our current perilous global system of fiat money in which nations seek to gain a trade advantage by lowering the value of their currencies.

Countries that do not know how to defend their monies and maintain their value risk attacks by speculators that can mean the collapse of a currency. Exacerbating global rivalries and antagonisms, this needlessly volatile environment gives new meaning to Colbert's vision of commerce as combat. Worse, it has held back the global economy and destroyed untold wealth.

Decades of Schizoid Monetary Policy

When it comes to money and trade, politicians are conflicted. Free trade has long been the official mantra. Policy makers may not talk about winning in combat—the more politely stated objective is usually to correct a trade deficit or achieve a so-called balance of trade. The bureaucratic euphemisms, however, boil down to Colbert-style protectionism: promoting exports that bring in more dollars or other hard currencies while limiting money- and "job-draining" imports that are believed bad for the economy.

Under the spell of this mercantilist mindset, a weak dollar—one that is cheap in relation to other currencies—is considered good because it makes foreign imports more costly and our exports more attractive. A strong dollar worth more than other currencies is considered bad because it makes imports cheaper and U.S. exports more expensive.

Since World War II, governments have wanted both cheap money and sound money. They face a quandary: weak money policies are considered a plus domestically because they encourage exports and are believed to stimulate the domestic economy, but too much money printing undermines one's currency and can incur the enmity of one's trading partners.

When he first took office, President Obama, who has done more to weaken the dollar than any other president in recent history, signaled through his soon-to-be treasury secretary Timothy Geithner that he was in favor of a *strong* dollar.

This is typical. Most administrations declare their intention to support a strong dollar—until they don't. Former Obama economic advisor Christina Romer conceded as much in a candid piece in the *New York Times*. She recounts that, after joining the administration, former treasury secretary Larry Summers advised her that in public statements the official line should always be that "the United States is in favor of a strong dollar," even though officialdom really considers a weak dollar more desirable.

Ambivalence over the issue of a weak-versus-strong dollar has long caused countries to lurch back and forth between loose and tight money. It was this widespread confusion, along with ignorance of the importance of sound money, that led to the breakdown of the Bretton Woods gold standard in the early 1970s and the fiat monetary system we have today.

Richard Nixon and the Triffin Dilemma

Richard Nixon and others at that time were worried about the consequences of what was known as the Triffin dilemma. In the early 1960s, the influential Belgian economist Robert Triffin wrote that with governments and large corporations around the globe relying on U.S. dollars as the world's foremost reserve currency too many dollars would flow overseas. This would create a balance of payments deficit for the United States that he and other neo-mercantilists believed was dangerous.

Hence the Triffin dilemma: if the United States were to restrict the outflow of dollars, Triffin and his supporters believed this would lead to a money shortage and less global growth. On the other hand, if the United States printed the dollars needed by the global economy, Triffinites thought the result would be a trade imbalance along with greater difficulty in maintaining the dollar/gold ratio.

The United States was also concerned about Japan and Germany, at that time America's foremost trade rivals. Both Japan and Germany had trade surpluses and were thought to possess dangerous levels of U.S. dollars, though they had very little by today's bloated standards. Americans were convinced that both countries were manipulating their currencies to boost exports and gain a trade advantage over the United States, which had begun to run a trade deficit by the early 1970s.

The dollar was indeed weakening, but not because of Triffin's scenario. The United States and other nations may have agreed to a gold standard as a result of Bretton Woods, but they did not understand the mechanics of how to maintain it and, subsequently, the importance of strictly adhering to it.

Both the administrations of Nixon and of his predecessor, Lyndon Johnson, were violators. Johnson ballooned U.S. spending to pay for the new entitlement bureaucracies of the Great Society, and also to wage the Vietnam War. His administration kept pressuring the Federal Reserve to keep interest rates low. There were more dollars circulating than the markets wanted. Moreover, the feeling was growing that the United States wouldn't, or couldn't, defend the Bretton Woods parity of $35 an ounce.

Seeing the world from the blinkered perspective of old-time mercantilists, Nixon and his advisors believed that the problem was a merchandise trade shortfall—the fact that the United States was buying more from countries overseas than those nations were buying from the States. This was a supposed signal of national weakness that they believed was depressing the dollar. Nixon and his advisors were convinced that keeping the greenback fixed to gold at its then-current ratio meant an overvalued dollar, allowing nations such as Germany and Japan to maintain a trade advantage. To them the answer was clear: the dollar had to be devalued.

The thinking was that freeing the values of currencies to "float" would give the United States and other governments more leeway to cheapen their money to correct such trade imbalances. Believers in floating exchange rates convinced themselves that fluctuations would be mild.

President Nixon's announcement on August 15, 1971, closed the "gold window." No longer would the United States redeem dollars for gold, in effect ending the gold standard. Temporary tariffs would be imposed on imports to turn around America's balance of payments, and a 90-day wage and price freeze was announced to control inflation.

The Bretton Woods system was formally pronounced dead in early 1973. The ending of the dollar's link to gold also ended fixed exchange rates for the world's currencies that had been pegged to the dollar. For the first time ever, there was no country on a gold standard.

Nixon insisted that his act of recklessness was necessary to help the economy by boosting exports. The Fed's money printing achieved its desired objective—at first. A false boom propelled Nixon to an easy win in 1972. The stock market peaked the following January.

Nixon's declared intent, as he put it, was to "stabilize" the dollar. In fact he had cut the world's monetary system loose from its anchor, giving the United States and other nations license to create money at will. A global money-printing binge ensued, further weakening the dollar as well as other currencies. Inflation took off.

Nixon likely came to regret the destructive forces that his policies had unleashed. Between 1973 and 1974, the Dow Jones Industrial Average lost 45% of its value. The Nixon Shock was responsible for the disastrous economic malaise of the 1970s, characterized by stagflation, a toxic combination of inflation and economic stagnation.

Nixon's ending of the Bretton Woods monetary system also helped give the United States and other countries the energy crisis. After the 1973 Yom Kippur War, Arab oil producers raised prices by 70%, followed by the Arab oil embargo. The rise in oil prices caused some people at the time to insist that the world was running out of oil. The cause, however, was the weak dollar. Nixon's price controls on gasoline, meanwhile, resulted in lines and rationing.

Seeing the surge in inflation, the Federal Reserve sharply raised interest rates. The gold price fell as the monetary base contracted. The economy stalled; unemployment shot up.

Nixon came under political fire and ultimately was forced from office under the cloud of the Watergate scandals. (His political position, though, had also been profoundly weakened by the economy.)

The ending of fixed exchange rates was a supreme act of mercantilism that ushered in a decade of stagnation and monetary chaos and laid the groundwork for the biggest economic disasters of recent times. It helped to bring on the stock market crash of 1987. And it gave us the destructive cheap dollar policies of the past decade that set the stage for the 2008–2009 financial crisis.

Floating exchange rates allowed the United States to gradually weaken the dollar under the George W. Bush and Obama administrations in the name of boosting exports and stimulating the economy. Those policies, in turn, fueled the catastrophic real estate and commodity bubbles—and eventual busts—that resulted in a debilitating drop in people's real incomes over the last decade.

The ending of the Bretton Woods standard forever changed the global financial system. But it wasn't just Nixon who was at fault. Almost all political leaders and economists of the time shared in the blame.

Post Bretton Woods: A More Dangerous World

The neo-mercantilists of the twentieth century may have thought that floating exchange rates would allow countries to correct perceived imbalances with their rivals and bolster their domestic economies. But the monetary system they created was more volatile than the one they had destroyed, with balance harder than ever to achieve.

When the world's currencies were pegged either to gold or to the gold-linked dollar, foreign exchange markets traditionally were like the money changers of old, converting currencies for governments, financial institutions, multinationals, and individuals transacting business across national borders. In the words of foreign exchange strategist Callum Henderson, "Between 1945 and 1970, currency speculation to all intents and purposes did not exist."

That all changed after the end of the Bretton Woods system. Bigger and more violent foreign exchange markets have seen a succession of monetary crises, shaking the economies not only of the United States and South America but also of Russia, Asia, and southern Europe.

In a 2000 study, researchers from Rutgers University, the University of California at Berkeley, and the World Bank analyzed data spanning 120 years of financial history and found that the "crisis frequency since 1973 has been double that of the Bretton Woods and classical gold standard periods and is rivaled only by the crisis-ridden 1920s and 1930s." This study was published eight years before the financial crisis.

The turmoil of the post–Bretton Woods era is what sent European nations scurrying for the shelter of a stable currency, setting the stage for the euro. The explosion of currency trading it has wrought has become a huge source of fees for banks. It has helped produce the market swings and giant windfalls so decried by Occupy Wall Street and others. In this dangerous world, monetary policy is deployed as a frequent weapon, nearly always with destructive consequences.

The Cudgel of Money

In his 2013 State of the Union address, President Obama talked about achieving trade that is "fair and free" through major initiatives with Asia and the European Union. In previous speeches, he made clear his underlying objective: to double exports within five years to revive a stagnant U.S. economy. Obviously the president isn't a dictator like Mao Zedong, who can simply command the economy to make a "Great Leap Forward." Such statements are generally understood as declarations of monetary policy. Obama was signaling that he would continue the strategies of lower interest rates and quantitative easing that have produced a dramatic drop in the value of the dollar.

Obama is only the latest American president to use currency as a weapon. Over recent decades, many of his predecessors, usually goaded by Congress, have similarly sought to increase exports by weakening the dollar.

Monetary protectionism even cropped up during the Reagan years. Egged on by an increasingly protectionist Congress, treasury secretary James Baker steadily drove down the dollar, a result of his obsession with U.S. trade deficits with Germany, Japan, and other countries. Following the announcement of a large U.S. trade deficit on October 14, 1987, Baker declared that the answer was that the dollar would have to decline further. His remarks were followed by a sickening slide in the stock market that culminated in Black Monday on October 19, 1987, when the Dow Jones Industrial Average lost 508 points, more than 22% of its value, in a single day. Congressional legislation and a weaker dollar nearly did to equities what the Smoot-Hawley Tariff with its sweeping trade protections did 58 years before, triggering a world trade war that set off the Great Depression. This time, however, the United States backed down and a crack-up was avoided.

Apocalypse When?

Given the violence of the post–Bretton Woods environment, it's no surprise that the worldwide monetary expansion and financial crises of the past decade have increased anxieties to new levels. This has been reflected not only in the high price of gold, but also in the recent spate of disaster predictions. Even some seasoned observers see the potential for a crisis more devastating than the meltdown of 2008. A few have gone so far as to predict the monetary equivalent of a world war.

Forbes.com contributor Eamonn Fingleton has envisioned such a doomsday scenario. Quoting economist Paul Craig Roberts, he writes that the collapse of the dollar could create an apocalyptic situation in which "shoppers in Walmart will feel they are in Neiman Marcus."

In his book *Currency Wars*, investment strategist James Rickards reveals that the Pentagon actually brought together academic and financial experts to explore how such a scenario might unfold. The group was instructed that "the only weapons allowed would be financial—currencies, stocks, bonds, and derivatives." Attendees were asked to imagine "a global financial war using currencies and capital markets instead of ships and [planes.]" Rickards describes today's monetary environment as "a new version of seventeenth-century mercantilism in which corporations are extensions of state power," and in which nations like China, Russia, and others will use devaluations and financial instruments such as derivatives as "financial weapons of mass destruction."

Noted investor Jim Rogers is so worried about the possibility of a new inflationary disaster and credit collapse that he moved himself and his family to Singapore.

The fears of Rogers and others have been prompted not only by the global environment, but also by developments in the United States. Many are legitimately alarmed by the United States' unprecedented level of government debt, its momentous money-printing initiative, and its economic stagnation. They are concerned as well by political contention at home and the appearance of weakness abroad. These anxieties have translated into mounting concerns about the future of the dollar.

Could the dollar really come under attack and suffer a total or near-total collapse like the Thai baht or more recently the Turkish lira?

The Chinese are sufficiently worried to have called for the "de-Americanization" of the world financial system and for abandoning the dollar as the primary reserve currency. In the last several years, they have virtually stopped adding Treasuries to their reserves.

Chinese officials also proposed jettisoning the dollar in favor of a little-used global currency called special drawing rights (SDRs)—known informally as "paper gold." SDRs were created by the International Monetary Fund in the 1960s as an alternative to the dollar and gold to deal with the Triffin dilemma. Their value today derives from a market basket of four currencies: the U.S. dollar, the yen, the euro, and the pound.

That such scenarios are being considered reflects the dangers we all face. A new and more destructive monetary crisis is on the way unless policy makers come to their senses and abandon ridiculous ideas such as the trade deficit. The real danger today is not the trade deficit but rather the deficit of understanding about trade and money.

The Trade Deficit Fallacy

Just about no one questions the neo-mercantilist assumption that imports are supposedly money-draining job destroyers while exports that bring in money are wealth creators. A nation's trade deficit is considered the equivalent of a company losing money, and a trade surplus is analogous to a profit. A trade deficit is therefore viewed as a sign of economic weakness.

This misguided perception has even influenced how the government computes gross domestic product (GDP). Since the 1930s, exports have been calculated as increasing GDP;

imports are regarded as subtractions. Another puzzling computation is that government spending is calculated as a *positive* contribution to GDP—something that would be news to anyone who had ever lived in the Soviet Union.

Yet trade deficits and surpluses have historically reflected little about the health of an economy. Neo-mercantilists overlook the fact that the United States has had a merchandise trade deficit for roughly 350 of the last 400 years. America ran a trade surplus during the Great Depression of the 1930s, for all the good that did. It has run trade deficits generally in more prosperous times, such as the late 1990s. That's because in those environments the United States is seen as a desirable market that's rapidly growing and *consuming*. People want to sell to America. The fact that the United States buys products and services from other nations doesn't mean it is weak; it means that the U.S. economy is strong and has the wealth and resources to buy what others are selling.

All of us incur trade deficits in daily life. When you go to McDonald's and buy a Big Mac, you have a trade deficit with McDonald's. You're buying from the restaurant, but it's not buying from you. No one gets upset. McDonald's may get your money, but you get the Big Mac. You get something in return.

Forbes magazine has a trade deficit with our paper supplier. We buy more paper from them than they buy subscriptions or ads from us. The fact that we have a trade deficit with our supplier doesn't say anything about our health as a company. It only says that we have a need for paper.

The myopic focus on the trade deficit ignores the fact that transactions don't take place between nations; they take place between the people and companies within those nations. America's imports or exports reflect the needs and wants of people at any given time. For example, in 2008 Reuters reported that a major part of the U.S. trade deficit with China consisted of $2.74 billion in "oil country tubular goods"—for example, pipelines.

Why did the United States need so much steel pipe? Primarily because of the increase in shale gas exploration made possible by hydraulic fracturing and technical advances in oil drilling, which spurred greater demand. American entrepreneurs and producers were mobilizing to meet the nation's demand for energy. They bought pipes from China, and citizens ended up with greater access to much-needed energy. That's not a deficit; that's a plus.

A sizable part of supposedly foreign trade in fact takes place within U.S. companies. Much of America's commerce abroad takes the form of foreign affiliate sales—movement of goods and services between a U.S. corporation's global subsidiaries. More than half the imports ostensibly responsible for the U.S. trade deficit come from the foreign divisions of *American* companies, according to the U.S. International Trade Commission.

In today's global marketplace, there's really no such thing as an American product or a Chinese product. In one study, researchers from the U.S. International Trade Commission and Columbia University estimated that the share of foreign (that is, non-Chinese) content in China's exports is about 50%. The iPhone assembled in China, for example, wholesales at about $180. While considered a Chinese export, Chinese labor accounts for only about $6.50 of its cost. The device is made of parts from a number of Asian and European countries.

With all of the iPhone's imported parts, the sale of just one may increase the U.S. trade deficit by around $180. Does that mean America loses? Hardly. Consider that the device sells for around twice its cost. Apple's profit, and the gain to the U.S. economy, therefore, exceeds the trade deficit.

Restricting Apple's, or any other company's, international trade is as counterproductive as keeping Ford Motors from buying critical components from domestic suppliers because Ford might have a trade deficit with those companies. America doesn't win in any sense of the word. It loses because U.S. companies are rendered less productive, less innovative, and less efficient.

Nor does a deficit with a trading partner necessarily indicate that a country is blocking U.S. exports. Daniel Griswold, director of the Cato Institute's Center for Trade Policy Studies, points out that the United States runs a bilateral *surplus* [our emphasis] with Brazil, which is relatively protectionist, while we run deficits with Canada and Mexico, which are almost totally open to U.S. exports thanks to the North American Free Trade Agreement.

What about the argument that trade deficits mean the United States is losing jobs to cheap labor overseas? Dan Griswold reminds us that, in the prosperous 1990s, the U.S. trade deficit practically tripled. Industrial production and manufacturing output, meanwhile, dramatically increased. The lesson, he writes, is that:

> Trade deficits do not cost jobs. In fact rising trade deficits correlate with falling unemployment rates. Far from being a drag on economic growth, the U.S. economy has actually grown faster in years in which the trade deficit has been rising than in years in which the deficit has shrunk. Trade deficits may even be good news for the economy because they signal global investor confidence in the United States and rising purchasing power among domestic consumers.

The very idea of a trade deficit is the invention of theoreticians. It is meaningless.

What the Trade Deficit Doesn't Measure

For all the public angst over the trade deficit, most people have a hazy idea of what this number actually measures. Trade deficit numbers are reported in balance of payments data released by the Department of Commerce. The statistic is included within a category called the "current account," which measures international trade in goods, services, investment income, and unilateral transfers such as foreign aid and remittances.

The problem with focusing on the current account is that it is only a partial indicator of U.S. overseas economic activity. It doesn't measure, for example, when a U.S. company sets up an office in another country to manufacture products there.

The trade deficit doesn't capture the *flow of capital*—that is, what Americans are investing in other countries or, conversely, foreign investment in the United States. "Capital flows," analyst Marc Chandler points out, "are larger and more important than trade." To ignore them, he tells us, misses the bigger picture: "America is richer, better, and stronger than it was before the late 1970s and early 1980s when it began recording a sustained current account deficit and became a debtor nation again." He concludes, "The current account shows the value of goods and services that cross national borders. It doesn't show anything else."

Remember Adam Smith. There can be no "deficit" in a trade because it is a reciprocal exchange. The United States isn't just buying from companies or individuals outside its borders. Like those who purchased a hamburger at McDonald's, they are getting something in return.

What America gets in return for its overseas purchases and investment is measured by two largely overlooked balance of payments indicators that measure the flow of capital into the United States: the capital account and the financial account.

University of Michigan business professor and American Enterprise Institute scholar Mark Perry notes that U.S. cash outflows for imports, income payments, foreign asset purchases, and unilateral transfers are offset by cash inflows from exports, income receipts, and asset sales. He explains that, in 2012, for instance:

> There was a $3.4 trillion cash outflow from the US as American consumers, businesses and governments purchased goods, services and assets from abroad, and as US businesses and governments made income payments to foreigners (e.g. dividends and interest) for investments they previously made in the US, and there was a $3.4 trillion cash inflow to the US as foreigners purchased American goods, services and assets, and as foreign businesses and governments made income payments to Americans for assets owned abroad. . . . Once we account for all international transactions that took place last year, the cash inflows from abroad of $3.4 trillion paid to Americans exactly equaled the $3.4 trillion in cash outflows paid by Americans to foreign recipients.

The Cato Institute's Dan Griswold makes a similar point. Not only is America's trade deficit balanced by a foreign investment surplus—the foreign money flowing into the country also "keeps long-term interest rates down, prevents the crowding out of private investment by government borrowing, and promotes job creation through direct investment in U.S. factories and businesses."

Those American dollars flowing overseas, therefore, are doing anything but creating imbalances. They are being used to facilitate commerce across borders—transactions between people who create wealth both overseas as well as in the United States. America benefits from goods and services Americans buy from people in other countries. Foreigners, in turn, benefit from U.S. dollars, which help grow their economies—and which they plow back into the United States by investing in its businesses, stocks, bonds, and real estate.

Who's Really Doing Currency Manipulation—and Why It Doesn't Work

Too few politicians of any ideological persuasion fully get it on trade. Shortly after taking office, President Obama made it clear that he shared Washington's preoccupation with imbalances and deficits. Backed by 130 members of Congress, the president called upon China to revalue its currency to "a more market-oriented exchange rate." (Translation: raise the value of the yuan so that Chinese imports would cost more, making U.S. exports more competitive.) There was much talk at that time that if China did not comply, the United States would respond by imposing tariffs on Chinese products. But the U.S. government never followed through. That was probably because the charges of currency manipulation were false.

The numbers tell the story: Between 1995 and 2005 China's exports to the United States increased *sixfold*. Yet the dollar/yuan exchange rate did not change.

During most of that time, the yuan was pegged to the dollar. Since 2005 it has been pegged to a basket of currencies. The yuan's value relative to the dollar increased 21% between 2005 and 2008. Chinese exports to the United States indeed cost more. Despite this, Chinese imports continued to grow vigorously for the simple reason that Americans wanted to buy them.

The heated accusations about currency manipulation totally miss the point. Trade is ultimately about the needs of people, not exchange rates. If any nation manipulates currency, it is the United States. As noted, since the early 2000s both the Bush and Obama administrations have deliberately weakened the dollar to spur exports. (As we noted, former Fed chairman Ben Bernanke, a strong believer in a weak dollar trade policy, was a Bush appointee before he was tapped by Obama for another term.)

The Reagan administration constantly fought with Japan and Germany over the strength of the yen and the deutschmark. So did every other administration since Dwight Eisenhower. For all the fireworks, Johns Hopkins economist Steve Hanke notes that these United States–initiated feuds have historically failed to have much effect on the supposed trade problem.

For example, the United States for decades has pressed Japan to strengthen the yen. The value of the dollar compared with the yen slid from 360 yen per dollar in the 1970s to as low as about 80 yen to the dollar in 2012. This depreciation, however, has accomplished little. The United States still continues to run trade deficits with the Japanese. Nor did a strong yen end the problem of competition from cheap Asian exports. All it did was weaken Japan, opening up the door to other Asian nations, such as Korea and Taiwan.

The indignation over currency manipulation may make for good headlines, but the charges are more bluster than fact. The bottom line: currency wars over fake issues like trade deficits are to no one's advantage. If the U.S. government really wants the Chinese to act with more fairness, it should get them to reduce trade barriers. What about China forcing U.S. companies to reveal trade secrets in exchange for trading relationships? Or Chinese partners stealing from American companies? Those are the real issues.

The Obama administration's focus on the yuan/dollar relationship is a waste of time. As we saw with Japan and the yen, revaluing one's currency ultimately fails. Once producers, importers, and exporters recover from the shock, they recalibrate prices to reflect real-world values. One ends up with the same trade imbalances. Meanwhile trading relationships suffer and growth and incomes decline—the inevitable consequence of a needlessly weakened dollar.

Could the Euro or Another Currency Replace the Dollar?

Given the uncertainties of U.S. monetary and fiscal policies, and the equally uncertain world monetary environment, some have raised the question: Could the euro eventually rise up to replace the dollar as the world's leading currency? Despite all the recent controversy over the euro, it's a question worth asking. After all, the euro has become the second-most-traded reserve currency after the dollar. It was created, in part, as an alternative to the dollar on the global markets. Unlike the paper gold the Chinese have proposed to replace the dollar, the euro has a track record and is real money. Why couldn't it supplant the dollar?

Before answering, a little history. The euro was launched in 1999. Its spiritual father was Canadian Nobel Prize–winning economist Robert Mundell, who believed that a single, shared currency would promote trade within the European community and increase investment by facilitating the flow of capital. He also felt that a major currency that was a potential rival to the dollar would force the United States to embrace monetary stability and a sound dollar.

From the beginning, critics have distrusted the euro. Many doubted that European nations with different political traditions and cultures could successfully share a single currency. The misunderstanding intensified in the last several years when overextended nations including Greece, Cyprus, Italy, and Portugal teetered on the brink of insolvency. Several countries have had to be bailed out by the International Monetary Fund, the European Central Bank, and the European Union. These events have been mistakenly reported as a "euro crisis." But the euro is anything but the cause.

The turmoil in Europe is the result not of the euro, but of bad economic policy that combines excessive taxation, overspending, and stifling regulation. Imagine if the overextended states of Illinois and California were to default on their bonds. Would that mean that they would leave the U.S. dollar zone and adopt new currencies? The sovereign debt crisis is no more a euro crisis than the recent fiscal meltdowns of some states in the United States are a dollar crisis. Greece, Cyprus, Italy, and Portugal have had fiscal problems for many of the same reasons that states such as Wisconsin and New Jersey have nearly had a meltdown: their taxes have been too high, their government bureaucracies too large, and their public employee salaries and pensions unsustainable.

Critics also say that Europe shouldn't rely on a single currency because countries have different fiscal policies. They believe that, without a central political authority to impose uniformity, these differences will undermine the euro. The debt woes of Greece, Portugal, Spain, and Ireland should in no way threaten the existence of the euro, however, any more than Illinois's or California's profligate ways should threaten the dollar's existence.

Forbes.com contributor Louis Woodhill got it right when he wrote that a European "'fiscal union' is no more necessary for the long-term survival of the euro than it is for the long-term survival of the metric system. 'The euro' is a unit of measure, like 'the meter.' It is the unit of market value used within the euro zone."

What about predictions that Greece will eventually seek to solve its problems by abandoning the euro or that the euro itself will collapse? Woodhill rightfully calls such suggestions "insane." Remember that for money to work, people must have faith in it as a reliable unit of measurement based on marketplace experience. Greece would never abandon the euro, Woodhill tells us, because its own currency would be so much worse:

> The mere *threat* of a return to the drachma would precipitate bank runs and the collapse of all Greek banks. No one—and definitely not suppliers of imports— would be willing to hold the drachma, which would be a currency that was *designed* to be devalued. A "drachmaized" Greek economy would simply disintegrate.

People have also assailed the euro for the same reason they are afraid of gold: because it makes it more difficult for nations to devalue their currencies. Do you think that Greece or any nation can solve its economic problems through devaluations that destroy the wealth of its citizens?

In reality, any euro crisis is a central banking crisis. The system could have worked just fine had the European Central Bank pegged the euro to maintain a constant value. Instead the misguided policies of the region's Eurocrats have allowed it to become another roller-coaster fiat currency like the dollar.

For all its problems, there is a real need for the euro, which is why most nations in the European Union, with the notable exception of Great Britain, have now adopted it. And in many ways it has succeeded. Former *Wall Street Journal* top editor George Melloan reminds us that the euro has made transactions in Europe's close-knit nations many times easier. Two decades ago, he writes, if you needed to make a quick trip to a neighboring country:

You had to exchange your Belgian francs for French francs, German marks, or Dutch guilders, paying a commission to a money changer. Exchange rates were in constant flux, which meant that traders had to hedge exchange risks at a cost that also was passed on to consumers. And competition across borders, which was the point of the Common Market from its infancy, was inhibited by the fact that there was no single standard of value.

Robert Mundell and other advocates of the euro hoped that the European currency would provide shelter from post–Bretton Woods volatility. Little did they realize that Europe would behave as badly as the United States.

Why the Dollar Will Remain the Leading Currency—for Now

We're more optimistic about the euro than some of its critics. But the European Union's currency—or for that matter, the Chinese yuan, also known as renminbi—are still light-years away from becoming the dollar's equal. No question that the dollar has suffered a loss of prestige, but it is still unlikely that it will lose its leadership position in the global marketplace. We say this because of the nature and meaning of money. History has shown that capital flows to countries with a stable currency. The United Kingdom became a financial power after the founding of the Bank of England in the seventeenth century spurred the development of capital markets and eventually led to the adoption of a gold standard.

The dollar became the currency of global business not as a result of the Bretton Woods conference, or of any conference. It is the world's foremost currency because it arose from the market, as real money always does. People around the world use dollars because the U.S. economy is the biggest in the world and its capital markets are the deepest, the most liquid, and the most innovative. If you're a government, a corporation, or a major investor, you wouldn't want to do business with Fiji dollars, Argentine pesos, Brazilian reales, or for that matter Russian rubles. You probably wouldn't even want the yuan. Those currencies offer far less opportunity to invest your money on a major scale.

The global business community still prefers the dollar because there is no better alternative. An estimated two-thirds of existing $100 bills reside outside the United States. Since the banking crisis, U.S. currency holdings outside the United States have not decreased; instead, they have dramatically increased. Before 2008, about 56% of U.S. currency resided outside the United States. After the financial crisis, that percentage actually rose to around 66% in 2012.

Many contracts today between non-U.S. parties are denominated in dollars.

Countries that do well, such as Switzerland, Singapore, and Hong Kong, have (by today's standards) generally sound money fixed to the dollar or to a basket of currencies.

For a variety of reasons, China's idea of an artificial reserve currency—even one called paper gold—is not likely to succeed in the global market. Remember our definition of money: it is a tool that arises from real-world transactions. Paper gold did not. Like the bitcoin, SDRs were artificially created. Pegged to a collection of fluctuating currencies, paper gold derives its worth not from real-world transactions, but from bureaucratic fiat.

Could a new monetary order emerge within the next decade, when some predict China will become the world's largest economy? Possibly, but China has problems: an overbearing government, widespread corruption, the lack of financial markets to fund small businesses, and a weak legal system.

The U.S. economy continues to be a magnet for foreign investment not only because of its size but also because of its business environment: historically, the United States has offered a pro-market climate based on reasonable taxation, the rule of law, and a court system that can be relied upon to enforce contracts and protect property rights. These things are taken for granted in the United States, but they are often not found even in many developed countries. Investors and entrepreneurs in America generally have not had to contend with the kinds of problems often encountered with capricious governments.

America's debt/GDP ratio has risen alarmingly. But, as we noted, it is worse in other developed countries, including, most notably, Japan.

The fear that the United States is destroying its traditional advantages with the federal government's high spending and regulatory onslaught is well founded. It is certainly true that the Federal Reserve and the U.S. Treasury Department have badly mismanaged the dollar. But the other major central banks have done no better. For now, the dollar wins by default.

There Would Be No Dilemma with a Stable Dollar

The Chinese and others are right to worry about the consequences of today's runaway U.S. debt and an ever-weakening dollar. The root of the problem, though, is that the United States and most other countries do not appreciate the importance of sound money—and what it takes to maintain it.

The doomsday scenarios that we mentioned earlier in this chapter could be avoided with a stable dollar. Dangerous as they may be, today's sky-high levels of government debt are not unprecedented. Great Britain, for example, had a huge debt after the War of Spanish Succession in the early 1700s: 260% of GDP. That nation also took on enormous debt during the subsequent Seven Years' War, and later, as a result of the 20-year war with Napoleon. Yet Great Britain was able to emerge in the nineteenth century as the greatest industrial power in the world because of its stable currency and capital markets. Both facilitated economic activity and produced a growing revenue stream for government that was not frittered away with reckless spending. In this way, Great Britain was able to grow its way out of a giant debt burden. In the century before World War I, its debt as a percentage of GDP went from 200% to 27%.

The Monetary Base: A Tool for Stability

The dollar may be more vulnerable today than it has been at any other time in recent history. But most of today's problems could be solved by a return to stable money. Even if, before a return to gold, the dollar were to come under attack in a currency war, it is possible to defend against the kind of assault that brought down the Thai baht and endangered other Asian currencies. The Russians showed this when they successfully defended the ruble in 2009. Unlike the Thais, they didn't buy currency on the foreign exchange market and then unload it back into their economy. They reduced the monetary base, in addition to raising interest rates.

If the Fed continues to taper and scale back on quantitative easing, the United States does not have to be on a collision course with hyperinflation. Respected Stanford University professor Ronald McKinnon proposes that the Fed taper by announcing a schedule of gradually increasing short-term interest rates. With rates higher than zero, banks would have more of an incentive to resume lending. In this way, the Fed could carefully funnel money back into the economy—with a watchful eye trained on commodity indicators to avoid releasing too much.

The problem would be most swiftly remedied, of course, if the dollar were relinked to gold. The United States demonstrated this during the early years of its existence: America's finances were in a state of disarray after the wild inflation resulting from massive money printing during the American Revolution. Then, thanks to the efforts of Alexander Hamilton, the young country reformed its finances. Along with raising revenue from tariffs and excise taxes, the government adopted a gold-based monetary system. Soon international capital from the Dutch and other investors started to flow into the young republic, fueling its historic growth.

We should also not forget that the United States had an even more staggering debt ratio than exists today after World War II: 122% of GDP. But at the same time the economy had stable money. By the end of the 1960s, debt as a proportion of GDP had fallen sharply to 34% of GDP.

Debt is not a death sentence, if you get the economy right and if you understand money.

THE NUGGET

The only real deficit is not enough trade.

CHAPTER 4

Money Versus Wealth

Why Inflation Is Not a Good Thing

It isn't the gold we have that makes us rich. It's what
we make, our know-how, our productivity. So long as
this country produces more and better, the world will
continue to want what we make.

—MALCOLM FORBES

IN NOVEMBER 2013, JANET YELLEN, WHO WAS SOON TO
succeed Ben Bernanke as head of the Federal Reserve, tes-
tified at her Senate confirmation hearing about her views
of the economy, the role of central banks, and recent Fed policies, including the gargantuan monetary expansion known as
quantitative easing (QE). The job of chairman of the Fed, the
leading central bank, is probably the most powerful nonelected
government position in the world. Its actions have a major
impact on the lives not only of Americans but also of people
throughout the world.

The media covered the hearing with only tepid interest, as
though Yellen were just another midlevel bureaucrat. The real
focus that week was the disastrous rollout of President Obama's
Affordable Care Act (popularly known as Obamacare). For

weeks, controversy had raged over what had gone wrong with the government's new health insurance initiative and what was needed to fix it. Even media long supportive of Obama were proclaiming that the program wasn't working.

Little such media indignation, however, was directed at another government failure mentioned at the Yellen hearing, one with implications more far-reaching than Obamacare: the inability of the Fed's historic monetary stimulus, quantitative easing, to restore the economy.

This massive injection of liquidity, *the largest monetary expansion ever*, was a disaster more momentous than the launch of Healthcare.gov. Five years and three rounds of quantitative easing had produced miserably feeble GDP growth of just under 2%, about half the level of a decade earlier. The biggest monetary stimulus ever had produced the weakest recovery from a major downturn in American history.

Combined with the zero interest rates of the past several years, quantitative easing should have delivered a charge to the economy sufficient to revive Keynes himself. Since QE started in late 2008, the Federal Reserve had increased its balance sheet from $900 billion to $3.7 trillion in 2013. Around the time of Yellen's confirmation hearing, required bank reserves had already reached $124 billion. Excess reserves—the money above and beyond the required reserves that banks are allowed to lend—were a staggering $2 trillion and rising, many times the normal level.

The problem was that QE also involved the arcane strategy of suppressing interest rates known as Operation Twist. As mentioned, the Fed normally lowers—or raises—short-term interest rates. But under Operation Twist, it was buying bonds to suppress long-term rates as well. The real "twist" was that instead of stimulating job creation, Operation Twist was doing the opposite. It was directing credit to certain sectors of the economy—the federal government, large corporations, and the housing sector—away from the small businesses that have traditionally been the economy's job creators. Because of post–financial crisis legislation, the Fed was also paying banks to hold on to their excess reserves.

In other words, QE was working against a recovery. Job creation was at its worst level since the 1930s.

Yet because the media and policy makers are uncomfortable with the subject of monetary policy, there was little of the robust questioning and debate about QE that swirled around the Affordable Care Act. There have been no headlines like "Federal Reserve Stimulus Disaster" or "QE Rollout a Miserable Failure."

Monetary Obesity Is Not Healthy

We need food to live. But too much food leads to unhealthy obesity. The same applies to money. We need money for commerce. But just as too much food can be bad for your health, an oversupply of money can undermine the health of an economy.

If expanding the monetary base was the way to economic vitality, Zimbabwe would be the richest country in the world. When that country first became independent in 1980, the Zimbabwe dollar was worth more than the U.S. dollar. In the early 2000s, after redistributionist reforms led to the destruction of the country's agricultural economy, the Zimbabwe government responded to the crisis with a manic printing of money. The result was a hyperinflation second only to that of Hungary after World War II. By 2011, Zimbabwe was printing 100-trillion-dollar bills that became a hot novelty item among collectors. Eventually it had to abandon its currency and start over.

The story of monetary expansion is not a story of wealth creation but rather of wealth destruction. History contains countless examples: from the eighteenth-century French de-bacle of the Mississippi Bubble, described later in this chapter, to the wild colonial inflations preceding the American Revolu-tion to the German hyperinflations of the early 1920s and af-ter World War II to the 1970s U.S. stagflation. Over the past decade, reckless monetary expansion has rocked countries like Venezuela and Argentina. In the United States, it led to the col-lapse of the housing market, the 2008 financial crisis, and sub-sequent global stagnation.

Keynesians and monetarists are on the wrong side of his-tory. Increasing the supply of money cannot create prosperity because that is not how wealth is created. Wealth and growth come from *innovation*. Henry Ford's mass production of the au-tomobile, for instance, transformed society by creating jobs in entirely new industries, from fast food to auto repair and even to home building. (Car ownership made the suburbs possible.)

Over the last several decades, we've seen this kind of job creation as a result of the personal computer. Twenty years ago, there were no jobs in "social media" or in designing Internet sites, or in retail stores devoted to selling things like iPads.

Keynesians, however, are convinced that monetary expan-sion spurs economic activity and employment. There may be a growth spurt. But much of the activity, like the feverish home buying and mortgage lending that took place as a result of the cheap dollar in the early 2000s, is artificial. And as we saw with the housing market, it ultimately collapses.

Excess liquidity also slows growth by distorting credit mar-kets and impeding capital creation. Expanding the money sup-ply encourages the misallocation of resources.

When governments destroy the value of money, one can no longer trust prices. People make bad decisions. Like misguided hikers who have been given a bad map or a corrupted GPS de-vice, the economy can end up wandering in circles, stagnating like Spain in the Middle Ages or the United States in the 1970s. Or, as in Weimar Germany or Zimbabwe, the economy can go over a cliff.

Why Hasn't There Been More Inflation?

Keynesians and monetarists largely dismiss today's fears of the inflationary effects of QE and the weakening dollar. Economist Paul Krugman, with his usual note of negativity, accuses advocates of stable money of "inflation hysteria." In her Senate testimony, Janet Yellen deflected concerns with bureaucrat-speak, insisting that "at this stage, I don't see risks to financial stability" from current Fed policies. It is true that despite the immense injection from QE, the United States has yet to see severe, across-the-board rises in the cost of living. According to the Consumer Price Index, the rate of increase in 2013 got as low as 1.1%.

CPI numbers, however, don't reflect the price rises people have been experiencing. Meat prices are the highest they have been in about a decade. Gas prices have come down from their very highest highs, but the price of a gallon of gas is about double what it was less than 10 years ago. Consumers are also seeing plenty of price hikes in other places. Financial analyst Michael Sivy wrote in *Time* magazine that he was shocked to discover the price of ink cartridges for his printer increased by 25% in less than one year.

He and others believe that prices are rising faster than government statistics indicate because of changes in methodology that have caused the Consumer Price Index to understate the rate of inflation. CPI metrics change so frequently that measurement methods, in the words of investor and financial commentator Peter Schiff, bear "scant resemblance" to what they were just a few decades ago.

Schiff created a market basket of essential goods needed for daily living—such as eggs, milk, gasoline, and bread—and compared their price changes to CPI statistics for the same period. Between 2002 and 2012, the CPI reported a total of 27.5% inflation. But the prices of goods in Schiff's market basket increased more than 44%.

What would inflation be today if CPI statisticians were using the old metrics? John Williams, economist and founder of American Business Analytics & Research, features charts using CPI methods of the 1970s and 1980s on his website Shadow Stats.com. He comes up with an annual inflation rate that ranges from as low as 5% to as high as 10%.

Prices rise and fall, as we've noted, for any number of reasons—from changes in supply and demand to increases in productivity. To what extent do the recent price increases have to do with the weakening of the dollar? The best place to look for the answer is gold prices. Gold is the purest indicator of the dollar's value because the supply and demand of the precious metal do not vary dramatically from one year to the next. Gold is not vulnerable to weather like agricultural commodities or to sudden surges in supply or demand that affect oil and gas prices.

Gold prices, as we all know, have increased to stunning levels in the past several years. They have come down some, but in early 2014 the price of gold was three times what it was in 2003; it took 200% more dollars to buy gold than it did a decade ago. In other words, our money is worth much less.

Commodities have also risen sharply. The Thomson Reuters Continuous Commodity Index (CCI) measures six categories of commodities, including energy, grains, meats, and precious metals. From December 2008 to November 2013, the CCI increased from around 370 to 506, an increase of nearly 37%.

On Forbes.com investment advisor Richard Finger voiced the widespread concern about the economy's inflationary direction: "Nobody knows the ultimate denouement of money printing on this scale. Germany tried 'abnormal' money printing in the early 1920's after WW I and the result was hyperinflation, the collapse of the German economy, and the rise of Hitler."

What will happen as the Fed continues to pile more money on top of hyperinflation-level bank reserves? The answer is that we're in uncharted territory. Forecasting disastrous inflation may be the equivalent of refighting the last war—an analysis too closely based on events of the past. Indeed, something different may be happening: a historic decline into a corrosive environment of stagnant growth. Instead of a deadly pneumonia, we may be experiencing a chronic disease that saps away America's traditional vitality. Either prospect is destructive and underscores the need for a stable dollar.

The Danger of a Little Inflation

Right now the Fed is scaling back the amount of bonds it buys each month and hinting at future interest rate increases. Nonetheless the monetary base remains enormous by historic standards. Keynesians, including IMF officials, central bankers, and finance ministers, have of late been beating the drums for "a little more inflation." In an eyebrow-raising article titled "In Fed and Out, Many Now Think Inflation Helps," Binyamin Appelbaum in the *New York Times* suggested in the fall of 2013 that the Fed under Janet Yellen would expand the monetary base enough to spur price increases. According to the *Times*, Yellen believes:

> A little inflation is particularly valuable when the economy is weak. Rising prices help companies increase profits; rising wages help borrowers repay debts. Inflation

also encourages people and businesses to borrow money
and spend it more quickly.

The story quoted a Harvard economist who proposed expanding the monetary base to achieve an inflation rate of around
6%. He made this astonishing statement: "A sustained burst of
moderate inflation is not something to worry about. *It should be
embraced* [our emphasis]."

Proponents of QE make a distinction between severe inflation, which they see as unlikely, and moderate inflation, which
they think can be a good thing. The notion that there can be
harmless inflation is a toxic fallacy. The real estate bubble of
the early 2000s that brought on the 2008 stock market panic resulted from the weakening of the dollar that took place in the
early and mid-2000s before quantitative easing.

Whether the rate is 2% or 12%, inflation fundamentally
distorts market behavior because it impairs the critical signals provided by the price system. People who see prices going
up rapidly will start buying on the mistaken assumption of increased demand. Or else, sensing trouble, they'll seek to shelter
their money. Either way, events can easily spiral out of control.

In the words of noted historian Amity Shlaes: "The thing
about inflation is that it comes out of nowhere and hits you."
She gives the example of 1972, when "all appeared calm . . .
before inflation jumped to 11% by 1974, and stayed high for
the rest of the decade." Inflation similarly shot up, almost overnight, after both world wars.

Germany suspended its gold standard and started running
the printing press in 1914 at the start of World War I. But it
took six years for a real hyperinflation to get started. Inflation
was moderate at first. The dollar and gold price of the mark
improved sharply in 1920–1921. Shlaes tells us, "Many financial analysts thought the Weimar authorities weren't producing

enough money." A *New York Times* headline at the time declared: "Tight Money in German Market: Causes of the Abnormally Rapid Currency Deflation at Year-End." In actuality, Shlaes writes:

> The Germans didn't know it, but they had already turned their money into wallpaper; the next year would see hyperinflation, when inflation raced ahead at more than 50% a month. It moved so fast that prices changed in a single hour. Yet even as it did so, the country's financial authorities failed to see inflation. They thought they were witnessing increased demand for money.

Prices, however, continued rising. Finally, Germans lost faith. The mark began to collapse. "Disillusionment," warns Shlaes, "can come as fast as a gust."

The Absurdity of the Phillips Curve

Policy makers insist on stoking inflation because of their rigid belief in the Phillips curve, the unscientific and unproven theory that price increases are the way to the Holy Grail of full employment.

Back in the 1950s, William Phillips, a New Zealand economist, helped promote this idea with a graph that became known as the Phillips curve. It showed the supposed correlation between inflation and unemployment. According to Phillips and his fellow Keynesians, vigorous growth corresponded to price increases, while lower inflation correlated with higher jobless levels. In other words, there was a trade-off between inflation and employment. Stable money, they concluded, is bad for the economy.

Advocates of this preposterous theory maintain that raising or lowering inflation is like adjusting the climate controls on a thermostat. Just as you'd use your climate control keypad to raise or lower the temperature in your living room, loosening or tightening up on the money supply, they believe, can increase or decrease the level of employment.

Seven Nobel Prizes have been awarded to economists whose work disproved the Phillips curve: F. A. Hayek, Milton Friedman, Robert Lucas, Robert Mundell, Finn Kydland, Edward Prescott, Edmund Phelps, Thomas Sargent, and Christopher Sims. Yet Keynesian policy makers and pundits cling to this idea, despite the Fed's $4 trillion balance sheet expansion that has left labor participation rates at a 35-year low.

Economic historian Brian Domitrovic pointed out on Forbes.com that "inflation and unemployment regularly move in tandem." They don't move the way Keynesians would have you believe. In the inflationary boom/bust era of the 1970s and early 1980s, unemployment reached higher levels than during the financial crisis. The very opposite was the case in the 1980s. After Ronald Reagan cut taxes and stabilized the dollar, in Domitrovic's words, "inflation and unemployment both rappelled down a cliff."

The United States has had what could be characterized as "full employment"—jobless rates of under 5%—during eras of stable or relatively stable money. Two dramatic examples are most of the 1920s and 1960s.

Cheapening the value of money is not the way to create real, sustainable employment. Jobs are created in a healthy economy when entrepreneurs start companies like Starbucks or Staples that succeed in the marketplace. They get capital to expand and hire more people.

This is not what takes place in an inflationary economy. There may be some job creation—Germany had low unemployment during its hyperinflation of the 1920s—but the burst of activity is the result of false market signals and misdirected resources that come from government's distortion of money. It is ultimately artificial and unsustainable. Very little new wealth ends up being created, and sooner or later much more is destroyed.

Former congressman Ron Paul sums it up: "If governments or central banks really can create wealth simply by creating money, why does poverty exist anywhere on earth?"

Stimulus or Redistribution?

The Appelbaum *New York Times* article about the advantages of inflation draws a different picture. The paper reported that plenty of people on Main Street as well as in Corporate America would actually *welcome* inflation. In fact, the reporter suggested, they could barely wait for it to get started:

> The school board in Anchorage, Alaska, for example, is counting on inflation to keep a lid on teachers' wages. Retailers including Costco and Walmart are hoping for higher inflation to increase profits. The federal government expects inflation to ease the burden of its debts.

It is true that some people benefit, at least at first, from inflation's burst of activity. But, as we've pointed out, very little new wealth is being created. It is simply being transferred from one group in the economy to another.

Murray Rothbard, noted economic historian, made the point that inflation favors "firstcomers," those who are the earliest recipients of the new money. They include not just retailers like Walmart and Costco, singled out by the *New York Times*, but also countless others who benefit when people start spending the government's newly created money. The losers are "late-comers" who are slower to receive the inflationary money. They generally belong to fixed-income groups such as retirees and people on salaries.

Forbes.com contributor Richard Finger puts it bluntly. The Fed's low-interest-rate, easy money policies, he says, "punish the virtuous, the millions of responsible savers. . . . They can no longer count on decent risk-free returns for retirement."

Bill Taren, a Florida retiree, found that his retirement account at his credit union paid a measly 0.4% interest. Meanwhile inflation was averaging 2.8% in 2012. Horrified by his dwindling savings, he and his wife decided to stuff their money under their mattress. He explained that at least that way "we can see the cash when we want."

Debtors Win, Creditors Lose

The seventeenth-century philosopher John Locke was among the first to observe that inflation rewards debtors who are able to pay what they owe with less valuable money, while stiffing creditors who get paid back in less valuable currency. In his words:

> Whether the creditor be forced to receive less, or the debtor be forced to pay more than his contract, the damage and injury is the same, whenever a man is defrauded of his due; and whether this will not be a public failure of justice thus arbitrarily to give one man's right and possession to another, without any fault on the suffering man's side, and without any the least advantage to the public, I shall leave to be considered.

Government, of course, is the biggest debtor of all. By diluting the value of your money, it gets extra money to spend—or to pay its debts. As Keynes famously acknowledged, inflation is a stealth tax whereby "government can confiscate, secretly and unobserved, an important part of the wealth of their citizens."

Uncle Sam also gets to pay back bondholders, such as China and others that have bought U.S. Treasuries, in cheaper dollars. This is especially true with QE, thanks to record low interest rates under Operation Twist that are saving Washington hundreds of billions of dollars, which it would otherwise have had to pay to bondholders.

Richard Finger calculates that if the U.S. government paid normal historical rates of interest on its $17 trillion national debt instead of the Fed's current rock-bottom rates, it would be facing, he calculates, an additional $500 billion interest expense.

In other words, lower interest rates as a result of QE mean a *$500 billion windfall* for Washington—money that makes it easier for politicians to keep spending. For example, $500 billion is nearly enough to cover benefits paid to participants from all of Medicare, which amounted to $536 billion in 2012. And it is many times the amount the administration needs to keep expanding the food stamp program, which now costs around $80 billion a year.

Manias, Bubbles, and Distortions

Weakening a currency may produce activity that looks like wealth creation. But real wealth creation, as we've noted, comes from meeting genuine needs of the marketplace—inventing new technologies like the iPad or the flat-screen TV that improve productivity and raise standards of living. Activity that results from monetary policies intended to stimulate an economy, on the other hand, is a response to artificial price signals and is usually misdirected.

In the inflationary 1970s, for example, higher prices fostered the mistaken perception that developed nations were running out of energy. The price of oil went from $3 a barrel to almost $40. Capital flooded oil production. The number of workers in the energy industry soared. The same thing happened in the last decade. Since 2008, the number of employees in the oil and gas industry has increased by over 30%. This was only partly due to the surge in exploration accompanying the growth of hydraulic fracturing technology ("fracking"). It was also on account of the herd or bubble mentality created by inflation.

There are two kinds of bubbles. The first takes place naturally in a free economy when people jump on a promising technology, like the PC boom in the early 1980s or auto manufacturing in the early twentieth century (or, for those who remember the 1950s, the hula hoop craze). People start new businesses in a promising sector until it gets too crowded, and some of them fail. They can set the stage for later success, like Apple's failure with its Newton handheld device, which paved the way for smartphones and other mobile devices. Forbes publisher Rich Karlgaard calls such ventures "noble flops."

The second kind of bubble is created when people respond to inflationary price signals. Money tends to flow into protective investments instead of into entrepreneurial job-creating ventures. How does buying a bar of gold translate into production and economic growth?

During the German hyperinflation of the 1920s, Germany's panicked citizenry bought every hard asset they could get their hands on, including diamonds, works of art, and real estate. Adam Fergusson noted in his classic chronicle of the era, *When Money Dies*, that families bought pianos even if they didn't play them. The act of buying was a form of speculation. People were rushing to put their money in possessions with value, because they didn't know what their money would be worth the next day.

Inflation also misdirects money in other ways—for instance, by sending it into nonproductive investments like tax shelters. They were a way of life during the 1970s, when inflation kept pushing people into higher tax brackets. Seeking to avoid "bracket creep," tax filers invested in everything from producing azaleas and almonds to mink and trout farms. Markets were distorted by activity that took place solely for the purpose of tax avoidance. Movie production soared, as did the amount of vacant office space. Tax shelter madness also helped fuel the collapse of the savings and loans in the 1980s.

Most tax shelters were eliminated with Ronald Reagan's tax reform of 1986. In the low-tax, low-inflation years that followed, there was little need for them. Just a warning: if the Fed attempts to engineer a little inflation, mink farming and other tax schemes may soon make a comeback.

The Subprime Mortgage Meltdown: The Twenty-First Century Mississippi Bubble

Though widely blamed by politicians and the media on predatory lending, the subprime mortgage disaster of 2008 that started the worldwide financial crisis was the twenty-first century's answer to the eighteenth-century inflationary debacle known as the Mississippi Bubble—the result of a loose money scheme engineered by the Scottish mathematician John Law.

The extremely colorful Law was the author of a tract titled *Money and Trade Considered, with a Proposal for Supplying the Nation with Money*. It made the Keynesian-style argument that increasing the supply of money would boost trade, employment, and production. After serving time in prison for killing a romantic rival in a duel, he escaped to France. Using his aristocratic connections, he managed to convince the French government that his expansionary scheme was the answer to the crushing debts left over from the reign of Louis

XIV. Law was appointed to the powerful position of controller-general of finances, where he got his chance to put his loose money theory into practice.

Law consolidated France's trading companies into a monster monopoly known as the Mississippi Company. Owning a vast swath of what today is the central United States, the public-private company sold shares to investors throughout Europe. A mania for New World real estate ensued. Law had also created a virtual central bank that pumped immense amounts of liquidity into the French economy. France's total money supply exploded. Inevitably, investors lost faith in Law's overhyped New World scheme. Combined with a roaring inflation, the bubble burst, devastating creditors throughout Europe and nearly bankrupting France. Law was forced to flee the country.

The subprime mortgage meltdown of 2008 contains more than a few echoes of the Mississippi Bubble. As with John Law's French debacle, the crisis was the result of excessive amounts of liquidity created by a central bank, the Federal Reserve, that ended up fueling giant government-created enterprises. Here the culprits were Fannie Mae and Freddie Mac, the mortgage companies originally created and later spun off by the U.S. government.

Responding to political pressures for affordable housing that intensified under the Clinton administration in the 1990s, Fannie Mae and Freddie Mac set out to make housing loans more available. They did this through the securitization of mortgages—the risk-spreading practice of buying and bundling mortgages and selling them to investors as mortgage-backed securities.

As the push for affordable housing accelerated, Fannie Mae and Freddie Mac were bundling increasingly risky subprime mortgages. In the early 2000s, the loose money policies of the Bush administration poured gasoline on a fire that had already started to burn. In an attempt to stimulate the economy after 9/11, the Fed, in a series of steps, lowered the federal funds rate to 1%, and the banks loosened their lending standards.

Between 2000 and 2003 the monetary base grew at levels equivalent to the inflationary 1970s. The dollar price of gold moved upward. The size of the subprime mortgage market grew 200%.

Inflation's herd instinct took hold among buyers and sellers. No longer were home buyers asked for the traditional 20% down before buying a house. "Stated income loans" became common. They were also known as "no-doc" or "liar loans" because borrowers could give just about any income figure and it was rarely checked. Little wonder just about everyone wanted to get in on the action. A homeless man in Saint Petersburg, Florida, managed to buy five houses. Speculators rushed into the market. The weak dollar corrupted pricing information, leading people to believe that housing prices and demand could only go up. If that homeless investor defaulted? No big deal. The houses would be worth more than his mortgages.

The bubble started to deflate when the Fed started to raise interest rates, which reached 5.25% in June 2006. Hundreds of thousands of foreclosures shook major financial institutions that were the holders of this debt, setting off a chain of events that led to the collapse or forced sale of major Wall Street houses and commercial banks.

Making matters worse was the recent reestablishment of the accounting regulation known as *mark to market*, which forced banks to unnecessarily write down the value of their capital. Mark to market made banks holding subprime mortgages look even more troubled than they actually were, attracting the attention of short sellers who threw bank stocks into a death spiral. (When mark-to-market accounting was drastically changed starting in March 2009, the bear market promptly ended.)

The financial panic in the fall of 2008 nearly took down the U.S. financial system and pushed the global economy into the severest economic crisis since the Great Depression. Alex Pollack of the American Enterprise Institute points out that much of what was destroyed was artificial wealth created by inflation. "A lot of the . . . wealth," he explains, "was an illusion—an illusion created by the housing bubble." The collapse in housing prices brought inflated prices back down to reality. He concludes, "So in fact, the wealth didn't disappear: it was never really there in the first place."

John Law had to flee France in disgrace. In contrast, Federal Reserve chairmen Alan Greenspan and Ben Bernanke, whose easy money policies led to the housing bubble, made a great deal of money writing memoirs and giving speeches, and their institution at the heart of the debacle, the Federal Reserve, ended up with vast new powers unprecedented in American history.

Monetary Expansion and Income Inequality

In the storm of recriminations following the Panic of 2008, Occupy Wall Street held months of street protests in New York City and around the country decrying the pain caused by the crisis and assailing the financial sector for reaping seemingly disproportionate gains. The demonstrators were protesting free enterprise. But the Fed was the real culprit.

A little-appreciated reality of inflation, confirmed by a succession of studies, is that it increases income inequality. One Northwestern University researcher found a significant relationship between the expansion of the money supply and the amount of income inequality as measured by indicators of income inequality like the Gini coefficient.

While a weakening dollar hurts people on fixed incomes, monetary expansion delivers windfalls to certain sectors of the

economy, like the financial industry, among the first to benefit from the Fed's bond buying. In September 2012, when Ben
Bernanke announced that the Fed would buy around $40 bil-
lion in mortgage-backed securities per month for the next three
years, Wall Street was ecstatic. Markets closed at their highest
level since 2007.

Not everyone was as enthusiastic. The dollar, that barometer of investor jitters, took a hit: the price of gold jumped to
$1,772 an ounce, and the dollar's value fell in relation to other
currencies.

Anthony Randazzo, director of economic research at the
Reason Foundation, put it this way, "quantitative easing has
made it cheaper for the government to borrow, has artificially
propped up the housing market (making it take longer to recover), and has dramatically manipulated the distribution of
capital in financial markets. And the economy has not been in
recovery."

Windfalls for Authoritarians

Another largely overlooked consequence of the dollar's decline
has been massive wealth transfers to commodity-producing
nations often hostile to the United States. Remember, when
money is devalued, people invest in commodities and hard assets. Advocates of energy independence should be angered to
learn that, thanks to the weakening dollar, the oil-producing
countries of the Middle East, Venezuela, and Russia have reaped
gains in the hundreds of billions of dollars.

The giant windfalls are not due to America's increasing use
of foreign oil. Consumption has actually been decreasing because of fracking, which has opened up new domestic energy
sources. More money has continued to flow to oil-producing
nations because of the cheapening dollar—resources that could

have gone to job-creating investments, research into medical technologies, and cures for diseases.

Before the end of the Bretton Woods standard, from 1947 to 1967, the dollar price of a barrel of oil rose at an annual rate of less than 2%. After Richard Nixon freed the dollar to float, oil producers started sharply raising prices. On January 1, 1974, the Organization of Petroleum Exporting Countries (OPEC) raised the dollar price of a barrel of oil from $4.31 to $10.11.

Forbes contributors Ralph Benko and Charles Kadlec calculated in 2011 that if the United States were still on the Bretton Woods gold standard:

> A barrel of oil today would sell for less than $2.80 a barrel, and the price of gasoline would probably be around 30 cents a gallon. The increase in the price of oil in the past 45 years is not due to OPEC. It is due to a fall in the value of the dollar.

They quote Keynes: "Those to whom [debauching the currency] brings windfalls, beyond their deserts and even beyond their expectations and desires, become 'profiteers' who are the object of hatred of the bourgeoisie, whom inflationism has impoverished, not less than of the proletariat."

The Real Effect of Artificially Lowered Interest Rates

There's another reason that loose money policies fail as a stimulus. Governments and larger enterprises may be able to borrow more, but the smaller entrepreneurs who are the economy's foremost job creators often end up with less access to capital, because credit usually ends up being rationed.

The Fed's monetary policies were a critical reason for the credit drought that persisted for more than five years after the height of the financial crisis. Industrialist Lynn Tilton, CEO of Patriarch Partners, complained in 2013 to the *Wall Street Journal* that the reason "we haven't seen a sufficient number of startups" is that "there's not a lot of financing right now."

Congresswoman Cathy McMorris Rodgers and others say that the Fed's zero interest rates were the reason bank lending was so tepid for so long. "This seems counterintuitive," she acknowledged. However, "there's a strange logic to it":

> With the private sector engulfed in so much uncertainty . . . banks are reducing credit to businesses, while increasing their purchase of government debt. The banks take in low-cost funds from the Fed and then lend it back to the government at a higher rate. This produces a small profit that—when done on a large enough scale—can become quite lucrative, indeed.

The misallocation of credit was also encouraged by QE's Operation Twist strategy of pushing down longer-term rates by purchasing long-term Treasuries and mortgage-backed securities. For the first time not only short-term but also long-term rates were at near-zero levels.

Distinguished economist David Malpass, Stanford University economist John Taylor, and a growing number of others make the disturbing observation that these Fed purchases have badly skewed credit markets. QE's focus on buying longer-term bonds means that mainly large companies end up getting cheap credit. Also benefiting are those so-called government-sponsored mortgage enterprises Fannie Mae and Freddie Mac, the originators of mortgage-backed securities. As mentioned, the federal government also benefits from lower interest rates, which allow it to run up deficits at virtually no cost.

In the meantime, commercial banks get Fed-created excess reserves and earn interest on those deposits. Bond underwriters and traders benefit too. Everyone benefits except smaller businesses that mostly rely on credit, along with ordinary citizens who are savers and investors, who are being paid the lowest interest rates ever.

The credit rationing that is a result of this process inhibits the formation of new capital needed to finance the Apples and Googles of tomorrow. Stock markets may reach dramatic highs and lows, but in the end they produce lower returns for investors during periods of unstable money. There's lots of activity, but it amounts to much less than it would have in a system with a stable dollar.

Meanwhile, Average Net Worth Is Declining

The artificial windfalls created by loose money can create the *appearance* of prosperity. After all, aren't people getting rich? Many may appear to be, but society as a whole is getting poorer. The cheapening of money destroys the purchasing power of every dollar you earn. It reduces the value of assets owned by individuals and businesses. Today's dollar buys less than 20% of what it did in 1971. In 2014, it was worth just 17 cents in 1971 dollars.

Findings by the Pew Research Center attest to this decline in the dollar's purchasing power: the median net worth of households headed by Americans 35 and younger has plunged from $11,521 in 1984 to just $3,662 in 2009—an astonishing 68% decline in wealth.

Thanks to improvements in technology, we may have a higher standard of living today, but a middle-class family with two incomes can barely afford what a middle-class family with one income did in the late 1960s and early 1970s. Kadlec and Benko point out:

When the dollar was as good as gold, working people—
not just rich people—prospered. Between 1950 and
1968, real median incomes of males rose steadily,
climbing to $32,310 from $19,989 [in 2009 dollars].
That's an increase of 2.7% a year. But ever since 1968,
real incomes went flat. Incredible as it may seem, the
debasement of our dollar has taken away every penny of
nominal pay increase for 41 years, leaving the median
income in real terms in 2009 at $32,184, virtually the
same as it was in 1968.

The dollar's decline is not the only cause of this. Over the
past four decades, state governments as well as the U.S. federal
government have steadily piled on taxes. Federal payroll taxes
have soared. Couples have found that their combined salaries
push them into higher tax brackets. States and municipalities
have boosted property and sales taxes. A number of states have
imposed income taxes since the 1960s. By one count, Uncle
Sam imposes more than 50 taxes on Americans. Little wonder
that it takes two incomes to do what one could have done 40
years ago.

Loose Money Addiction: Cautionary Tales

When talking about the perils of weak money, advocates of
stable money frequently use the addiction analogy. Because it
enables government borrowing and spending, it's easy for politicians to become dependent on artificial liquidity. As with all
addictions, however, there are consequences, and ultimately a
price to pay. Monetary expansion can be hard to stop. Politicians don't like to face the political costs of clamping down on
inflation, especially when its false prosperity comes to an end.

In the early 1980s, the Fed under Paul Volcker swiftly boosted interest rates to draconian levels to end inflation. Texas's oil-based economy slid into depression. Big oil companies had to merge to stay alive; numerous wildcatters went under. Other parts of the country dependent on agriculture experienced a similar upheaval. Anger at the Reagan administration turned Iowa from red to blue.

The cure for inflation can be bitter medicine, but the alternative is long-term malaise and decline. More than a century ago, Argentina was the eighth-largest economy in the world, a vibrant frontier nation much like the United States. But the Argentine government in the twentieth century resorted to manic money printing to finance its welfare state. In recent decades, Argentina has endured a succession of currency crises with hyperinflation that has reached as high as 5,000%. It's hard to know definitively what the inflation rate is today because the administration of Cristina Fernández de Kirchner in Argentina has long been suspected of faking the numbers. The government actually tried—and failed—to make it a crime for anyone outside the administration to publish an inflation figure that contradicts its own statistics. Private sources put the annual rate at about 25%, more than double the government's numbers.

Argentina's devaluations and flagrant dishonesty have all but destroyed public confidence in the Argentine peso. These days people literally go into the street to exchange pesos for dollars in black markets. The real-world value of the peso is said to be anywhere from 35 to 50% lower than the official exchange rate. The Kirchner government, however, has refused to stop trashing the nation's money, which would necessitate an end to manic spending. Its "solution" has been imposing capital controls in a desperate attempt to halt the flow of hard currency out of the country.

Without a reliable currency, meaningful investment in Argentina has become virtually impossible. Devaluations also mean exports that bring in less revenue and a slowing economy. In the fall of 2013, the nation's economy had stalled and was teetering on the brink of yet another major crisis.

The story is much the same in socialist Venezuela. The country has suffered 10 major devaluations since the early 1980s. Under the late president Hugo Chavez, the bolívar was devalued 992%. This ocean of easy money has only managed to meet the short-term needs of the country's voracious government. Ultimately, it is never enough.

Decades of cheapening money have devastated Venezuela's economy and impoverished its people. Venezuelans have all the cheap gas in the world, which costs about 12 cents a gallon. However, they can barely afford cars or anything else. The *Financial Times* reported in 2013:

> The currency is woefully misaligned . . . a burger at McDonald's [costs] $12, two pounds of chicken $13 and a Volkswagen Golf $45,000. Buying a car—even at those exorbitant prices—is very difficult. Shortages are common for many staples: rice, oil, flour, milk, medicines and toilet paper—and cars. Even would-be buyers with money in hand need to join long waiting lists.

Brazil, along with a number of other South American countries, made an attempt in 1999 to wean itself from easy money and maintain a stable currency through "inflation targeting." The effort enabled Brazil to strengthen its currency and achieve a 7.5% growth rate in 2010. But the government's inability to stop spending, along with the strengthening dollar, has recently caused the Brazilian real to weaken along with the economy. Growth slowed to 1% in 2012.

Easy money sooner or later means stagnation, and not just in South America. One sees the same phenomenon in nations flooded with excess liquidity as a consequence of the "resource curse." Loose money from an overabundance of natural riches translates into economic lassitude.

Saudi Arabia, for example, is a massive welfare state. The jobless rate is nearly 11%. Ninety percent of the employees in private companies are expatriates. The situation is so bad that the Saudi government now fines companies that have too many foreign employees. One of the characteristics of countries with easy wealth is that people are not motivated to take jobs they may perceive as having low pay or being less than desirable. They don't have the drive to innovate or move up in the marketplace, because there is no need.

Why have the Middle Eastern region's immense oil riches failed to produce the growing entrepreneurial enterprises you find in nations like Singapore, Taiwan, South Korea, and Israel, countries with far fewer—or even no—natural resources? Why are there no high-tech or textile industries of the kind you'd find in those countries? The reason is that nations that rely on the riches from natural resources rarely develop the habits of commerce that are the real engine of wealth.

Tight Money Causes Problems Too

As mentioned, Keynesians see the economy as a closed system, an engine. In reality it operates more like a Rube Goldberg contraption. A single event sets off a succession of unintended consequences. This is why monetary bureaucrats get into trouble when they try to act as puppet masters.

We saw this in 1997 when the United States cut taxes. Among the highlights, the Clinton administration cut the capital gains tax from 28% to 20% and barred new Internet taxes.

The economy took off, as did the stock market. Demand for the dollar rose. The Fed didn't meet the demand by supplying enough dollars. The gold price fell. The central bank inadvertently began a deflation. Commodity prices tumbled. Corn, for example, plunged from over $5 a bushel in 1996 to under $2 a bushel in 1999. Oil got as low as $10 a barrel. Agriculture and traditional manufacturing buckled.

The result: investments moved away from those traditional sectors, and not because of genuine market forces. Where did investment money go? Into the tech sector. Thanks to the growth of the Internet, technology was in the midst of a boom. The Fed's tight money set off a chain of events that ended up inflating this boom at the expense of traditional industries.

In early 2000, the Nasdaq hit 5000, a level it has not yet touched since. Shortly thereafter, stocks started to wobble. The high-tech bubble was starting to deflate. By 2001, the economy had slid into recession.

Had the Fed allowed the economy to recover on its own, we might not be writing this book. But naturally, it didn't. Faced with the bursting of the tech bubble in 2001, two weeks before the inauguration of incoming president George W. Bush, Federal Reserve chairman Alan Greenspan changed course and began loosening. He cut rates from 6.5% to 6%.

He should have stopped easing when gold reached $350 an ounce. When the precious metal went above $400 an ounce in late 2003–2004 it was clear that the economy was going in an inflationary direction. But he continued lowering interest rates that were now inflating the housing bubble. We all know where things went from there.

Greenspan might have been able to avoid some of this had he kept an eye on the price of gold. But he did not appear to do so, which was surprising given his past support of gold-based money. In addition to being an anchor of value, the price of gold is a vital barometer whose fluctuations tell you if there is too much, too little, or the right amount of money in the economy.

Unfortunately, not only Greenspan but also nearly all recent Fed chairmen have failed to appreciate the importance of gold as a barometer. Decisions are made too often on what are essentially hunches—and what the political climate is.

All this raises the larger question: Should the Federal Reserve really be in the business of fine-tuning the economy? The Fed was conceived during an agricultural era, when banks making crop loans could face seasonal cash squeezes during harvest time. It was supposed to provide a source of liquidity and also, like the Bank of England, be a lender of last resort. That is a very different role from the one that it has today: attempting to modulate normal business cycles.

Equilibrium is the pipe dream of academicians. In real life, the economy is not an engine, but a dynamic, serendipitous stew of human actions, needs, and desires. Unpredictable events constantly arise to thwart the earnest intentions of bureaucrats. The Fed—indeed, any government bureaucracy—is no more capable of successfully orchestrating the economic activities of millions of people than it would be to control the weather.

THE NUGGET

To paraphrase Ron Paul: if printing money created wealth,
there'd be no poverty left on earth.

CHAPTER 5

Money and Morality
How Debasing Money Debases Society

Lenin was certainly right. There is no subtler, no
surer means of overturning the existing basis of society
than to debauch the currency. The process engages
all the hidden forces of economic law on the side of
destruction, and does it in a manner which not one
man in a million is able to diagnose.

—John Maynard Keynes

AMONG THE GREAT IRONIES IS THAT LORD KEYNES, THE
foremost proponent of monetary stimulus, penned one
of the most famous and powerful summations of the
societal disarray that occurs when money is destroyed. Keynes
wrote these words in 1919, shortly before Germany's inflation
flared up into the Great Disorder, the hyperinflation and social
breakdown that preceded the rise of Adolf Hitler. He was convinced that there was a distinction between extreme inflation
and more moderate levels, which he believed would stimulate
an economy. History soon proved him tragically wrong.

By providing a common standard of value that facilitates trade among total strangers, money promotes the cooperation and trust vital to commerce. Unstable money that can't be trusted undermines the market's common perception of value, creating distortions and uncertainty that disrupt transactions, making trust harder to establish. Transactions become more difficult or cannot take place. Or they appear to be unfair. In the most extreme situations, people eventually lose faith in the system—and in each other.

A Classic Scenario of Malaise

Noted investment strategist Dylan Grice points out: "History is replete with Great Disorders in which social cohesion has been undermined by currency debasements." The destruction of money has always brought with it social malaise. From the decline of Rome to the French Revolution to the German hyperinflation to—more recently—the U.S. stagflation of the 1970s and Argentina in the present day, the scenario has been the same. It has been marked by scapegoating, corruption, social unrest, and increasingly coercive government. In the worst cases, such as in Weimar Germany, the destruction of money has led to political extremism and the rise of dictators.

Because developed nations have not recently experienced Weimar-level inflation, most people consider the possibility of a Great Disorder to be extremely remote. But that has also been true of past disasters caused by the destruction of money. People are slow to recognize what is taking place. Monetary blogger Paul Hein compares the gradual breakdown to the heating of water in the pot containing the frog. Sooner or later, he says, "the situation becomes unbearable."

Given the bloating of the world's monetary base over the past decade, nothing can be ruled out. Indeed, some observers today fear that the water may be reaching a boil. They point to the global financial crisis, largely overlooked hyperinflations of close to Weimar magnitude that have recently occurred in Zimbabwe and Syria, and the general unrest throughout the Middle East as being part of a four-decade worldwide decline of trust that has resulted from the shift to fiat money and the Fed's weakening of the dollar.

A Fissure at Society's Core

Locke observed centuries ago that the debasement of money drives a fissure into the core of society by defrauding both lender and borrower. Not only economic but social trust unravels when this fundamental relationship is destroyed. The financial crisis was very much a Lockean betrayal of trust that started when the Fed pulled out the rug from under borrowers by raising artificially low interest rates. Homeowners who could no longer afford their homes stiffed lenders, producing a wave of foreclosures. The resulting collapse of major financial institutions took the wealth of millions down with them. This in turn triggered the stock market panic of 2008 that set off a worldwide destruction of trust that ricocheted from one continent to the next. In Europe, bank failures and bailouts shook the confidence of global investors, helping bring on the EU's sovereign debt crisis.

This worldwide loss of faith swiftly turned to rage: riots and street protests rolled across the world—from Latvia, Germany, Turkey, France, and Austria to Great Britain, Ireland, Italy, Spain, and Greece. Anger in the United States erupted in the form of Occupy Wall Street protests.

By fueling inflation, the Fed's weak dollar also contributed to a meltdown of trust in the Middle East, where Tunisian protests over soaring food prices led to the mass unrest of the Arab Spring.

ETM Analytics, a South African investment advisory house, has issued reports called Riot Alerts, which predict the world's most likely trouble spots. The firm is able to forecast unrest based on nations' rates of "monetary abuse." Syria, suffering nearly 200% hyperinflation, topped the list in February 2013, followed by Argentina, South Africa, Egypt, India, and Turkey.

In the case of Syria, hyperinflation has been caused by its civil war. ETM's analyst Chris Becker explains, however, that monetary malfeasance is generally "the catalyst or trigger for the ultimate flare-up of unrest and violence."

Turning Society Against Itself

Weak, unstable money inflames perceptions of unfairness. People with fixed incomes struggling with rising prices in an uncertain economy become enraged when they see others appear to get rich through speculation or crony capitalism, not honest effort.

It is no accident that income inequality was an emotional issue in the United States even before the financial crisis—since the Fed started weakening the dollar. In 2012, a poll by the Pew Research Center found Americans to be more polarized than at any time during the past 25 years. "Nearly all of the increases have occurred," the study reported, "during the presidencies of George W. Bush and Barack Obama."

In the words of Dylan Grice, during times of monetary expansion "the 99% blame the 1%; the 1% blame the 47%; the private sector blames the public sector, the public sector returns the sentiment—the young blame the old, everyone blames the rich—yet few question the ideas behind government or central banks."

He warns: "What we've effectively done with this . . . money printing exercise is to turn society against itself."

The Symbiosis of Money and Trust

Money promotes trust by providing a stable unit of measurement people in the market can agree upon, that is the basis of transactions between strangers. But it's not just that money is the foundation of trust. The converse is equally true: *social trust depends on stable money*.

George Mason University economist Bruce Yandle tells us:

> Practically all market transactions depend on some degree of trust. . . . Consider some simple actions. I fill the tank of my car with fluid from a pump at a 7-Eleven store I have never visited, trusting that the fluid passing through the hose is gasoline. I walk into a large TESCO superstore in Prague, a store and company I have never patronized, and buy a supply of groceries, including fresh fruit, soups, and coffee. I consume the items without a second's concern about their safety. I e-mail my broker and tell him I want to buy a thousand shares of stock . . . [though] I have never checked the firm's financial strength. . . .
>
> Trust is somehow rooted in individuals. Within all these examples, truth telling and promise keeping are typical features of ordinary commercial life. The marketplace is infused with trust.

Economist and political philosopher Francis Fukuyama defines trust as "the expectation that arises within a community of regular, honest, and cooperative behavior, based on commonly shared norms, on the part of other members of that community."

Fukuyama notes that societies with high trust tend to be better wealth creators. What he calls "high trust societies" (examples include Germany, Japan, and the United States) tend to be better at forming corporations and have prospered more rapidly than lower trust societies that have relied more heavily on smaller family businesses.

Money promotes trust not only by acting as a common measure of value, but also through the mechanism of credit. After all, what is credit—a loan based on a promise of future re-payment—but the financial expression of trust?

To see the interrelationship between money, credit, and social trust, one need only compare various nations' bench-mark interest rates. They tend to be higher for troubled economies. Contrast the rates in 2014 for high-inflation Argentina (15.0%), Belarus (26.0%), and Myanmar (11.3% and more recently 10.0%) to those in nations with lower inflation and higher trust such as Norway (1.5%) and Australia (2.5%). Or better still, contrast them to the 3% yields on long-term bonds that prevailed in the nineteenth century during the global economic boom that took place during the classical gold standard era, a time when money was considered as good as gold.

Unfortunately, the relation of money to social trust is seldom fully appreciated. This has been especially true since the financial crisis, during which money and finance have become almost synonymous with greed.

There is a strong correlation between periods of social unrest and periods of monetary volatility. The four-decade destruction of the dollar is also a story about the destruction of trust. More than one study has shown an overall decline of faith in the system since the early to mid-1960s, even before the destruction of the Bretton Woods standard. Various factors have contributed to this slide, including assassinations, the Vietnam War, and the rise of the counterculture.

Social trust has taken especially sharp dives during the double-digit inflation of the late 1970s and during the weak dollar expansion of the last decade that culminated in the financial crisis.

In addition to being an economic catastrophe, that worldwide event was a destruction of trust from which we have yet to recover.

How the Financial Crisis Exemplifies the Corruption of Trust

The financial crisis that began in the United States and tore through the global economy began with the corruption of fundamental mechanisms of money and credit that are part of what Bruce Yandle calls the market's "trust technology." Instruments like credit ratings, he explains, are "assurance mechanisms" vital to the "truth telling and promise keeping" that establish trust and allow the economy to function.

The Fed's lowering of interest rates and the monetary expansion of the early 2000s, combined with pressures from affordable housing regulations, he tells us, impaired the market's trust-assuring capabilities by damaging this critical infrastructure. As a result, loans were made to people who would not normally have received them. This in turn led to financial institutions bundling tainted loans in the mortgage-backed securities they sold to investors.

Trust-assurance mechanisms like bond credit ratings were also compromised by the politicized environment. Finally, when the Fed raised interest rates, Yandle writes, "politically distorted assurance devices failed to function," setting off a wave of foreclosures.

The reinstatement of mark-to-market accounting regulations, which forced banks artificially to undervalue their loan portfolios, provided a tipping point. The return of this toxic regulation caused banks holding subprime mortgages to look more financially precarious than they were in reality. Attacks by short sellers sent bank stocks into a death spiral, setting off the

Panic of 2008–2009 and the crisis of confidence in the financial system.

The painful memory remains with us: several of the nation's largest financial institutions that were supposedly "too big to fail" collapsed, merged, or, in the case of Citigroup and AIG, were temporarily taken over by the government, which seized most of their equity. The Dow Jones Industrial Average lost 7,600 points, or 54% of its value, in 17 months.

For weeks, financial institutions were virtually paralyzed. Some people withdrew their money from banks and brokerages and many more wondered if they should. An incipient wholesale panic of withdrawals from money market funds was halted when the Fed temporarily guaranteed their values. But this crisis of trust was only just beginning.

From Foreclosures to Sovereign Default

The collapse of confidence in the system brought about by the weakening of the U.S. dollar set off a seismic reaction quickly felt around the world. Bailouts and bank seizures took place in countries from Great Britain to Germany to Ireland. The contagion helped trigger the sovereign debt crises in the euro zone that began months later in 2009.

Many observed at the time that some banks were in better condition than was widely perceived. But this reality meant little. A Deutsche Bank economist told the *New York Times*, "In this day and age, a bank run spreads around the world, not around the block. Once a bank run is underway, it doesn't matter anymore if you have good loans or bad loans. People lose confidence in you."

Greece, hit hard by the ensuing global recession, revealed that its government deficit was twice what was previously reported. The prospect of a Greek government default on its bonds—which were owned by global investors, especially European banks in general and French financial institutions in particular—terrified the financial markets, igniting doubts about the creditworthiness of other European governments—especially Portugal, Italy, Ireland, and Spain.

Greece and other troubled nations suffered a series of downgrades on their bonds. Eventually Standard & Poor's rated Greece an "SD"—a selective default, indicating the country was unable to meet all of its financial obligations. Shaken bond buyers caused interest rates to skyrocket throughout Europe. Greek 10-year bond yields reached an astonishing high of nearly 49% at the height of the crisis in March 2012. Soaring borrowing costs pushed the region's troubled governments to the brink of insolvency. Greece eventually ended up in a bailout agreement engineered by the European Union, stiffing its bondholders for 50% of their loans.

The global contagion that started with a crisis of trust in the U.S. subprime mortgage market created new antagonisms in the euro zone. Greece was blamed for out-of-control borrowing and spending. Germany was resented for refusing to bail out Greece and pushing a solution that relied on private bondholders. The United States was condemned as responsible for the crisis. China, with its growing economic strength and ownership of the debt of so many troubled governments, was feared by everybody.

The Middle East: Weak Money Fuels the Fire

The destruction of trust produced by the Fed's tsunami of global liquidity did not end with Europe—it inflamed tensions in the Middle East as well. Remember, as the value of money declines, investors look to preserve their wealth. Money flows into commodities like oil and agricultural products, jacking up the price of essentials like fuel and food. In 2010 the United Nations Food and Agriculture Organization (FAO) Food Price Index reported a 25% surge in prices. People around the world blamed the jump on supply shocks from drought, poverty, and wars. But the real cause was the flood of loose money from the Fed.

The 2010 Tunisian street demonstrations that set off the Arab Spring protests were largely over food prices. The unrest then spilled over into Egypt, where the consumer price index had jumped 18% in 2009, compared with 5% in 2006. The country has since seen the toppling of the Mubarak and the Morsi governments and remains in flux. Unrest also increased in Iran, where the inflation rate had surged to an official rate of 25% in 2009, nearly twice its level several years earlier. The real level was probably twice that.

At the G-20 meeting in Paris in 2011, finance ministers expressed fears that U.S.-driven global inflation was threatening global stability. George Melloan was among those who made the connection between this unrest and QE. He acknowledged in the *Wall Street Journal*: "Probably few of the protesters in the streets connect their economic travail to Washington. But central bankers do."

To appreciate the depth of political upheaval created by the 2008 financial crisis, just tally the power shifts that occurred in its wake. In addition to the turmoil in the Middle East, 13 out of 17 European governments changed over as a result of the initial financial crisis. In the United States, the stock market panic in September 2008 reversed the slight lead of John McCain and helped sweep the far-left Barack Obama into office.

From Balance Sheets to the Streets

Throughout history, an extreme loss of trust in money has often turned into a hunt for scapegoats. When things go wrong, loose money—or, for that matter, tight money—is rarely seen as the cause. People look for someone to blame. As Keynes observed, "Those to whom the system brings windfalls, beyond their deserts and even beyond their expectations" become "the object of hatred" and are despised as "profiteers."

In his widely cited piece on great disorders, Dylan Grice reminds us that every inflationary period has been marked by vicious campaigns against supposed villains. The Romans in the third century blamed the Christians for the inflation caused by their own ruthless debasement of the denarius. Great Britain's witch trials in the sixteenth and seventeenth centuries and the French Revolution's Reign of Terror in which 17,000 people were slaughtered both coincided with periods of monetary debasement. And during its hyperinflation, Germany blamed the Jews.

In the immediate aftermath of the 2008 financial crisis, people from all sides questioned the fairness of the government propping up the financial sector with taxpayer money while people were losing their homes, jobs, and savings. Almost daily, politicians excoriated Wall Street greed, predatory lenders, and speculators. Condemnations of "fat cats with corporate jets" became mainstays of the political rhetoric.

In Europe, the story was much the same. Greek prime minister George Papandreou condemned speculators for driving down the value of his country's bonds. In Great Britain, protesters attacked the home of Fred Goodwin, the former head of the bailed-out Royal Bank of Scotland, who had been widely vilified as a symbol of banker incompetence and greed. Protesters sounded Occupy Wall Street themes in a written message that declared: "We are angry that rich people, like [Goodwin], are paying themselves a huge amount of money and living in luxury, while ordinary people are made unemployed, destitute, and homeless. . . . Bank bosses should be jailed. This is just the beginning."

There are some who have suggested that such rage is more than a response to the redistribution of wealth brought about by the distortion of money. The late Nobel Prize–winning Bulgarian writer Elias Canetti, who wrote about the emotions of crowds, offers a provocative, if unsettling, explanation of the psychology of the extreme scapegoating that occurred in the wake of Germany's monetary collapse. As a representation of toil and human action, it can be argued that money is not simply a medium of exchange, but rather an expression of self. When Germany's money collapsed, that society, he believes, reacted to the trauma of this "depreciation" by responding in kind:

> The natural tendency afterwards is to find something which is worth even less than oneself, which one can despise as one was despised oneself. It is not enough to take over an old contempt and to maintain it at the same level. What is wanted is a dynamic process of humiliation. Something must be treated in such a way that it becomes worth less and less, as the unit of money did during the inflation.

Occupy Wall Street: Players in a Classic Drama

In 2011, when Occupy Wall Street protesters started a two-month encampment in Zuccotti Park in New York's financial district, they were playing out the scenario of unrest that follows a debasement of money. Sounding age-old themes of inequality and injustice, their demonstrations quickly spread across the United States and then into a few European cities as well. A Detroit protester voiced the typical lament: "The financial architecture . . . is bad for more people than it is good for. This system is rigged for a very few."

Demonstrators staged a "Billionaires Walking Tour" to vent their rage outside the homes of JPMorgan Chase chairman and CEO Jamie Dimon, News Corporation CEO Rupert Murdoch, industrialist David Koch, and financier John Paulson—all of whom were assailed as symbols of the 1%.

The media blamed this breakdown of social trust on Wall Street greed. They should have blamed the Fed.

Along with boosting the monetary base to breathtaking levels, QE was delivering big gains to the financial sector. We have noted that the Fed's purchases of long-term Treasuries and mortgage-backed securities channeled credit to government and large corporations at the expense of loans to new and small businesses. Matthew Taibbi complained in *Rolling Stone*:

> Ordinary people have to borrow their money at market rates. Lloyd Blankfein and Jamie Dimon get billions of dollars for free from the Federal Reserve. They borrow at zero and lend the same money back to the government at two or three percent, a valuable public service otherwise known as "standing in the middle and taking a gigantic cut when the government decides to lend money to itself."

The problem, however, wasn't cheating by Wall Street but Fed policies that were attempting to revive the economy by doing the very thing that had brought on the crisis—pumping still more liquidity into mortgages. Meanwhile, people with moderate and lower incomes were continuing to struggle in a sluggish economy that QE had failed to revive.

For once, Paul Krugman wasn't wrong when he complained in 2013 that the nation was seeing a "rich man's recovery." "The rich," he writes, "have come roaring back":

95% of the gains from economic recovery since 2009 have gone to the famous 1%. In fact, more than 60% of the gains went to the top 0.1%, people with annual incomes of more than $1.9 million. Basically, while the great majority of Americans are still living in a depressed economy, the rich have recovered just about all their losses and are powering ahead.

He observes, "I guess I'd note that a large proportion of those super-high incomes come from the financial industry, which is, as you may remember, the industry that taxpayers had to bail out after its looming collapse threatened to take down the whole economy."

With Less Trust Comes More Government

In nations with chronic monetary instability, distrust of commerce is a way of life. A perfect example is Greece, whose policy makers were chronic currency debasers before embracing the euro. Joining the euro zone pushed the Greek government to stop inflation—though not spending. This legacy of monetary dysfunction has corrupted the country's political and economic life, in addition to undermining basic civility.

When entrepreneur Demetri Politopoulos returned to his native Greece from the United States to start a brewery, his products were vandalized, his tires were slashed, and he received taunts and threats. Given the deeply ingrained cultural hostility to commerce, one can readily see how unemployment in Greece is nearly 28%.

In Argentina, the poster child for the perils of inflation, *empresario*, the word for businessman, has come to mean *criminal*.

This toxic destruction of trust almost always brings with it increasingly capricious and draconian regulations. People turn to government when they feel they can't trust each other.

Argentina has virtually paralyzed its economy with countless arbitrary and politically driven regulations—including, at one point, a ban on imported books.

In Europe and the United States, there is a growing push for "macroprudential" strategies in monetary and financial regulation. This approach would give central banks and financial regulators sweeping new powers aimed at assessing entire markets and preventing bubbles before they happen. European central banks are already beginning to adopt such a preemptive— and dangerous—approach. Noted economist John Cochrane in the *Wall Street Journal* worries about the future of the United States entrepreneurial economy in the shadow of an increasingly powerful and capricious macroprudential Fed:

> How will homebuilders react if the Fed decides their investments are bubbly and restricts their credit? How will bankers who followed all the rules feel when the Fed decrees their actions a "systemic" threat? How will financial entrepreneurs in the shadow banking system, peer-to-peer lending innovators, etc., feel when the Fed quashes their efforts to compete with banks?

Given that finance was already the most regulated sector of the U.S. economy (that is, the numerous regulations and bureaucracies of Sarbanes Oxley, Dodd-Frank, not to mention countless preexisting securities laws and other constraints), today's calls for still more control look less like real efforts at reform and more like the kind of politicized strictures common in places like Argentina and Greece. They're part of the aftermath of political scapegoating and payback that ensues when the corruption of money destroys trust.

Indeed, Washington's punitive mood was clear in 2013 when JPMorgan Chase was forced by the Obama Justice Department to accept a $13 billion settlement—the largest fine ever paid by a company to the government and the equivalent of half the firm's annual profit. The "offer you can't refuse" allowed the world's largest bank to avert a lawsuit over its sale of mortgage securities to investors—the same investment vehicles that continue to be sold by Washington's creations, Fannie and Freddie, and that the Fed has bought as a result of quantitative easing.

The historic fine is in addition to the $18 billion JP Morgan has already spent defending itself against investigations by at least seven federal agencies since the financial crisis. Holding 50 meetings per month with regulators, the bank's senior executives have become virtual hostages to Washington. The *Wall Street Journal* reported in 2013 that the firm was nearly doubling its risk and compliance team to 15,000 people from 8,000 the year before, spending another $5 billion on compliance.

Critics gloated that the company got what it deserved. In truth, job-seeking Americans were the losers. Instead of JPMorgan Chase's billions being used as capital to back the next Apple or Google, the money went into the pockets of bureaucrats, funding broken websites and flailing bureaucracies.

Demoralization and Malaise

The intensified government controls on finance and capital that are typical reactions to the destruction of money neither restore trust in a currency nor revive an economy. Instead, they cause it to sink even deeper into stagnation and pessimism. During the 1970s' stagflation in the United States, Jimmy Carter encapsulated this despair in his famous "malaise" speech:

> The symptoms of this crisis of the American spirit are all around us. For the first time in the history of our country a majority of our people believe that the next five years will be worse than the past five years. Two-thirds of our people do not even vote. The productivity of American workers is actually dropping, and the willingness of Americans to save for the future has fallen below that of all other people in the Western world.

Inflationary despair is evident today in India, a longtime monetary abuser that was hit with rampant inflation after the economy slowed and the United States announced its intention to taper and raise interest rates. As a result, investors abandoned Indian bonds in favor of U.S. debt, setting off a slide in the value of the rupee, which reached a record low in 2013. The Indian government raised the benchmark interest rate to nearly 8% and imposed controls on overseas investment, going so far as to ban the import of duty-free flat screens by airline passengers.

Once known as the new tiger of Asia, India has seen its growth slip from around almost 9% in the early 2000s to below 4% in the fall of 2013. The country's vast subsistence population has been hit hard by rising food prices. India's growing middle class, a success story for the last two decades, is for the first time expressing pessimism about the future. Alam Srinivas, author of the book *The Indian Consumer*, told the *Washington Post* that the inflation "was a huge shock for the middle class. There was a sense that nothing could go wrong." One student said that she had postponed her plans for the future and was now "focused on simply surviving."

President Obama sounded the same grim themes in his 2013 speech on income inequality, the pessimism of which is characteristic of monetary malaise:

> It's not surprising that the American people's frustrations with Washington are at an all-time high. . . . Their frustration is rooted in their own daily battles—to make ends meet, to pay for college, buy a home, save for retirement. It's rooted in the nagging sense that no matter how hard they work, the deck is stacked against them. And it's rooted in the fear that their kids won't be better off than they were.

Unlike his predecessor Jimmy Carter, who acknowledged the role of inflation in the nation's woes, President Obama, like so many others in Washington, has failed to see a link between the problems of the 99% and wealth-destroying monetary policies. When the president complained that "the basic bargain at the heart of our economy has frayed," he could have been talking about what happens when the Fed weakens the dollar.

Debasing Public Morality

In 2013, Theodore Dalrymple described in *City Journal* how the debasement of currency "corrodes the character of people":

> It not only undermines the traditional bourgeois virtues but makes them ridiculous and even reverses them. Prudence becomes imprudence, thrift becomes improvidence, sobriety becomes mean-spiritedness, modesty becomes lack of ambition, self-control becomes betrayal of the inner self, patience becomes lack of

foresight, steadiness becomes inflexibility: all that was wisdom becomes foolishness. And circumstances force almost everyone to join in the dance.

Monetary blogger Paul Hein put it succinctly: "If there are no standards for money, other standards will fade away as well." The distortion of market trust mechanisms that are the unintended consequence of fiat money sooner or later are likely to produce deliberate transgressions of trust on the part of governments, institutions, and individuals.

Not only social unrest but corruption is a symptom of the reckless debasement of money. Big inflators like Syria, Argentina, and Zimbabwe typically score high in perceptions of corruption on Transparency International's annual Corruption Perceptions Index.

With the worldwide destruction of money, it is no surprise that corruption is on the increase. Transparency International's 2013 annual Global Corruption Barometer, which reports on corruption in 107 countries, found that 53% of people surveyed believe that corruption has increased or increased a lot over the last two years.

Examples seem to be everywhere:

- Turkey, which has been trying with some success to get inflation under control, was rocked by unrest in 2013 because of a government graft scandal. It eventually forced Prime Minister Recep Tayyip Erdogan to replace 10 ministers in his cabinet.

- In tiny Belarus, where inflation reached nearly 60% in 2012, bribes are necessary for admission to prestigious state universities that confer degrees in fields such as law and medicine.

- Russia's English language RT Network reported that inflation in 2011 meant the average cost of a bribe in that country "more than tripled."

In 2012 Barclays Bank and 15 other global financial institutions admitted to artificially lowering the London Interbank Offered Rate (LIBOR), the short-term interbank interest rate used when banks lend to each other. The banks were accused of manipulating rates initially so that their traders could profit when trading derivatives. Later, they pushed the rates downward to make their balance sheets appear stronger during the financial crisis. In the United States, the United Kingdom, and the European Union, banks had to pay fines totaling more than $6 billion.

If the system had had stable money, LIBOR's ethical breach would probably never have happened. Fluctuating currencies create the volatility that necessitates derivatives. Economist David Malpass noted: "The instability of exchange rates and the interest rates backing them create the need for complex derivatives and floating-rate financial instruments." In other words, the environment that encouraged banks to manipulate their interbank rates would not have existed. Barclays' self-protective manipulation of LIBOR would also probably never have taken place, because the financial crisis would not have occurred.

Sound money would have likely prevented other acts of desperation, such as the looting of private bank accounts that took place during the Cyprus financial crisis in 2012 and 2013. To help pay for a bank bailout, the Cypriot government, at the behest of Germany, the International Monetary Fund, and the European Union, imposed one-time taxes on the accounts of the country's bank depositors. It confiscated nearly half of the uninsured accounts over 100,000 euros of customers at the Bank of Cyprus. Voicing the stunned disbelief felt by many at this unprecedented confiscation of personal property and violation of trust, investor Jim Rogers declared to CNBC "What more do you need to know?":

> Think of all the poor souls who just thought they had a simple bank account. Now they find out that they are making a "contribution" to the stability of Cyprus. The gall of these politicians.

Gaming the System

It's not just governments and banks that stiff citizens and walk away from their loans. The destruction of money corrupts social trust and morality among ordinary citizens as well. In 2011, in the wake of the financial crisis, the *New York Times* ran an astonishing story, "They Walked Away and They're Glad They Did," a sympathetic look at people who had decided to abandon their mortgages in the wake of the financial crisis.

One pharmaceutical employee told the paper that three years after he bought his Los Angeles home, it was now worth nearly $250,000 less than what he paid for it: "We looked at how much my home was under water, how much I'd lost thus far and how much I would continue to lose until I started to break even. . . . And that could be 20 years away. It was a no-brainer." This man had enlisted the help of YouWalkAway .com, a service that specializes in "Intelligent Strategic Default." According to the *Times*, the process of walking away from a $300,000 loan was fairly routine:

> The company charges clients an enrollment fee of $199 to $395, and monthly membership fees ranging from $29.95 to $99.95, depending on which assistance plan a homeowner chooses. Then it essentially coaches clients

through the process of walking away from their mortgages, helps them figure out which threatening letters to pay attention to and which to ignore and provides access to lawyers versed in each state's property laws.

YouWalkAway.com's CEO Jon Maddux appeared to dismiss any moral concerns about helping people turn their backs on their loans: "I think as more and more people know someone that's done it, they know that, O.K., these people have moved on, they kind of pushed the reset button, and they're starting over."

The *Times* quoted a Harvard University housing expert who backed them up: "If your home is a financial asset, and it's financially rational to walk away, that's what you do."

It's Not Just Mortgages

Students cannot walk away from their loans as easily as homeowners whose houses are under water. Their lender, Uncle Sam, can garnish their wages. An increasing number, however, are choosing to do so; default rates are at their highest levels since 1995, according to the Department of Education.

Just as liquidity pumped into housing created moral hazard in the mortgage market, the Fed's monetary expansion over the last four decades has indirectly undermined morality in the market for college loans. Between 1996 and 2006, real federal aid—including grants, loans, and tax credits—has skyrocketed, increasing by 77%, from $48.7 billion to almost $86.3 billion. Aid (mostly federal) per full-time student increased 43%. The cost of college has risen commensurately: the per-pupil cost of tuition, fees, room, and board has increased 29% at private four-year schools; 41% at public four-year institutions.

As *U.S. News and World Report* reported, the loans for many young people have been "a gateway drug to destructive financial behavior." The magazine describes how one student used his loans to fund an expensive lifestyle that allowed him to purchase "a Jeep, stereo equipment, televisions and more. What he didn't spend, he invested, and lost." After graduation he faced unemployment and loan payments that were double his rent.

No surprise that, with tuition debt reaching $1 trillion, one of the complaints of the younger Occupy Wall Street protestors was the student loan crisis. They have a point. Loose money corrupts more than market truth telling. What kind of society sells a lifelong burden of indebtedness to people inexperienced with money who are at the beginning of their working lives? Loan sharks and drug dealers who create debt and dependence get put in prison. But the federal government gets to call its enabling of debt "financial aid."

Mortgages and student loans are the most extreme examples of the increase in consumer debt that has taken place in the era of fiat money. Since 1971, the last year the dollar was linked to gold, the ratio of total consumer debt to GDP has trended upward, from 12% to around 17.5% in 2013.

The personal savings rate, meanwhile, has trended downward, from 13% to under 5% today. When people are unable to save, they have greater difficulty planning for retirement or handling emergencies. They can't build wealth and move ahead. Little wonder so many people today are so angry.

The Crime Connection

The stealth thievery of monetary debasement trickles down too. The late journalist Henry Hazlitt is among many who have observed the relationship between crime and loose money. In his words, "Reward comes to depend less and less on effort and production." Therefore, "corruption or crime [seems] a surer path to quick reward."

The murder rate in inflation-racked Venezuela is 79 per 100,000, more than twice that of neighboring Colombia, a nation with a long history of violence. An estimated 1 million people have left Venezuela in a little more than a decade.

Under the Kirchner government, Argentina has also seen an increase in violent crime. Capital controls have forced Argentines to store their cash at home, resulting in a rash of home invasion robberies.

With monetary expansion beginning to drive up prices in the United States, crime has begun to increase. In 2012 the National Crime Victimization Survey by the Bureau of Justice Statistics reported the first rise in violent and property crime in two decades.

Researchers say that this is typical. A study in the journal *Economics Letters* found that since 1960 there has been a consistent correlation between the U.S. crime rate and the Misery Index, an indicator measuring inflation and unemployment.

Inflation has actually been found to have a stronger connection to crime than joblessness. One study by German and American researchers found that inflation had far and away the greatest effect on property crime, greater than variables like manufacturing employment. The authors write: "the answer leaves no room for interpretation. Almost all of the impact of the three macroeconomic variables falls on the inflation rate."

Richard Rosenfeld, a sociologist at the University of Missouri–St. Louis, wondered why the catastrophic 2008 economic recession, with its soaring jobless rates, did not produce an increase in crime. Crime in fact decreased. Rosenfeld now believes that the reason was that when the economy took a dive, the United States experienced the first serious deflation in 50 years. In 2010 prices began to rise—and crime did too.

From 2010 to 2011, the inflation rate doubled from 1.6% to 3.2%, according to the Consumer Price Index. Shortly thereafter, the Bureau of Justice Statistics announced a sudden increase in crime categories across the board. This supports the observations of Rosenfeld and other researchers who have found a lag to exist between inflation and the onset of crime—an increase in inflation tends to be quickly followed by an increase in crime rates.

America in the Twenty-First Century: A Declaration of Dependence?

Fiat money undermines social morality by facilitating the reckless expansion of government. It allows ambitious politicians to get votes by creating new and larger bureaucracies that create dependence and corrupt markets. Four decades of fiat money have facilitated enormous government borrowing that has produced today's dangerous level of government debt—and America's welfare bureaucracies and entitlement culture.

When Richard Nixon severed the link to gold in 1971, the total U.S. federal debt stood at $398 billion, 34% of GDP. Today, it tops $17 trillion, over 100% of GDP—large enough to cause the nations of the world that are holding U.S. bonds to worry about America's future solvency, and large enough for the rating agency Standard & Poor's to downgrade the nation's credit rating in 2011.

Federal payments to individuals for programs such as food stamps have exploded. Before the 1970s, it was around 21% of federal spending. Today it's around 70%. Almost half the U.S. population no longer pays income taxes.

The Supplemental Nutrition Assistance Program (SNAP), formerly the food stamp program, has more than doubled between 2008 and 2012, from $37.6 billion to $78.4 billion in fiscal year 2012. Housing assistance is near an all-time high of $55 billion. Medicaid, which had been rapidly increasing before the administration's healthcare law, is set to explode. David B. Muhlhausen and Patrick D. Tyrrell of the Heritage Foundation write:

> Americans have reached a point in the life of their republic at which the democratic political process has become a means for many voters to defend and expand the "benefits" they receive from government. Do Americans want a republic that encourages and validates a growing dependence on the state and a withering of civil society?

With more people than ever dependent on government and an economy growing at the lowest rate for a recovery ever, many today wonder whether America may be entering an era of economic decline resembling that of Spain in the Middle Ages, whose overly loose money from its mineral wealth encouraged idleness and corruption and discouraged enterprise.

The Spanish had problems with big government too. British historian J. H. Elliott wrote of *arbitristas*, Spanish reformers who saw "at the heart of their country a vast court, a monstrous tumour swelling larger and larger, and relentlessly consuming the life of the nation. The court and the swollen bureaucracy were crying out for reform."

In the recent battles over the federal budget that led to the partial government shutdown in 2013, media coverage of the debate focused narrowly on debt and deficits. The fight, however, really was over larger questions: Should America be allowed to continue down the road to more spending and dependency? Do we want to suffer the consequences of again raising the ceiling, increased borrowing, and pressures for still more monetary expansion that would further erode the value of the dollar?

The Lesson of Rome

Lawrence Reed, president of the Foundation for Economic Education, believes that there are lessons to be learned from ancient Rome, whose destruction of money caused a gradual erosion of the social and political order that led to the fall of the empire. Rome's monetary and societal debasement began "when the people discovered another source of income: the political process—the State." In a powerful speech to the 2013 Freedom Fest, he told attendees:

> Roman coinage was debased by one emperor after another to pay for expensive programs. Once almost pure silver, the denarius by the year 300 was little more than a piece of junk containing less than five percent silver.

The Roman Empire became a welfare empire. The result was a raging inflation. Like today, savings vanished. Businessmen were vilified. Increasingly overbearing government strangled the private economy. And finally:

> By 476 A.D., when barbarians wiped the empire from the map, Rome had committed moral and economic suicide. Romans first lost their character. Then, as a consequence, they lost their liberties and ultimately their civilization.

Will that be us?

THE NUGGET

*When people stop trusting money,
they stop trusting each other*

CHAPTER 6

The Gold Standard
How to Rescue the
Twenty-First Century
Global Economy

Time will run back and fetch the Age of Gold.
—John Milton

You cannot have a gold standard system in the future if
nobody knows how to do it.
—Nathan Lewis, *Gold: The Monetary Polaris*

FREEING THE DOLLAR FROM GOLD WAS SUPPOSED TO MAKE
the United States stronger. Instead it has made the
country weaker. It has eroded America's wealth and
has jeopardized its leadership position as the world's strongest
economy.

Something has to be done.

There is a growing consensus that the U.S. monetary system is broken. A 2013 Rasmussen poll found that an astounding 74% of American adults are in favor of auditing the Federal Reserve and making the results public. Only 10% oppose it.

A substantial number believe the Fed chairman has too much power over the economy. Momentum is building on Capitol Hill for a reevaluation of the role of the Federal Reserve System.

People are seeking solutions. We mentioned earlier the movement for alternative currencies. Lately there has been a push for another option that, until very recently, few people in policy circles would seriously entertain: a return to stable money through the use of a gold standard.

Gold.

Calls for a new gold standard are gaining support. The people are leading the way. Gold and silver coins are now accepted legal tender in the state of Utah. The states of Georgia and Montana have outlined ideas to allow the use of gold as payment in certain sectors of the economy.

Rep. Kevin Brady, chairman of the Congressional Joint Economic Committee, and Sen. John Cornyn are pushing a bill to create a bipartisan commission to conduct a thorough examination of monetary policy. Brady's bill is attracting sponsors in both the House and the Senate. Already, Rep. Ted Poe, another Texas Republican, has submitted a bill with a proposal for a new gold standard.

When the Cato Institute, a libertarian think tank, held an event discussing gold in the summer of 2013, the meeting drew hundreds of journalists, academics, entrepreneurs, key congressional staffers, and other policy thought leaders. Many had never before been interested in the subject of a gold standard. Ralph Benko, who edits the Lehrman Institute's *The Gold Standard Now* and is a Forbes.com columnist, marveled at the attendance, declaring, "This was no ordinary event. It may, in retrospect, be seen as the gold standard's Woodstock."

A return to gold-based money is not yet front and center on the national agenda. The policy establishment still dismisses it

as radical. But history has shown time and again that great social changes begin as seemingly radical ideas.

Why Gold?

We need gold because, as we've emphasized throughout this
book, gold is the best and the only way to achieve truly stable
money. Relinking the dollar to gold would eliminate the economic volatility and monetary crises that have been the consequence of fiat money. It would stop the erosion of our wealth
that is taking place today as a result of Fed-engineered inflation.
With a gold standard, *there would be no inflation*. That's right.
We said it and we mean it. As critics so often misunderstand, no
inflation does not necessarily mean an end to price instability.
Prices, as we've explained elsewhere, will continue to rise and
fall in response to changes in supply, demand, and productivity. As well they should. Gold would allow prices to convey real
market values, not Fed-distorted ones.

In other words, gold would enable money, for the first time
in decades, to completely fulfill its role as a facilitator of transactions, unimpeded and undistorted. People conducting business in the marketplace would have a tool that really works.
Commerce would boom.

That happened in the late nineteenth century, when most
nations, inspired by Great Britain's spectacular economic success after tying the pound to gold, spontaneously adopted a
gold standard. The global economy experienced an explosion in trade, capital creation, and investment that remained
unmatched for the next 100 years. Gold worked then because
leaders and governments didn't violate the rules, as their suc-
cessors did in the twentieth and twenty-first centuries. They believed in the principles of sound money. A gold standard would

deliver a stimulus to the United States and the world economy that Fed bureaucrats could only dream of.

Gold Takes the Politics out of Money

Gold takes decisions about the value and supply of money out of the hands of bureaucrats whose judgment is too often in error or driven by politics. Bureaucrats can no more guess the need for money than central planners could run an economy in the days of the Soviet Union. Seemingly sophisticated equations and various measures of money can never anticipate what people actually do.

The job of a government's central bank would simply be to maintain a stable gold price. In a gold standard system, the price of gold acts as a barometer. It indicates whether there is too much liquidity in the economy and whether we're heading toward inflation or if there's too little liquidity and possible deflation.

The demand for money reflects the ever-shifting actions and desires of billions of people in global markets, many of whom are reacting to thoroughly unanticipated events. Gold prices convey these changing needs better than anything else.

Why isn't the United States on a gold standard today? There are a number of reasons. The traumas of World War I and the Great Depression spurred the rise of neo-mercantilism and a new infatuation with activist government. If government could win wars by mobilizing the economy, many believed, imagine how society would benefit from its vast powers in peacetime, including greater control over money.

Then there are the hostile myths about gold that, like barnacles, remain stubbornly attached even today. Allegations range from "there's not enough gold in the world" to "the price of gold is too volatile" to even that "a gold standard constitutes the price fixing of money."

You'll also hear accusations that the gold standard caused the Great Depression and later created pressures leading to the end of the Bretton Woods system. That's like blaming a skyscraper's implosion on the tools used to build it, not on the violations of building codes that caused the collapse.

Debunking the Myths About Gold

Money simply reflects conditions in an economy. Like those construction tools, gold has repeatedly been blamed for economic destruction caused by obstacles that governments place in the way of commerce. First and foremost was the U.S. enactment of the Smoot-Hawley Tariff, which we will discuss later in this chapter. Placing onerous taxes on thousands of products, that toxic act of protectionism started the global trade war that triggered the Great Depression. Countries then deepened the slump with ghastly increases in taxes. A wave of devaluations followed. Nations, desperate to revive their economies, cast aside the wisdom of sound money.

Gold opponents also believe a peg to the precious metal opens up the United States and other nations to runs on gold supplies. This isn't true either. The focus on gold's supply (or the lack of it) is the same mistake made by mercantilist monarchs who thought gold in and of itself constituted wealth. As we emphasize in this chapter, gold's power lies in its effectiveness as a *measure*. A gold-based system can work even if a country doesn't own a single ounce of gold.

Gold Doesn't Mean a Fixed Supply of Money

Gold is far less rigid than most people realize. It is both flexible and stable. Contrary to the common perception, it allows the monetary base to grow, or to shrink, in response to transactions and monetary demand while preserving the value of money. A gold standard no more means a fixed supply of money than a use of the metric system means there has to be a fixed number of rulers.

Why Not Silver or Something Else?

Why gold? After all, as we've discussed, many commodities throughout history have been used as currency. Gold, however, is the best way to sound money because it maintains its value better than anything else on earth. It is to stable, long-term purchasing power what Polaris, the North Star, is to determining direction—that is, an unchanging fixture, a constant.

Gold is indestructible. You can freeze it, heat it, smash it or burn it, but you cannot destroy it. It doesn't rot. It is not prey to termites or rodents or disease. Its chemical composition never changes nor does its weight if you melt it down. Gold is tough but malleable enough to be shaped into coins or bars. Unlike the fei that we mentioned earlier, the precious yellow metal packs considerable value into a tiny amount of space, making it easy to use and transport.

Gold is not subject to droughts or abundant harvests that can produce the supply shocks experienced by wheat or corn. It is not consumed or burned like oil or natural gas. Gold is mostly used for jewelry and other ornaments and as a reserve of value. Gold has some industrial uses and was once employed by dentists for fillings in our teeth. But these have little effect on supply, constituting a fraction of the amount of gold mined each year.

All the gold that has been mined is still in existence, over six billion ounces. Experts estimate that more than 90% of it is accounted for today. The rest is either buried in the ground, having been lost by careless owners, or lying at the bottom of the ocean. As Roy Jastram put it in his classic work *The Golden Constant*, "The ring worn today may contain particles mined in the time of the Pharaohs."

Even the massive influx of gold and silver from Spain's New World colonies resulted in price increases averaging only 1.7% a year. Giant finds such as the California and Australian gold rushes of the late 1840s, as well as the enormous South African discoveries of the 1890s, resulted in relatively mild supply spikes that never exceeded 5%—and the growth rate quickly returned to normal.

Beautiful to behold, gold has been treasured by all nations and cultures since human beings first walked the earth. It has intrinsic value. Other commodities have intrinsic value—oil, for example, is referred to occasionally as "black gold." The petroleum supply, however, fluctuates far too much to be of use as a monetary anchor, not to mention the disadvantages of bulk, storage, and perishability.

What about silver? For centuries, silver had a close ratio to gold; 15 to 16 ounces of silver were equivalent to an ounce of gold. The currencies of China and India were once fixed to silver. But in the latter part of the nineteenth century demand for silver declined with the increasing use of paper money. Improvements in mining technology also enabled supplies to increase. The value of silver to gold began to fall. By the mid-1890s, the ratio was about 30 to1. Today it is in excess of 60 to 1.

Every alternative to a gold standard has been tried, including no standard at all. If something were superior—another commodity or a basket of commodities—we would have found it. And so the answer to the question *Why gold?* becomes self-evident: in 4,000 years of human experience human beings have found nothing better. History shows that a gold-based monetary system is frequently abandoned, but it always reemerges. Always.

No Better Stimulus than Gold

Janet Yellen, Ben Bernanke, and other Keynesians have forgotten the global economic expansion that took place from the 1870s until 1914, during the era of the worldwide gold standard. In a unique interlude of monetary harmony, European nations, Japan, and the United States linked their currencies to gold.

The move toward the worldwide gold standard era began in the late 1600s in Britain with the Great Recoinage debate of 1696. Britain's currency had been debased by wear and tear, as well as by the age-old practice of coin clipping favored by governments as well as counterfeiters. They would slice precious metal off the edges of coins, and the shavings could then be melted down into bars or currency.

Almost 50% of the precious metal was missing from British coins by the end of the seventeenth century. It was decided that, to avert a monetary crisis, Britain would melt down and remint the damaged money. Traditionally such an occasion was an opportunity for a devaluation. British treasury secretary William Lowndes wanted the coins reissued at a far lower value. John Locke, the esteemed political philosopher, argued that such a devaluation was a violation of natural law, equivalent to an arbitrary seizure of property. The eminent Isaac Newton also opposed debasement, considering it an affront to science, a moral transgression no different from counterfeiting.

Parliament's eventual decision not to devalue was a victory for advocates of sound money. Newton, as Master of the Mint, formally fixed the pound to gold in 1717 at the once-famous rate of three pounds, seventeen shillings, and ten-and-one-half pence to an ounce (£3.89), a ratio that stood unchanged until 1931.

When it tied the pound to gold, Britain was a second-tier nation. Soon all of that would change.

Great Britain Leads the World into a Golden Era

By the end of the Napoleonic wars in 1815, Great Britain emerged indisputably as the world's major power and global center of innovation. The industrial revolution, gaining momentum since the early 1700s, reached full speed. Great Britain gave us such innovations as steam engines, steam-powered trains, and mass-produced cotton fabrics, to name a few. The city of Manchester became to manufacturing what Silicon Valley is today to high technology.

The United States underwent a similar metamorphosis after adopting sound money. Reckless money printing during colonial days and the War for Independence had left the finances of the young republic a shambles. Alexander Hamilton, the first secretary of the treasury, realized that the only hope for recovery lay in a system based on sound money. Among other initiatives, Hamilton established a mint with a dollar fixed by law to a specific weight in gold. The value was fixed at \$19.39 per ounce. (In 1834 it was slightly devalued to \$20.67.)

Overnight the economy sprang to life. Capital poured in from the Dutch and also America's former enemies, the British. Barely a century after Hamilton's reforms, the United States was the premier industrial power in the world, surpassing even Great Britain. This growth took place despite a chaotic banking system bogged down by politics and burdened with government restrictions.

Inspired by the success of Great Britain and to a lesser extent the United States, other nations began to follow their example. By the end of the nineteenth century, Germany, Italy, Spain, France, Russia, Japan, and even Greece all adopted gold-based money.

The Era of the Classical Gold Standard

The era of the classical gold standard was a unique interlude in history. It saw an explosion of trade and innovation that, in many respects, has yet to be equaled even today. Rarely in human history has there been such an increase in population and living standards—or such a free flow of people and capital. Money was not the only factor in the global boom; by discrediting mercantilism, Adam Smith and his fellow free-market thinkers had helped still the heavy hand of government in the economy. The nineteenth century was an era of economic freedom, with no restrictions on the flow of capital.

London became the world's center of finance. British investments played a significant role in the development of the United States and numerous other countries. Railroads, factories, and agricultural enterprises proliferated throughout the world, including India, Argentina, China, Malaya, and Africa.

This explosion of capital helped trade flourish despite a flurry of protectionist tariffs in the latter part of the nineteenth century. Enormous strides in shipping and the technological advances of the industrial revolution were raising living standards, bringing new products and services at lower prices to people around the world. The invention of refrigeration, for instance, meant a country such as Argentina could grow immensely rich by exporting beef in greater volumes and more cheaply than ever before. International trade as a proportion of global economic activity wouldn't reach the levels of 1914 again until almost a century later in 1996; capital flows, not until 1999.

Advances in the United States were particularly impressive. Between 1870 and 1914, real wages more than doubled even though the country had millions of immigrants. Agricultural output tripled. Industrial production, led by Andrew Carnegie's application of new steel technologies, surged a jaw-dropping 682%. Tens of thousands of miles of new railroad tracks criss-crossed the continental nation.

The United States was hardly alone in experiencing such spectacular growth. Russia saw increases in oil and steel output after adopting a gold standard in 1897. The country became a magnet for foreign investment, especially from its ally, France. Russian bonds became a staple of the French bourgeoisie. The country also became the world's biggest exporter of grain, with the highest economic growth rate in Europe on the eve of World War I.

Contrary to the myth long perpetuated by the communists, Russia was moving in the right direction economically and was on the way to industrialization without communism, which retarded development and killed tens of millions of people.

No longer was military power the way to riches. Thanks to trade and the free flow of capital, smaller countries like Norway, Switzerland, and Holland with lesser armies—and lower military budgets—enjoyed higher standards of living than Germany or France.

By providing a shared standard of value and facilitating global trade, the worldwide gold standard also helped break down longstanding barriers between nations that had been adversaries. For example, France got a significant portion of its coal, the chief source of energy at the time and a critical component of explosives, from its archenemy Germany.

The era's focus on commerce also helped calm tensions between the warring nations of Latin America. Capital poured into the region, mostly from Great Britain. New opportunities attracted millions of immigrants who were more interested in bettering their lives than in battling their neighbors. The incidence of warfare in South America declined so that by 1914 peace, not war, was the rule. The British author and Parliamentarian Norman Angell remarked in 1913:

> Just note at what is taking place in South America. . . .
> These countries, like Brazil and Argentine, have been
> drawn into the circle of international trade, exchange
> and finance. . . . *It is not because the armies in those states*
> *have grown* that the public credit has improved. Their
> armies were greater a generation ago than they are now.
> It is because they know that trade and finance are built
> upon credit.

Other examples of interdependence abounded. The naval rivalry between Great Britain and Germany did not prevent the owners of Germany's growing merchant marine from insuring their ships with British companies in London.

The pre–World War I era was no utopia (working conditions in factories were harsh by today's standards) and saw plenty of political agitation, but it was in retrospect a remarkably positive time, unrivaled in history. Unfortunately age-old forces of nationalism and political antagonisms eventually won out over the advances of commerce. Tensions between Austria-Hungary and Serbia set off the chain of events leading to World War I. Germany and Austria-Hungary, among others, had long military traditions. The military castes of both countries, particularly Germany, failed to grasp the fact that trade, not military muscle, is the true source of power. Few leaders at that time could have ever imagined that just a century later a commercially successful Germany with a significantly smaller army would be the dominant power in Europe, while Russia with a far larger military would lag behind.

Lower Interest Rates, Cheaper Capital, Gangbuster Growth

In today's command-and-control system of fiat money, lowering interest rates requires an act of largesse from a central bank. Under a gold standard system of sound money, interest rates naturally fall. That's because lenders can expect to be repaid in money that has not declined in value.

The cost of capital dropped dramatically in Great Britain after Newton tied the pound to gold in 1717. The Crown had previously rued the fact that it had been unable to borrow money at the low rates obtained by the fiscally prudent Dutch. In 1694 the newly created Bank of England lent the government of William III 1.2 million pounds at 8%. That was considered a concession to the new king, but it was far higher than the 4% rates the Dutch were paying.

After Great Britain adopted gold-based money, however, the government could issue bonds (called stock in those days) with no maturity at a rate as low as 3%. By the late 1800s that rate went down to 2½%. Between 1821 and 1914 the average yield of British government bonds—called Consols—that had no maturity was 3.15%.

The peg to gold also meant that Great Britain was now a better investment. Before the pound was linked to gold, fiat money had enabled a free-spending monarchy. A gold-based pound, however, signaled that Parliament—specifically, the taxpayers who made up the House of Commons—was firmly controlling the purse strings. (Unlike today's Keynesians, they knew that money didn't come from the tooth fairy.)

Nathan Lewis writes that lender confidence soared in the nineteenth-century gold standard era: "Interest rates worldwide converged to low levels. British debt was perceived to have the lowest risk of either credit default or currency devaluation. Other governments' debt traded with a small risk premium."

The story was much the same in France and the United States: yields on French government debt started out at about 15% when the Bank of France was established in 1800. They slid to 3% by 1902. As for the United States, Lewis writes:

> The market recognized that gold indeed served as a superlative standard of stable value—that it was money *par excellence*, as Karl Marx wrote in 1867. Currency stability in turn engendered economic stability and provided the reliable foundation for all financial and economic activity.

Investors were so confident during the gold standard era that in 1896 Northern Pacific Railroad issued a 150-year bond at an interest rate of 3%!

The explosion of wealth creation that took place during the worldwide gold standard era was no anomaly. From 1946 to 1970, under the gold-based Bretton Woods system, U.S. industrial output surged 209%, an average of 4.8% a year. In the post–gold standard era this growth dropped dramatically: industrial production increased 159% between 1970 and 2012, a little more than 2% a year; in the period of 2000 to 2012, it rose a total of 7%.

No Credit Rationing

Under a gold standard the cost of money will be somewhat higher than it is today—after all, you can't get much lower than zero interest rates. But the Fed would no longer be artificially suppressing interest rates with its price controls. The result: credit and capital would be more widely available. Smaller businesses will get loans at an affordable cost instead of getting no credit at supposedly near-zero interest rates. For most job-creating small businesses, credit in recent years has been a lot like government-rationed healthcare—supposedly free, but much of the time you can't get it.

A Return to Government Accountability

Gold makes governments *accountable*. Having to maintain a stable monetary value makes it harder to turn on the printing press to pay for political promises or to buy votes. Governments have to turn instead to borrowing and higher taxation, actions that require popular support. In other words, gold discourages the profligacy possible with fiat money by assuring that spending has consequences. Gold standard advocate Daniel Ryan explains:

> Government can still borrow, but they can't use the central bank to sidestep the consequences of excessive borrowing that every other borrower has to face: higher interest rates. A gold standard would forbid quantitative easing. Thus, a gold standard puts a lid on the shenanigans politicians like to use for political gain. We've all seen the effects of leaving monetary and fiscal discretion in the hands of politicians and their appointees: chronic inflation and chronic government debt. Had there been a gold standard, government debt would have never gotten out of hand like it has.

Government finance was never as self-restrained as it was during the classical gold standard era. With European nations becoming increasingly democratic and dependent on consensus, budget expenditures therefore had to be of a more careful nature. Germany, for example, badly wanted to boost spending for its military to compete with rivals France and Russia, which were improving their armies. It also wanted a navy to rival Great Britain's. But the German government was constrained by the fiscal discipline imposed by the gold standard.

Germany spent only around 2 to 3% of its GDP on its military—a far lower percentage compared with the size of its economy than what was spent by nations like France (3 to 4%). The numbers, in other words, suggest that it could have easily spent more. In a sense, the prewar gold standard saved the Allies. Germany came within a whisker of winning the war in its early weeks. Without a gold standard, it is very likely that Germany's military outlays, and its military strength, would have been far greater.

Even without a gold standard, stable money fosters fiscal discipline, though to a lesser degree. We saw this during the Clinton administration, which generally maintained a steady dollar. In his book *The Agenda*, Bob Woodward quotes the president's incredulous reply when told by his advisors that, before spending to stimulate the economy, he first needed to cut a record-high national deficit. To do otherwise would imperil demand for the government's bonds and its ability to borrow. According to the book, the president exclaimed, "You mean to tell me that the success of the program and my re-election hinges on the Federal Reserve and a bunch of f****** bond traders?"

Top Clinton advisor James Carville told the *Wall Street Journal*: "I used to think if there was reincarnation, I wanted to come back as the president or the pope or a .400 baseball hitter. But now I want to come back as the bond market. You can intimidate everybody."

Because it would mean a return by government to fiscal accountability, the idea of gold-based money has traditionally struck fear into the hearts of many proponents of big government who wrongly equate stable money with austerity. As we've pointed out, this is not true: Otto von Bismarck began the modern welfare state in Germany during the era of the classical gold standard. Great Britain likewise enacted a series of social welfare programs before World War I.

At the same time, Europe's great powers also were able to afford large military establishments. It was amazing to see how small military budgets as a proportion of countries' gross domestic product were before World War I. Great Britain, for example, was famous for its navy, yet its naval outlays were relatively small at less than 2% of GDP.

Gold allows governments to do more with fewer taxpayer dollars. It would lower the cost of capital for government as it would for the broader economy. Washington could more easily service its debt. There would be the added benefit of more tax revenue because the economy would flourish under a gold standard, especially when combined with a sensible tax and regulatory system.

A gold standard would allow government to deploy money more efficiently. It doesn't necessarily mean lower spending, because in a vibrant gold standard economy the tax base would be bigger.

Real Money Means Real Prices

Sound money via a gold standard would mean that median incomes would once again rise in real terms. When you have fiat money, as we've discussed, prices go up and real salaries go down. You're getting paid in money that is worth less and less.

A gold standard would obliterate inflation. From 1821 to 1914 the cost of living in Great Britain went up 0.1% a year. Compare that to the double-digit rate of inflation in the United States between 1971, when the link to gold was severed, until

1983, when that bout of inflation was conquered. Since then the average rate has been above 3%, based on the highly imperfect CPI calculations. In the real world it's higher; for example, a gallon of gas in the United States in 1971 could be bought for as little as 30 cents a gallon. Today it is around $3.50 and has been far higher.

Eliminating inflation is not the same as price stability. Prices will continue to fluctuate with gold-based money, but they would do so in response to changes in supply, demand, and productivity.

We're not saying that gold would mitigate the normal industry shakeouts that can sometimes occur or that it could prevent market distortions created by bad government regulation or excessive taxation. Gold-based money, however, would enable the market's system of communication to convey the *true* worth of goods and services being exchanged. In other words, price signals would be free of distortion.

Under a gold-based system, prices would tend to drop more than they do today because there would be lower commodity prices. Food and energy prices would likely be lower, as would the prices of goods and services that make heavy use of those commodities. Lower fuel prices, for instance, would cause airfares to drop. Imagine how much less punishing winter would be with half the fuel cost.

Gold would have prevented the housing bubble and other imbalances that have occurred in response to price signals distorted by the ever-weakening dollar. Oil would not have skyrocketed from $3 to nearly $40 a barrel in the 1970s, nor would there have been the exploration mania and eventual crash in the 1980s. Gold-based money would have spared us the other inflationary disasters in farmland, copper, commercial real estate, and gold prices—and the busts that followed when the Fed tightened and markets came back down to earth.

George Soros May Have to Find a New Job

A single fixed exchange rate under a gold standard would drastically reduce speculative trading and the windfalls it produces. As we've mentioned, much of the speculation that takes place in today's financial markets is a response to the volatility produced by the collapse of the Bretton Woods gold system.

Capital and brainpower instead would be directed into ventures that meet people's real-world needs and desires. No more tax shelters and protective investments. After all, why would you need to invest in gold unless you make jewelry or want to wear it? Society would benefit.

We had a taste of this after the early 1980s through much of the 1990s, an era of semi-sound money when the price of gold, despite ups and downs, averaged around $350 an ounce. The United States became a world leader of innovation. Cocktail chatter turned from tax shelters to tech investments. The Dow Jones Industrial Average surged 15-fold from under 800 to over 11,000. Short-term interest rates came down from their height of around 21% to 5%. The interest rate of long-term government bonds dropped from a high of 15.75% in 1981 to a little over 6% in the 1990s.

The Reagan boom saw huge job creation after inflation was conquered in 1982: in the rest of the decade 20 million jobs were generated. U.S. growth during this period exceeded the size of the West German economy, the third largest in the world. George Gilder has observed that the United States created more private sector jobs during that era than in all of Europe and Japan put together.

This occurred despite the economic depressions that took place in energy, agriculture, and commercial real estate. The U.S. economy in the 1980s was liquidating the malinvestments of the 1970s and roaring ahead with investments in technology, media, autos, and other sectors. There was more capital for productive ventures because of the lower price of lending and borrowing that came about with more stable money. The 1980s saw the rise of the personal computer, telecommunications technologies like fiber and cellular, cable television, and other innovations. America's share of the global GDP moved upward.

The boom continued under the Democrats in the 1990s. The Clinton administration was, for the most part, a sound dollar administration. Then the George W. Bush administration started the United States on the road to a weak dollar policy, and all of us continue to live with the consequences. Despite the abundance of anti-Bush rhetoric, the Obama administration has only doubled down on the loose money policies of his predecessor.

A return to the sound dollar policies of Reagan and Clinton would mean more wealth creation through innovation. Forbes .com political economy editor John Tamny points out that, if the United States returned to gold, people like George Soros—or, for that matter, Paul Tudor Jones or John Paulson—could not amass such immense fortunes from speculation; they would have to channel their energies elsewhere.

Had Nixon never freed the dollar from gold, Tamny believes: "It's a fair bet . . . that the three (along with many of their numerous competitors) would have grown rich through the creation of efficiency-boosting software, a cure for cancer, and transportation advances that would make today's cars look positively pedestrian."

The Gold Standard: Four Possibilities

How do we get there from here? Implementing a gold standard would require choosing one of several systems of gold-based money. Most people are probably not aware that there are several different gold standard systems. Two have been put into practice: *the classical gold standard*, which was used by the world's largest economies from 1870 to the outbreak of the First World War in 1914, and the *gold exchange standard*, which was used after both world wars. Another two have been proposed: a *100% gold-backed currency* and what we call *the gold price system*.

Each has its critics and supporters. But in all, gold is the yardstick of value. We thought a quick guide would be useful, since you are likely to hear more about them in the near future.

The Classical Gold Standard

The classical gold standard was the system established by Great Britain and later used by others during the nineteenth century. Countries pegged their currencies to a particular weight of gold. Anyone could take gold to a bank and exchange it for currency at a fixed rate, or they could swap money for gold. Governments during the classical gold standard era possessed gold reserves: gold bars. Most also had bonds denominated in foreign gold-based currencies.

Gold coverage—the ratio of gold reserves to the monetary base—varied and fluctuated in each country. Convertibility, however, was sacrosanct. A drop in a nation's gold reserves meant countermeasures had to be taken, such as raising interest rates to attract short-term money and perhaps cutting spending or raising some taxes to demonstrate fiscal prudence.

Contrary to myth, trade balances weren't needed for the system to work. Great Britain routinely had enormous trade surpluses and was proportionately the greatest capital exporter ever. The United States, by contrast, routinely experienced trade deficits and was a major capital importer. Yet the dollar remained successfully fixed to gold.

As we've noted, the classical gold standard was destroyed by the First World War. The breakup of the German, Russian,

Austro-Hungarian, and Ottoman empires produced numerous new countries with their own currencies and central banks, making the system harder to implement.

More critically, there was also the mistaken perception that wartime inflation had created a gold shortage—not enough gold to restore the kind of gold-backing prevalent before hostilities. Such a fear stemmed from the longtime misguided focus on the supply of gold rather than how it functions. Had nations simply pegged their currencies at the postwar value, gold could have resumed its role as a standard of measurement. The imagined shortage would have quickly disappeared. Instead the solution was to abandon the existing system in favor of a new one: the gold exchange standard.

The Gold Exchange Standard

The gold exchange standard was seen as the answer to the supposed gold shortage because it required fewer nations to hold gold than under the classical gold standard. The U.S. dollar and the British pound would be directly fixed to gold, but other countries could forgo using gold bars and instead link their currencies to dollars and pounds. Government reserves would include not only gold, but also U.S. and British government bonds.

Countries didn't mind this. Unlike piles of gold, bonds paid interest. Reserves could grow effortlessly. If nations wanted more gold, they could redeem their dollars and pounds to get it.

Gold standard purists then and today, however, were appalled by the substitution of debt for gold in government reserves. Believing that countries needed to hold physical supplies of gold, they considered such a use of leverage inflationary, little better than a pyramid scheme. Critics claim to this day that such flaws helped encourage an excess of credit creation that produced the disaster of 1929. This was an incorrect reading of what was occurring in the market, which was rising because of an incredible surge in corporate profits. The cause of the Depression was the U.S. enactment of the Smoot-Hawley Tariff, which we discuss in greater depth later in this chapter.

Another gold exchange standard, the Bretton Woods system, emerged in the waning days of World War II, as we noted earlier. At that time, the United States owned more gold than the rest of the world's governments combined. So only the U.S. dollar was fixed directly to the precious metal, redeemable in gold bars solely by governments or central banks. Other currencies were tightly pegged to the dollar.

That was the problem. When Nixon closed the gold window in 1971, there was no gold-based currency in the world for the first time ever. This made resurrecting a new arrangement extremely difficult. Remember that the classical gold standard was preceded by Great Britain, the United States, and other nations having gold-backed currencies. The Bretton Woods gold standard would have worked if the United States had played by the rules and understood how to manage the system.

A 100% Gold-Backed System

Some gold standard supporters advocate a system where the currency is 100% supported by gold. That wasn't the case under a classical gold standard. Only a percentage of the money stock was covered; it was widely assumed that not everyone would simultaneously seek to redeem paper for gold. The system operated somewhat like our modern system of fractional reserve banking, under which banks loan out most depositor money, keeping only a fraction on hand as reserves.

For some of the same reasons that fractional reserve banking and its leverage have discomforted critics, some believe a gold standard demands 100% coverage. In a 100% system, gold would support the *entire* money stock, making it 100% redeemable. Supporters of a 100% system like it because they believe it eliminates the risks of bank runs and the system failure that might come with dependence on leverage. Banks would have to have gold reserves on hand to redeem 100% of depositors' money.

Advocates also claim that, since the global gold supply grows at about 2% a year, in line with long-term economic growth rates, a 100% system would not be deflationary. Sadly, they're mistaken. Here's why: Say you pegged the dollar to gold at the market price, which has been fluctuating at around $1,200 to $1,400 an ounce. Given that the United States holds 261 million ounces of gold that would mean the total monetary base—the currency in circulation and bank reserves on deposit at the Fed—could not total more than $325 billion. That would require a huge contraction in the monetary base and a deflation to end all deflations. Even before the Fed's QE binges, the monetary base was a tad under $900 billion. Today it is $4 trillion.

Some respond that we could take a page from Franklin Roosevelt, who devalued the dollar from $20.67 to $35 in 1934, and jack up the dollar price of gold to $10,000 or more an ounce. Then you'd end up with the opposite problem: Weimar-style inflation.

A more realistic variation of this idea would be a gold-based currency board. Currency boards have been around for over 150 years. A government simply uses a sound or widely used currency to back its own money. Its money is 100% backed by that other currency. Several countries use such a system today, including Denmark, Bulgaria, and Lithuania. Hong Kong has had a currency board tied to the dollar since 1983. In these cases, their monetary bases are made up of only euros and euro-denominated bonds plus some gold. Their central banks have no discretion. People can turn in the local currency for euros at a fixed rate, and vice versa. Their domestic money supplies are solely determined by the needs and wants of their own people.

So why not such an arrangement that is gold based? Johns Hopkins economics professor Steve Hanke, a world authority on currency boards who helped design them for Bulgaria and others, has outlined how such a system might work. Instead of a currency, such a board would "hold reserves in gold or in highly rated or liquid securities denominated in gold or fully hedged against changes in fiat-currency price of gold."

One could see how a currency board would work for a smaller country, but it would be impractical for a large country like the United States because of the difficulty of having a 100% backed dollar. And, as we have noted, it's not necessary.

The Gold Price System

This new version of the gold standard has been proposed in legislation introduced by U.S. Representative Ted Poe. It uses the precious metal as strictly a yardstick of value and does away with the need for nations to hold gold supplies. The system is the essence of simplicity. The dollar would be pegged to gold at, say, $1,200 an ounce. If the market price goes above that level, the Federal Reserve would engage in open market operations, selling bonds to extract reserves from the banking system until gold settled back to $1,200. Conversely, if the price went below $1,200, the opposite action would occur. The Fed would purchase bonds, which would put money back into the banking system. A strength of the gold price system, as Louis Woodhill has noted on Forbes.com, is that there is no way for speculators to attack the system by buying up supplies of gold. And as we've said, you don't need to hold any gold for the system to work.

The key challenge of this method is setting the gold/dollar ratio. Setting the price of gold at too low a level, such as $400 an ounce, risks delivering a deflationary shock to the economy, as happened in Great Britain in 1925. Probably the best method would be to take a 10-year or even 5-year average of the dollar/ gold price, mark it up 10% as insurance against deflation, and go with it.

A Gold Standard for the Twenty-First Century

If America is ever to attempt to restore the vitality of its economy, it must return to the tradition of sound money via a gold standard. Below we present a proposal for a new gold standard for the twenty-first century. It combines the fundamentals of the old systems, using gold as the yardstick of value, while avoiding the vulnerabilities: no more manipulating interest rates, no more misguided focus on the balance of payments, no worry about who buys U.S. debt, and no concerns if there's another big gold discovery.

The United States doesn't have to worry about stockpiles of gold. It simply must have the knowledge and the will to defend the ratio between the dollar and gold. The following list lays out the basic features.

A fixed dollar value that would be maintained by the Fed.

The twenty-first century gold standard would fix the dollar to gold at a particular price. As we mentioned, that price might be decided based on a 5- or 10-year average of recent gold prices, marked up as insurance against deflation. The Federal Reserve would use its tools, primarily open market operations, to keep the value of the dollar tied at that rate to gold.

The program would be phased in gradually.

The process need not run more than 12 months. The government should announce a certain date when the conversion to a gold standard will take place. A gradual phase-in will help markets prepare for the return to gold-based money. With no more fears of future inflation, a more natural gold price should re-emerge, making it easier to arrive at the gold/dollar ratio. The transition period would also enable financial institutions and investors to adjust expectations about future interest rates and alter investment strategies to reflect a new environment of stable money. Global markets would make similar adjustments. The dollar would be permitted to fluctuate against gold with a range of 1%, the rate used under the Bretton Woods system for currencies against the dollar.

The system would be backed up by law.

To minimize the inclination of central bankers to exercise "discretion," procedures governing the twenty-first century gold standard would be codified into law. This legislation should also bar the Fed from manipulating interest rates. The U.S. central bank could no longer use its tools to fix the federal funds rate, the interest rate banks pay to one another for borrowing reserves. The Fed could still set the discount rate that banks pay to borrow money from the Fed at its discount window. That charge would be set above free-market rates of similar maturities so that banks don't use the window to get a cheap source of money to lend out.

Barriers to alternative currencies would be removed.

Removing barriers to alternative domestic currencies would also help to keep Washington playing by the rules. The rise of competing currencies would be another signal to the Fed to defend the dollar. After all, people use U.S. dollars as a matter of convenience. To consider an alternative would mean a very real distrust of the dollar's integrity.

To permit currency diversity, no taxes or government fees could be levied on sales of gold and silver bullion, as is the case today. Capital gains taxes would also be a no-no. Onerous reporting rules that now afflict gold and silver bullion buyers would be prohibited. Individuals would be permitted to launch alternative currencies.

The convertibility of dollars into gold would be restored, if needed.

The twenty-first century gold standard would allow people to turn in dollars to the government to receive gold at a fixed rate and cash in their gold for dollars. Americans had that right, except in wartime, until 1933. They did not have it under the Bretton Woods system, when only central banks of other countries could redeem dollars for gold. This kind of convertibility, while not really necessary, would serve as one more safeguard to maintain sound money if the Fed does not do its legally mandated job of maintaining the dollar/gold ratio.

Instead of a formal gold cover of yesteryear, legislation for a new standard might specify that Uncle Sam would indeed be obliged to take dollars from all comers. In addition, the U.S. government would have to replenish its gold stocks if they fell below, say, 50 million ounces (the amount is 261 million ounces today). Washington's gold holdings would be audited yearly, as would the Fed itself. For its services, government would convert currency to gold at a fixed fee of 2% or more so as not to compete with private dealers.

Other currencies would be pegged to the dollar.

If the United States went to gold, other countries would likely fix their money to the dollar, if only for convenience. Numerous countries in Latin America and Asia already try to keep their currencies closely aligned to the greenback because doing so makes trading and investing with the United States much easier. Part of the task at hand would be to make sure that their central banks understand how to defend their ties to the dollar. (We've seen repeatedly, as in the Asian crisis of 1997–1998, how central banks lack the knowledge of how to defend their currencies from speculative attacks.) Of course, if a country wanted to attach its currency directly to gold instead of the gold-backed dollar, it could do so. The result would be the same: stable exchange rates.

The Fed would have a role, at least for now.

The Fed would continue to act as a lender of last resort and deal with panics that might arise from a 9/11 type of event.

Common Concerns About Gold

If a gold standard offers so many powerful advantages, some may ask, why hasn't the United States returned to it in the decades after Bretton Woods? One reason is that gold is ferociously dismissed by the Keynesians and monetarists dominating the policy establishment. Ronald Reagan, who created a Gold Commission in 1981, was a believer in sound money. Like John F. Kennedy, Reagan understood that, in the words of Kennedy, the dollar should be "as good as gold," that a great nation must have a sound currency. Unfortunately he was unable to prevail over his advisors who, with the exception of the noted economist Arthur Laffer (of the Laffer curve fame), were almost unanimously opposed to gold. Had he done so, we might have a gold standard today.

The lack of real discussion has allowed myths and misconceptions about the gold standard to persist. Below we list several concerns that are frequently raised.

Gold shows too much price volatility to be a reliable anchor.

Opponents point to gold price fluctuations as proof that a gold standard would mean price volatility. In 2010 Chris Beam worried in Slate.com:

> Gold is notoriously volatile—its price has doubled over the last two years. If the Federal Reserve were to simply fix the dollar to the price of gold on a given day and demand for gold changed drastically, it would wreak havoc on the economy. If the Fed pegs the rate too low, for example, people would want to trade their dollars for gold, forcing the Fed to raise interest rates in order to make dollars more attractive. Even if the Fed were to pick the rate correctly, it would still have to make adjustments based on the economies of the United States' trading partners. If the dollar is growing in value, but another country's currency is decreasing in value, yet both currencies are pegged to gold, something has to give—either one of the currencies has to inflate or deflate, or the exchange rate has to be adjusted.

Put aside the misunderstanding of exchange rates. (If two currencies are pegged to gold, their exchange rates, by definition, are fixed.) The writer doesn't get the point about how the gold standard fundamentally operates. The price of gold is volatile only when it has no link to the dollar. Remember, gold's intrinsic value makes it a refuge for investors fleeing unsound money. A good part of gold's price reflects anticipated future inflation and sheer uncertainty about what is to come. If the dollar were sound, there would not be the flight into, or out of, gold.

In 1980, when people feared that the United States was incapable of controlling an ever-worsening inflation, the dollar price of gold soared quickly from $220 to $850 an ounce. When emotions calmed, the dollar price fell to $300 an ounce. Gold shot to a record high of $1,900 an ounce in 2011. Since then the precious metal has come down considerably.

It is possible to pick a gold price that neither fuels inflation nor attempts to turn the clock back too far in time as Great Britain did after World War I. As for the concerns about our trading partners, remember that nations of the world voluntarily adopted gold standards following the lead of Great Britain in the 1870s—and their economies boomed.

There is not enough gold to have a gold standard today.

Critics complain that the United States has only about 261 million ounces of gold with a market price of roughly $325 billion. The monetary base is over $4 trillion, and the most commonly used money supply measure, M2, stands at almost $11 trillion. The total of M1, the most liquid part of the money supply, is $2.6 trillion. If the dollar were pegged to gold at its current value, they say, we would have to undergo a savage deflation that would make the British experience of the 1920s look like a sedate picnic.

What they don't recognize is that what makes gold work is not its supply, but rather its ability to provide a stable yardstick of value. You don't need to have piles of this precious metal for a gold standard to work. Even during the heyday of the classical gold standard, no country ever had 100% gold backing for its money. Great Britain often had very low amounts of gold backing the pound, and the amount there and in other countries varied widely. (As we've said, you don't even need to own an ounce of the yellow metal to have your currency linked to gold.) Previously we explained how a twenty-first century gold standard would work with our current supply. If the United States decided to have convertibility—to give people the legal right to redeem dollars for gold at a fixed rate and vice versa—the U.S. government still has enough of the metal to make such a system work, even with the Fed's bloated balance sheet.

A gold standard would be too rigid.

The misconception here is that a vibrant economy would be held back because a fixed gold price would tie government's hands, preventing growth in the money supply. Gold, however, is far less rigid than critics perceive.

From 1775 to 1900 the U.S. population grew from 4 million to 76 million. During that time, America's mainly subsistence agricultural economy blossomed into an industrial colossus. In the process, the global supply of gold increased a little more than threefold while the money supply in the United States mushroomed 160-fold even though the dollar was fixed to gold.

A gold standard allows the money supply to expand naturally in a vibrant economy. Remember that gold, a measuring rod, is stable in value. It does not restrict the supply of dollars any more than a foot with 12 inches restricts the number of rulers being used in the economy.

What if a crisis like a major financial panic demands an emergency injection of liquidity? The Bank of England developed the concept of the lender of last resort back in the 1860s under the classical gold standard. The Federal Reserve could easily fill the same function today if the United States reestablished a gold standard. At its discount window, banks could still put up sound collateral for emergency loans, preferably at an above-market interest rate so the borrowing institution would liquidate the loan as quickly as practicable. But such an event under a gold standard would be far less likely. As noted monetary expert Nathan Lewis wrote on Forbes.com, stable money has never caused a financial crisis.

Gold helped bring on and prolong the Great Depression.

The antigold narrative also blames the precious metal for the Great Depression. Supposedly, fears of creating a run on gold in Great Britain kept the United States from raising interest rates to curb its overheating stock market during the 1920s. The result, allegedly, was a credit bubble and falsely inflated economy that brought about the crash of 1929. Afterward, gold ostensibly kept governments from reviving their sliding economies.

Hogwash. The Great Depression was the tragic consequence of the Smoot-Hawley Tariff Act enacted by the United States in June 1930. Equity markets try to anticipate the future. This dreadful legislation was unprecedented, imposing an average 60% tax on over 3,000 import items. When it appeared that a destructive tariff of historic proportions might pass Congress, the stock market cracked and then crashed in September–November 1929. When, for a brief time, the tariff bill appeared it might falter, stocks rallied mightily, ending 1929 almost where they were at the beginning of the year. Then the monster came to life again and the slide resumed. Other countries, of course, noticed what was going on and prepared retaliatory measures.

The enactment of the Smoot-Hawley Tariff Act set off a worldwide trade war that was as disruptive to global commerce as the beginning of hostilities in 1914. Policy makers didn't know what hit them. Their responses, primarily tax increases, compounded the downturn. Great Britain raised income taxes in 1930 and again in 1931. Germany, particularly hard hit because it was dependent heavily on trade, imposed draconian taxes, deepening the slump. The United States passed a bill of massive tax hikes in the spring of 1932 that was made retroactive to the beginning of the year. Income tax rates were boosted astronomically, with the top rate going from 25% to 63%. Epitomizing the folly of it all was a stamp tax on checks, thereby encouraging people to withdraw cash from already beleaguered banks. This draconian legislation even included numerous increases of excise taxes on items such as candy and movie tickets.

Critics respond that when Great Britain went off the gold standard in late 1931, its downturn ended. Of course, as we have noted, devaluation can initially deliver a boost. But this eventually deepened the devastation by escalating the trade war. After London's devaluation, at least 20 countries quickly followed suit. The United States did the same in 1934, as did Italy and Belgium; France finally devalued the franc in 1936. These beggar-thy-neighbor devaluations, as they were called, were ultimately damaging to the global economy. In the end there were no winners. The experience compelled allied and neutral nations to convene in Bretton Woods, New Hampshire, in 1944 and create a new gold-based international monetary system.

A gold standard would be undermined by speculators.

Critics question whether it is possible to maintain a fixed dollar/gold rate in today's global markets, in which computer technology makes possible giant trades and sophisticated speculators have access to vast resources. In 1992, for example, the British pound was tied to the German mark. Speculators led by George Soros attacked sterling by borrowing pounds and then selling them to buy marks. When it appeared that Great Britain, to save the pound, might need to raise interest rates as much as 100%, the humiliated government caved and it floated the pound. Soros and others then sold their marks for a greater number of pounds than they had borrowed, pocketing billions in profits.

Wouldn't a gold-based dollar be similarly vulnerable? The answer is: not if nations know how to defend their currencies. How can they do this? By using their reserves to buy their currency and maintain its rate by reducing the monetary base.

In early 2009 the Russian ruble faced a speculative assault. Russia then bought rubles, its monetary base declined, and the attack on the ruble failed. The United States has plenty of assets to mount a Russian-style defense against an attack on a gold-backed dollar.

Setting a fixed dollar/gold ratio is price fixing and therefore anti–free market.

Having fixed weights and measures is essential for fair and free markets. We don't let markets each day determine how many ounces there are in a pound or how many inches there are in a foot or the number of minutes in an hour. Money, similarly, is a measure of value.

Setting a new gold/dollar ratio is too difficult.

Gold standard critics commonly cite the painful deflation that roiled Great Britain in 1925 after it made the mistake of pegging the pound to gold at its pre–World War I gold price even though wartime inflation had more than doubled the cost of living.

This mistake could have been avoided had Great Britain simply fixed the pound to gold based on postwar values. Compounding the government's error was that it left in place its high wartime taxes, which also depressed the economy. When it comes to setting a gold/dollar ratio, one needs to remember the famous quote from Thomas Wolfe: "You can't go home again."

A gold standard for the U.S. dollar has to be based on present-day values. The ratio shouldn't be fixed at, say, $35 an ounce or even the $350 that prevailed for much of the 1980s and 1990s.

The challenge in setting the price today, however, is that people in the last few years have been buying gold out of fears of inflation. The answer should be calculations that take into account forward markets in gold, in addition to the price of inflation-protected bonds. The key is to avoid too low a ratio. To ensure that nominal wages don't fall, a slightly high ratio is crucial. Whatever the method used, the key is to set a price so people know what the rules are and the economy can get growing again.

The gold standard isn't perfect. No system is perfect. But stable money has never ever brought about the systemic financial and monetary crises caused by fluctuating money. If we are ever going to meet the challenges and avert the crises that face us today, gold is the best hope there is.

THE NUGGET

Gold remains the monetary Polaris.
Every alternative has failed.

CHAPTER 7

Surviving in the Meantime

Protecting Your Assets from Unstable Money

Sell them and you'll be sorry,
Buy them and you'll regret,
Hold them and you'll worry,
Do nothing and you'll fret.

— Old Wall Street saying quoted in
Investing in One Lesson by Mark Skousen

B Y THIS TIME, YOU'RE PROBABLY WONDERING *WHAT NOW?* As you read this book, the value of your wealth is eroding. If you had $100,000 in cash in 2000 and did absolutely nothing, it would have been worth only around $74,000 in 2013. That's right, the value of your money would have declined by about 26%. And that is with the last decade's supposedly low rates of inflation.

We believe that the economic and social consequences of the continuing destruction of the dollar will sooner or later force the world to reawaken to the necessity of stable money.

But that hasn't happened yet. The question is what to do in the meantime.

The primary objective of investing today should not be about getting rich but *preserving what you have*. It is about survival. Ironically, one of the unintended consequences of the Fed's manipulation of money is that it has made traditional wealth preservation through savings accounts untenable. You can't just park your money in banks that barely pay interest. Washington policy makers constantly decry the evils of risk, but their regulations, not to mention the Fed's artificial suppression of interest rates, have forced all of us into vehicles and strategies with higher levels of risk in order to preserve our money.

The next question is: What is the best way to do it? Contrary to what some "experts" suggest, there's no surefire formula. Consider this grim reality: most professional money managers underperform the market. Few mutual funds consistently beat the Dow or the Standard & Poor's 500 Index (S&P 500). Since managers and individual investors make up the market, by definition they can't as a class exceed it. Unlike the situation at Garrison Keillor's Lake Wobegon, everyone can't be above average.

In the mid-1970s, when inflation was raging in the United States and around the world, *Forbes* magazine featured on its cover a block of ice in the desert sheltered by an umbrella. The title read: "Inflation: How to Protect Your Capital." In the first paragraph of the story we quickly confessed: "We cannot tell a lie. Given our tax laws and today's virulent rate of inflation, there is no reliable way for the individual investor to hang on to his capital, let alone expand it by investing. Hold on to your pocketbook if anyone tells you otherwise."

That unsexy but wise advice still holds true today. In an environment of monetary instability, the only sure thing is uncertainty. Even the smartest investors, though, can't avoid being hurt by economic disruptions caused by the unnecessary and unexpected missteps of government. In the ferocious volatility of the last decade, John Paulson, who famously made billions trading in derivatives by foreseeing the subprime collapse, eventually stumbled in 2011 and 2012.

Good News in the Near Term, but . . .

With the Fed's taper and its higher interest rates increasing the availability of credit, expectations in the near term are for a continuation of the recovery. Banks swollen with those astronomically high reserves have begun to resume lending. Whether this leads to the inflation that some fear depends on what happens at the Fed. Forbes.com contributor Louis Woodhill has accurately observed, "Right now, the Federal Reserve is conducting a completely discretionary monetary policy. . . . No one can accurately forecast a whim."

The stealth tax of inflation, however, is far from the only wealth destroyer that can eat away at your money. Others include the new taxes and regulations from the Affordable Care Act or the financial asset seizures by government that are becoming an alarming global trend. The kind of looting of people's assets that happened in Cyprus is also happening in other countries. There have even been calls in the United States for restrictions on retirement accounts—401(k)s—despite the fact that they are personal property.

We would like to help you navigate the treacherous rapids ahead. Our advice won't put you on the Forbes World's Billionaires list. In fact, there are only a relatively few investors on it. Most make fortunes through owning their own businesses or by financing the ventures of others. What the information and suggestions in this book will do, however, is help you preserve and build on your wealth.

Achieving this objective does not require access to sophisti-cated hedge funds, equity funds, or even venture capital funds. Nor do you have to strive to get in at the ground floor of red-hot initial public offerings. All you have to do is follow a few ba-sic steps. If you are truly a long-term investor you will do very well indeed over time if you follow the advice we are about to give you. In fact, you will do better than the vast majority of professional money managers.

The Panic of 2008–2009 proved that you don't have to be a survivalist in an underground bunker to be concerned about the potential for disaster in this era of unstable money. The dev-astating bear market that began in late 2007 and ended in early 2009 may not have been the apocalypse some had predicted. To many, however, it felt like something close to it: the two most prominent major stock indexes, the Dow Jones Industrial Aver-age and the S&P 500, lost about 54% in value, and hundreds of individual stocks lost a lot more. Real estate investment trusts (REITs), a favorite income-producing vehicle for millions of investors, plunged 75% as many appeared headed for collapse. Bank equities overall dropped 80% as shareholders in many such institutions were wiped out altogether. All this havoc in a mere 17 months.

The financial crisis was a lot like Hurricane Katrina: most people didn't recognize the full magnitude of what was com-ing. Just as it's good to have a hurricane preparedness kit, it also makes sense to practice financial preparedness.

Some Questions and Answers

How do I protect myself?

Our recommendation: 5 to 10% of your money should be in-vested in Treasury Inflation Protected Securities (TIPS), another

5 to 10% should be in cash, 5 to 10% should be in gold coins or bullion, and the rest should be in stocks. A few comments on each follow.

Treasury Inflation Protected Securities. These low-risk bonds are decidedly unglamorous. But because their par value rises with inflation, TIPS are a prudent investment in inflationary times. They have a fixed interest rate and pay investors semiannually. You can purchase them from the government through TreasuryDirect.gov. TIPS require a small minimum investment of $100 and are sold in $100 increments with 5-, 10-, and 30-year maturities.

Cash. To be ready for emergencies, 5 to 10% of your money should be in cash. Typically, in bear markets you end up with too much cash and miss opportunities when the market turns around. In bull markets people will borrow too much on their credit cards and get in trouble when there's a crunch.

Gold. When we say gold, we're talking about gold coins or bars. You should not own gold as an investment but rather as an insurance policy. When governments misbehave and undermine the integrity of your money, the real value of your traditional investments and savings vehicles will be eroded. But you can take comfort in the fact that your gold will move up in nominal value.

As we discuss later on, the experience of the last several years underscores how treacherous it is to treat gold as an investment vehicle. Think of the losses suffered by all the people who bought gold in the last couple of years in response to all those TV ads. In 2010–2011 there was real fear that the Fed's ballooning balance sheet would bring a repeat of the inflationary 1970s. When the Fed's quantitative easing failed to make it into the economy, gold prices dropped dramatically from their highs.

Having a small percentage of your money in gold is a hedge against a weakening dollar. For example, during the inflationary period that began in the late 1960s and ended in the early 1980s, gold shot up from $35 an ounce to a brief peak of $850 in early 1980. Meanwhile the real value of stocks had gone down.

The reason you don't want to treat gold like your traditional investments, though, is what happened afterward. The yellow metal crashed to under $300 in the summer of 1982 when the Fed was killing inflation. For the next two decades gold's price remained around $350 an ounce. Only a nimble speculator could turn a profit in such an environment.

Stocks. Despite all its volatility, the stock market is your friend. Stocks are excellent long-term investments, and they are fine short term. This may seem counterintuitive, given recent events including the horrific plunge of 2008–2009, heinous frauds like those perpetrated by Bernard Madoff, an unending array of insider-trading scandals, flash crashes and technology glitches that can actually close down markets, and alleged (and untrue) market rigging by high frequency traders.

Now let's look at this fact: for over 100 years, the average annual return on stocks is about 9½% a year—5% from price appreciation of shares and 4½% from dividends. This average includes the years of the Great Depression, the two world wars, numerous recessions, and countless stock market corrections.

Obviously the market doesn't achieve that 9½% average appreciation in a straight line. The Dow Jones Industrial Average went nowhere from 1966 to 1982. When you factor in inflation, it lost considerable ground. Another widely used index, the S&P 500, did better, but it was still no bargain. But eventually things turn around. From 1982 to 2000, the Dow appreciated *15-fold*.

Since 2000, stocks have been hit with two severe bear markets—2000–2001 and 2008–2009. The latter one was especially painful. Yet, by early 2014, stocks *more than doubled* from the lows of early 2009.

If you have the intestinal fortitude to ride the highs and lows, you will eventually be rewarded. Consider this: if in your mid-twenties you put $10,000 into stocks in a tax-deferred account such as an IRA, reinvested dividends and capital gains, and made no more direct deposits, you would have accumulated well over $350,000 by your mid-sixties. By the time you hit 70 you would have more than $500,000. Even with average inflation of, say, 3% a year, you come out ahead.

Let's say when you start to work in your early twenties you set aside $100 a month into your account. By the time you're 70, your nest egg would be worth almost $1 million. Albert Einstein supposedly said that compound interest is the greatest miracle. He was right.

Why are you still confident in the stock market with so much recent volatility, and with the economy so burdened by increasing regulation and constraints on enterprise?

Remember that the market has achieved 9%-plus annual average returns for more than a century. There was no greater disaster than the bear market of 1929–1932 that saw the Dow Jones Industrial Average go down almost 90%. Equities will take hits, but they always come back.

Stocks represent ownership of companies. In the United States, free enterprise always triumphs. The American people have exhibited an astonishing capacity to right the ship of state when it goes drastically off course. We're seeing this with the dramatic attitudinal shift toward freer markets and away from central planning taking place right now in response to the Affordable Care Act, nicknamed Obamacare, which to date has been the greatest failure of a social experiment since Prohibition. One thing this freedom-loving practical nation has never tolerated is failure.

Could the U.S. government *really* do away with retirement accounts like 401(k)s— or seize people's savings, as the government of Cyprus did in that country?

The Obama administration has made noises about restricting private retirement accounts like 401(k)s and IRAs as a prelude to laying its hands on some of that money. Washington may attempt this through new regulations that would be imposed by the new Bureau of Consumer Protection that was set up under the Dodd-Frank bill. Ensconced inside the Federal Reserve, this bureaucratic monstrosity has no accountability and no congressional oversight.

This agency will eventually be found unconstitutional. But in the meantime it can create plenty of mischief. The government could also renege on the promise of Roth IRAs, which right now let you save after-tax money and make later tax-free withdrawals by decreeing such monies as taxable.

We have already witnessed brazen looting of people's financial assets not only in Cyprus but also in Poland, Hungary, and Argentina. Chile, with a new hardcore socialist president, may make moves on individual social security accounts that were privatized 30 years ago.

In the United States, such an attempt to seize individual assets will give rise to a fierce reaction. Not convinced? Just look at what happens when attempts are made to suborn the Second Amendment, the right to bear arms.

Deciding on a Stock Investing Strategy

You should have two investing strategies. The first is a con-servative strategy whose objective is preserving and building your wealth for retirement. You have the time to do this, even if you're in your late fifties.

When investing your retirement funds, your goal should be to do as well as the market. Invest in the whole market and ride the ups and downs. The best way to do this is through index funds. They were invented by one of the great investing heroes of all time, John Bogle, founder of the Vanguard Group, now the second-largest mutual fund group in the world and a cham-pion of low management expenses. As a Princeton University undergraduate, Bogle noticed the distressing tendency of indi-vidual investors to lose out in the investing game because of ex-penses and chronically bad timing.

His answer: the first index fund, launched by Vanguard in 1976. It was designed to mimic a broad stock market index, the S&P 500. Initially greeted with derision, index funds to-day are immensely popular. They exist for all the major mar-ket indexes, as well as for numerous sectors of industries such as banks, pharmaceutical companies, and technology firms. There are index funds that encompass the entire global universe of publicly traded stocks and for the markets of scores of individ-ual nations. There are also bond index funds of all kinds: U.S. Treasuries; high-grade corporate bonds; junk bonds; short-term, intermediate, and long-term debt securities; and interna-tional versions.

The advantage of index funds is that the individual stocks aren't being actively traded as they are in a traditional mutual fund. Because they don't need an army of managers and ana-lysts, costs are lower. The expenses of Vanguard's S&P 500 In-dex Fund are only one-sixth of 1% (or 17 basis points) versus at least 1.5% for the typical mutual fund; for its Total Stock Market Index, which encompasses just about all traded stocks in the United States, the expense is also an ultralow 17 basis points. While compounding can give you miraculous returns over time, *expenses* compound as well.

Choosing an Index Fund

Go for broad-based index funds like the Vanguard 500, which has 500 equities based on the S&P 500 Index, or the Fidelity Spartan 500 Index Fund. The big question revolves around how index funds are put together, more specifically how one weighs each stock. Does a smallish stock count as much as, say, Apple? Vanguard and its followers did it by the market capitalization of each equity. The debates about index funds sound almost like medieval theology. No need to get caught up in them. Traditional index funds work just fine for our purposes.

Beating the Market

You can indeed beat the market by a strategy as simple as investing in an index fund: dollar cost averaging. With this strategy you buy a particular dollar amount of an investment on a regular schedule—typically every month—and stick to it. You do this regardless of what's happening in the market. Yes, prices will go up and down. That's precisely the point.

Into your retirement accounts, put in a certain amount systematically, say $100 a month. When the market turns down, console yourself with the knowledge that you're getting more shares for your money. Inevitably the market rebounds, usually when you least expect it. Your bonus: your gain is bigger.

Take this simple example: You put $100 in and buy 4 shares at $25. The next month, the market is down and shares are $20, netting you 5 shares. The month after, the market is horribly bearish and shares are selling at $10, giving you 10 shares. Now the market turns bullish with shares back at $25 and you buy 4 shares. After four months, with dollar cost averaging you own 23 shares worth $575. If the market had been stable, you would own 16 shares worth $400. Extreme? Of course, but the point is valid.

Now let's go to a real-world example. Say you started your monthly retirement program of $100 a month in early 2000 when the Dow peaked at 11,722 and stayed with it through 2012 (we leave out 2013, when the Dow surged 27%, to underscore our thesis). With dividends and capital gains reinvested, your investment would have appreciated 48% thanks to dollar cost averaging.

You might want your retirement money to be divided in half between stocks and bonds. Each year—and only once a year—you would recalibrate your portfolio to bring it back to that 50/50 balance. Say stocks that year surged and bonds bombed, so your portfolio is now 65% in your equity index fund and only 35% in your bond index fund. You would sell equity shares and buy bond shares to restore the ratio you want. You would do the same if you have divided your portfolio between U.S. and international stocks and bonds. The key here, as in all of investing, is discipline and consistency.

To sum up, index funds let you do what few money managers do—they let you do as well as the market. *Dollar cost averaging enables you to beat it.*

That's why you should take full advantage of every retirement vehicle you can, such as 401(k)s, including maximizing employer contributions, IRAs, and Keogh plans, which are available if you have self-employment income and can be utilized even if you also have a regular salary.

Indulging Your Inner Buffett

Your second strategy can be to indulge your "inner Warren Buffett." You might take some additional risk to see if, like the famous Forbes World Billionaire investor, you can beat the market—or achieve the more modest objective of meeting your own particular needs and wants. Put aside a percentage of your money that you don't need in the near term—or, in the worst case, that you could afford to lose—for investments with a little more risk.

This is where you can focus more on individual stocks. But indulging your inner Buffett doesn't require getting esoteric. Remember that very few succeed in beating the market. Charles Ellis, a noted money manager with an excellent long-term record, recommends that people approach investing the way they should play tennis: get over the fact that you are not going to make it to Wimbledon or the U.S. Open—except as a spectator. Just focus on getting the ball over the net and within the lines, period. Leave the fancy shots for others and you will do far better than if you try to act like the pros.

If you want to invest in individual stocks, then go for blue chips like Coca-Cola, which has raised dividends every year since it went public. These days "stodgy" blue chips also include the likes of Amazon, Google, and Apple. In general, you should aim for stocks with good dividends (high-growth, large-cap stocks like Amazon are an exception) and ride them up and down.

Industries to Focus on During Times of Inflation

Good places to look during inflationary times, at least initially, are in industries related to commodities and construction and other hard assets. One example: companies that make farm or construction equipment, such as John Deere and Caterpillar. Both did well in 2011–2012 and then faltered a bit. Caterpillar has since come back but has trailed the stock market.

Keep in mind that investments that do well in times of inflation are always part of the next bubble. As we've discussed, inflation misdirects capital to hard assets and commodities. In the early 2000s, housing did well—until it didn't. Mining companies did well but then were clobbered, especially gold mines. Steel companies blossomed and then took a hit. The same thing happened during the inflation of the 1970s. Those who did well with gold, oil, other commodities, forest products, farmland, and tax shelters took a beating in the 1980s.

If we do end up getting truly high inflation, you need to take an especially hard look at earnings. Remember, rising prices distort market signals. A company can appear to be doing well while the real reason for the "soaring" revenues may be inflation.

Do we really need to be protecting against inflation when the annual CPI increase was under 2% in 2013?

Remember what we said: if you started with $100,000 in 2000 and did nothing, your money would have declined in value by 26%. According to the CPI, inflation got as high as 4% in the past decade. Independent estimates put the rate significantly higher. Also it's not the annual rate but the total rate over time that eats away at your savings. It's like the reverse of compounded interest.

Investments for When the Fed Tightens

There's no simple investment solution when the Federal Reserve tightens, because the Fed can tighten in several different ways. One scenario is typified when the Fed deliberately tightens up on credit, as in the early 1980s when Paul Volcker's attempt to wring inflation out of the economy was successful, but it sent both the bond and the stock markets reeling. Another scenario is the inadvertent tightening that occurs when the Fed does not meet monetary demand, as happened in the booming economy of the late 1990s. This gradually hurt traditional manufacturers and commodities; when there's a shortage of cash, people sell commodities to raise it. We noted in Chapter 4 on inflation that the Fed's actions ended up adding fuel to the high-tech boom because investors, looking for opportunities in the United States, turned to high tech.

For investors this means: stay the course with your retirement money. With your other assets, proceed with caution.

The Importance of Taking the Long View

We can't repeat it enough: your emotions are your enemy when it comes to investing your money.

A powerful real-life example of how emotions are misleading is the bear market that began in late 2007 and lasted for almost two years. In January 2009, while the financial panic had ended weeks before, stocks experienced the most dismal performance since January 1933 in the pit of the Great Depression. February 2009 was no better: it was the worst February for stocks since 1933.

The media abounded with speculation about the potential for a repeat of the Great Depression. Stocks, with few interruptions, kept sliding and sliding, almost to the point of oblivion. The Dow Jones Industrial Average, as we noted previously, fell 89% before the sickening slump ended. It was a virtual wipeout of equity value. We've had nothing even approaching this descent before or since. And yet today, not even counting reinvestment of dividends, the DJIA is 40 times higher than its pre-Depression high.

Nonetheless, many people, seeing their lifetime savings shrinking so rapidly in the violence of a bear market that seemed to have no end, decided to pull some money out of the market before it was all lost. Gallows humor about 401(k)s turning into 101(k)s couldn't mask the psychological and financial devastation tens of millions of people experienced.

Then in March things suddenly turned around. Despite the policies of a new administration and the actions of the Federal Reserve, which gave the United States the weakest recovery from a sharp economic downturn in the country's history, stocks more than doubled. By 2013, the major indexes were exceeding their precrisis high. Real estate investment trusts and banks went up several-fold.

How many individuals who fled the market with some or all of their money during its darkest days got back in for this totally unexpected bull market? All too few. Mutual fund industry numbers tell the sad tale: investors continued to pull money out of equity funds until late 2012. Most parked their cash in no-yield money market accounts or in bond funds, in which the Fed's quantitative easing programs had created a bubble.

As the famous investor Sir John Templeton once put it: "Bull markets are born on pessimism, grow on skepticism, mature on optimism, and die on euphoria."

Daniel Kahneman, a noneconomist who won the Nobel Prize in Economics for behavioral finance, has noted the phenomenon of how when everyone is optimistic, when friends tell you how well they are doing, you tend to put money in the market. And when everyone is saying the sky is falling, you take your money out.

More Questions and Answers

Is the stock market today overvalued or undervalued?

In early 2014, stocks were fully priced. The price/earnings (P/E) ratio of the S&P 500 was at a healthy level. Having advanced so much, in order to advance further the market will want policy reinforcement such as a tax cut or simplification of the tax code, a progrowth budget deal, and/or a reform of the debt ceiling law that has incentives for spending restraint or regulatory moderation in antigrowth rules from the Obama administration. These are not likely. But barring a foreign crisis, earnings will grow and so will stocks, though at nothing like the pace of 2013.

Let us reiterate: don't try to be a market timer. You have no way of knowing when a long-term bear market or bull market will turn. In 1996 Fed head Alan Greenspan gave a headline-making speech in which he warned about market "irrational exuberance." The Dow was 6,437. Despite Greenspan's jeremiad, it went on to reach new highs in 1997, 1998, and 1999.

What are some key indicators of the health of the stock market?

Corporate earnings, and the prospect of them, drive markets. But not all profits are the same. One very useful measure of corporate profits is the National Income and Product Accounts (NIPA) issued by the Commerce Department's Bureau of Economic Analysis (BEA). It excludes nonoperating items such as dividend income, capital gains and losses, and deductions for bad debt. It is an excellent measure of companies' operating profits, certainly better than reported earnings, when companies naturally try to put the best face on things.

In the late 1990s, for instance, profits looked robust. But by the BEA's NIPA measure of earnings, profits peaked in 1997, not 2000. Reported profits were rising because of a surge in capital gains, not earnings from actual operations. This was a time of leveraged buyouts, divestitures, and IPOs. The wise investor would have sensed that the stock market was rising more than justified by the state of the economy.

Investors should also pay attention to the individual sectors of the market as broken out by Standard & Poor's. Are all the gains taking place in only one sector? That could be the sign of a bubble, as opposed to healthy economic growth. Before the dot-com bust, the late 1990s bull market was becoming more and more narrowly based, involving primarily high-tech companies. Much of the rest of the market was stalled or contracting.

Before the crash in 2008–2009, financial and housing stocks were on fire. The financial sector stocks were more than double what they were before the collapse of the Bretton Woods system. Although finance has been an innovative industry, nothing justified such a surge. It was clearly artificial, reflecting the increase in speculation and in the financial instruments that are a consequence of fiat money.

Austrian economist Joseph Schumpeter observed this during Austria's post–World War I hyperinflation, which was every bit as bad as Germany's. Vienna's glorious coffeehouses, which were on every corner, were replaced by banks. When the inflation ended, the banks went away and the coffeehouses returned.

How important is the price/earnings ratio when choosing individual stocks?

When stocks in a bull market reach a P/E of 20 or more, beware. A sound ratio is 15 or so. P/E ratios, however, are generally a useless indicator of value in bear markets when many companies, including good ones, are experiencing losses.

Investing in International Stocks

Countries whose economies are growing faster than the U.S. economy can appear to offer investment opportunities. The downside is greater volatility and higher risk.

Take the example of China. That country with its seemingly unstoppable economy would appear to provide countless investing opportunities. But look at the real picture in this graph. No, that's not a roller coaster but rather a chart of Chinese equities traded in Shanghai.

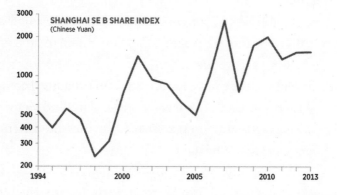

Potential investors awed by China's spectacular growth are too often blinded to the economic problems causing such ups and downs. For instance, China's still-communist government restricts where savers can park their money in addition to imposing various controls on foreign investing. Having an expanding economy doesn't mean that every stock benefits.

In fact much of China's growth comes from millions of small private companies that are essentially off the investment radar. Traditional banks often ignore them. These entrepreneurial enterprises get expensive financing from nontraditional sources such as street lenders. Listed equities do not include these small businesses.

To invest successfully in foreign equities one needs to understand a country's political and regulatory environment. The experience of Japan underscores how treacherous investing can be. In the 1950s and 1960s, Japan pursued extraordinary growth policies that kept the yen stable and spending in check (no more than 20% of GDP). The government cut taxes every year. Stocks surged.

Then in 1989, after a traumatic real estate bubble, Japan's government went off the rails. Savage tax increases were enacted. Spending went berserk. For several years the Bank of Japan adopted a deflationary monetary policy.

The country is still in a rut today. The Nikkei 225 peaked in 1989 at almost 40,000. A quarter of a century later, the Nikkei is at 15,000.

To minimize the risks of international investing, consider an index fund approach. Companies like Fidelity and Vanguard offer such vehicles for foreign stocks that include the entire world and the world sans the United States.

How About Bonds?

The conventional wisdom has long been that bonds are safer than stocks. Because a bond is a debt that gets repaid, you're less likely to lose your investment than with a stock, the value of which can sharply decline. The interest of bonds, unlike dividends, is guaranteed. There can be painful exceptions such as during periods of inflation, which knocks down the real value of both principal and interest. Political maneuvering can also affect bonds. For example, after the General Motors bankruptcy engineered by the Obama administration, bondholders were forced to lose far more than they would have in a normal, non-politicized restructuring; debt holders received a shellacking.

From the early 1980s until recently, bonds generally have had a great run upward, even outpacing stocks from time to time. But with the Federal Reserve winding down QE and its bond-buying binge, interest rates will be going up. Bond prices will be under pressure for the foreseeable future in this uncertain interest rate environment.

To guard against future inflation, put 5 to 10% of your money in inflation-indexed Treasury bonds. If you haven't dumped your munis, good. The worries of two years ago were overdone; there was not a tsunami-like wave of city and state insolvencies. A word of advice if you want to buy bonds right now: stay short term. Don't forget: *interest rates will be moving up.*

As with stocks, there are all kinds of debt issues from Treasuries to junk, from long to short durations. You now can get bonds from all over the world.

There are a handful of ways to deal with your urge to have bonds. One is to own a balanced fund like Vanguard's Wellington Fund that mixes debt with dividend-paying stocks and has low management expenses. Again, watch those expenses; Vanguard's expenses are usually among the lowest in the industry. Another option is to put money into a bond index fund that holds a wide range of debt. Depending on your age, you can go for funds that are short term, intermediate term, or long term. One exception is the present moment, as the Fed tries to wind down quantitative easing. Wait a year or two until the pricing in credit markets returns to normal.

Don't try to guess classes of debt in which to put your retirement money. Since 2008 junk bonds have done far better than higher-rated debt issues as investors reach for yield in an era of zero-interest rates. But they also get slammed hard in recessions.

A warning light: junk bond issuances were at a record high in 2013. Emerging market government debt was popular for a time and has fallen into disfavor as investors anticipate higher interest rates in the United States. So don't be a timer or sector picker. Go for a broad-range index fund.

Is Gold a Good Investment?

Gold is a great indicator of what's going on in the economy. As we noted, gold can also act as portfolio insurance against the effects of monetary malfeasance by governments. But gold is not an investment unless you're in the jewelry business. It is not similar to building a factory, opening a store, providing a new service, or creating a new product.

Most of the time, gold has been a loser compared to stocks. From August 1982 to February 2000 the Dow Jones Industrial Average increased 15-fold, a gain of 1,400%. Include dividends and the gain is even more impressive. Gold? It went nowhere. The same was true from the end of World War II until the Bretton Woods system was blown up in 1971.

From 2000 until the summer of 2011, gold went up sixfold. Since then, it tumbled over 35% while stocks went up 40%. The precious metal increases in its dollar price only when the United States is misbehaving monetarily.

Gold Mining Stocks

Gold mining stocks aren't the answer either. Since 2011 these equities have been slaughtered, down more than 50%. The marginal price, including depreciation, of mining an ounce of gold is nearly $1,200. What about gold-based exchange-traded funds (ETFs)? Several have been launched that own gold and whose price mimics the gold market. No worry about gold mine managements or buying and storing the precious metal. And no worries about the dealer charges you pay when buying gold coins. Some people who purchased coins as a result of those once-nonstop TV ads found themselves paying out-landish commissions.

While a handy tool, metal-based ETFs have yet to prove themselves in a severe crisis or panic. They will probably pass with flying colors, but you should hedge your bets by having most of your holdings in the real stuff.

Other Investment Vehicles: Commodities and Currencies

Most people get interested in commodities and currencies when the dollar becomes very uncertain. Commodities and cur-rencies can be bought on credit through your broker. You can lose a lot of money very quickly. Whatever a salesperson may tell you, surveys have found that most individual traders lose money in these markets. You are going up against people who make their living trading these things, which is stressful and fast-paced. Don't kid yourself about your ability.

When money is stable, the volume of commodity trading is lower. Institutional money managers also wouldn't treat com-modities as an investment class, as they routinely do today.

Real Estate Investing

Housing took on the mantle of a great investment vehicle when the dollar went off the gold standard. Again, this flawed per-ception is a response to the instability of fiat currency. A house is a very expensive consumer item. It is a place in which to live, not a substitute for investing. An investment in a successful new venture grows in value because it creates a new product or service. The price of a house may rise because of increased demand. And it may become more valuable if you invest in im-proving it. When you have an unstable monetary environment, hard assets like houses can benefit, at least for a while. But a house does not offer the same kind of growth potential as investing in an Apple or a Google would.

We saw all too painfully during the subprime crisis that a house is no surefire way to make money. Having to maintain a home means that there are plenty of hidden costs you may not have counted on. And people can get into trouble overborrowing to buy a house—or find themselves strapped by rising mortgage and property tax payments.

Should you buy a house and then rent it out? Only if you treat such an act as going into a business. Tenants can make you pull your hair out; they can sue you. Going into the rental business is not like buying a stock.

A house can provide the emotional satisfaction of having a place of your own. But, like gold, it is more of an insurance policy than an investment that provides the kind of growth potential you need to beat inflation.

Life Insurance

Permanent life insurance, which is also called "whole life," combines insurance with a savings vehicle. Unlike term life policies, this insurance does not expire; you have it for as long as you want right up until your death. And you can't be dropped if you fall ill. The cash value of a permanent life policy always goes up each and every year. Moreover this cash buildup grows tax-free. If you let the policy lapse, you will owe no tax unless the cash exceeds the total premiums you paid for the policy.

With a mutual insurance company, the annual dividends can be used to reduce the premium. Within several years, the policy will become self-sustaining. That is, the premium effectively disappears because the annual dividend will exceed the premium. How many years depends on the company's investment performance. You can borrow the cash portion at a specified rate of interest below what you would pay borrowing on your credit card, and usually below the margin rate that you would pay borrowing from your brokerage account.

Permanent life insurance is a great anchor in turbulent times—it's nice to know that whatever is happening, one financial asset continues to grow.

Many advisors are negative on permanent life, saying the product is too expensive because of commissions paid to agents who sell the policy. Critics assert that you would do better to buy term insurance and invest the rest of the money yourself. We disagree. Most people won't invest the alleged savings each year. Obviously not all companies are the same; you must examine credit ratings.

*   *   *

This chapter has covered some basic ways to protect your money. There are of course plenty of other investment vehicles. They include, to name a few, annuities, private equity, and hedge funds. In the back of this book we list some books that can help you go further in evaluating the tools and strategies that best meet your objectives.

Most people don't have the inclination or time to handle their investments on their own. They need a trusted advisor or advisors. Just as skilled athletes will use a coach, a trusted advisor can be helpful even for seasoned investors. John Schlifske, the CEO of Northwestern Mutual, likes to make that point this way:

> My [exercise] coach doesn't really tell me anything I
> don't already know. But with a scheduled appointment,
> I will do what I should do but might not if I didn't have

to meet with that coach at a particular time. The same principle is true of a trusted advisor. He or she will help keep you on your program.

Schlifske's advice is especially true in these times of turmoil. Everyone can use advice on the challenges and complexity of the myriad of financial questions raised by taxes, family, your business, and countless other topics.

There is no scientific formula for picking the right coach. You should do the obvious due diligence including researching fees, comments online and from friends, possible disciplinary actions, or promises that sound too good to be true. One axiom that famous money manager and Forbes columnist Ken Fisher emphatically emphasizes: make sure the custody of your securities is separate from your advisor. You want to know that what your statement shows is actually what you have.

THE NUGGET

When it comes to investing, emotions are your enemy.

CHAPTER 8

Looking Ahead

We cannot predict the value of our homes or prices
on the stock market from day to day. We cannot
anticipate illness or automobile accidents, the behavior
of our children, or the incomes of our parents. . . . We
are almost entirely incapable of predicting the future.

Yet economics purports to be strangely exempt
from this fact of life.

—George Gilder, *Knowledge and Power*

WHERE DO WE GO FROM HERE? THE GLOBAL OUT-
look is mixed. If the Federal Reserve continues
pulling back from its disastrous experiment in interest rate manipulation known as quantitative easing, more
credit should flow to small and new businesses. America's recovery should gain momentum. This will not only be good for the
United States but also for the European Union—where there
have been slight signs of growth—and the rest of the world's
nations. Regardless of forecasts by the naysayers, the United
States, at least for the time being, continues to be the engine for
the world's economies.

At the same time, the currency crises that have roiled emerging nations in response to the Fed's taper underscore the perils of
a fiat monetary system. Throughout this book we've explained

how money brings together strangers throughout the world, enabling them to work together and conduct transactions that meet the needs of people in the global marketplace. Currency crises resulting from the taper show how easily misguided monetary policies can cause this global cooperation and enterprise rapidly to unravel.

The woes in emerging countries remind us that, while the darkest days of 2008–2009 may have passed, the conditions that caused the catastrophe remain with us. The world will continue to lurch from one crisis to the next until we finally understand that the way to growth and a more prosperous future is not through weak money or tight money—but through sound money.

A monetary system based on sound and stable currencies is our best hope of finally achieving a genuine recovery, one that would usher in a new era of material progress that would lift living standards to unheard-of heights. We got a taste of the possibilities in the global economic expansion of the 1980s and 1990s when the United States had a somewhat stable dollar. The world experienced growth and prosperity that nearly rivaled that of the classical gold standard era of 1870–1914.

Bill Gates once predicted that by 2035 there would no longer be poor nations. For his prediction to come true—and for us to finally vanquish the malaise that we mistakenly call "the new normal"—the world monetary system must be anchored by a stable global currency.

The British pound performed that role in the nineteenth and early twentieth centuries. Since then the de facto world currency has been the U.S. dollar. Its destruction after 1971 has hurt the United States and the world economically and politically. This cannot be allowed to go on or we will face new and ever more turmoil that will imperil free markets and ultimately democracy itself.

Many of the major problems that plague us today, from anemic growth to high food and fuel prices to sovereign debt, have roots in distortions and volatility that are the by-products of fiat money. People instinctively sense that there's something wrong with our present system. The challenge is to convert this unease into knowledge, debate, and a demand for change. For too long, our thinking about money has been needlessly clouded by jargon, bad ideas, and political agendas.

Restoring Monetary Sanity

If we are to overcome the obstacles that face us, we, the people in the United States and around the world, must learn more about money. Such an understanding requires knowledge of some simple fundamental principles. Here's a recap of some key precepts:

1. **The foremost objective of monetary policy must be to maintain currency stability.** The only justification for central bank manipulation of the monetary base is to maintain fixed currency values. This is achieved most easily when there is a gold standard.

2. **Trade itself has nothing directly to do with the value of a currency; balance of payment deficits have no impact on an economy if money has a fixed value.** Media coverage of the emerging markets crisis in early 2014 was littered with numerous commentaries about the need for countries with a current account deficit to take corrective action. The obsession with the balance of payments deficit has for decades led to needless monetary devaluations, capital controls, and protectionist trade restrictions that have wreaked havoc around the world. This wrongheaded focus on the current

account and the overall balance of payments helped to give us the disaster of fiat money.

Adam Smith's fundamental insight about the mutual benefits of trade continues to be ignored. If a central bank correctly uses open market operations to maintain monetary stability, trade deficits would have no effect whatsoever on currency values or an economy.

When Turkey's lira came under speculative assault, the problem wasn't the current account; it was political turmoil and a loose monetary policy. Turkey responded by more than doubling its interest rates, a move that slowed its domestic economy. This would not have occurred had Turkey adjusted its monetary base to keep the lira at a stable level.

What about so-called hot money pouring into a country—or, conversely, large amounts pouring out? Again, the right countervailing monetary policy should be able to deal with the problem. If a central bank adjusts the monetary base, it can maintain stability. Remember our story about Switzerland. When enormous amounts of money—primarily euros, but also dollars—flooded the country to buy the Swiss franc during the euro and sovereign debt crises, the Swiss responded by putting a ceiling on how high the franc could increase in value against the euro. A relatively stable value was maintained and Swiss exporters avoided further harm.

3. **Printing money is not creating wealth.** Had mercantilist monarchs succeeded in turning lead into gold, they still would have failed to create wealth. Gold would have become so plentiful that it would have lost its value. Enough said.

4. **Beware of the false growth that comes from monetary stimulus.** Not all growth is what it appears. The Great Inflation of the 1970s did have periods of seemingly good

GDP expansions, but they were false advances. The debasement of the dollar led to massive investments in energy, commodities, farmland, and commercial real estate. All experienced horrific downturns in the 1980s when inflation was conquered and the malinvestments were liquidated. We see the same phenomenon at work today. Commodity-oriented economies such as Brazil, Russia, and South Africa have similarly experienced false booms.

In the early part of the 2000s, excess liquidity created by the Fed and other central banks enabled otherwise less-than-prime creditors like Greece and Turkey as well as millions of home buyers in the United States to borrow vast amounts of money. Manipulating or devaluing the currency, or, for that matter, boosting government spending, might raise GDP in the short term. But this activity is a response to distorted market signals and is always false and unsustainable.

5. **Loose money can damage an economy without a big, immediate rise in the cost of living.** In the popular mind and in the minds of most economists, inflation means rising prices as reflected by the Consumer Price Index (CPI). As we have painfully learned from the housing meltdown, loose money can produce destructive asset bubbles without a big across-the-board rise in the CPI and 1970s-style inflation. Debasing money always leads to unpleasant consequences, although the symptoms are not always the same.

6. **There is no such thing as price stability.** Even when there is stable money, prices for goods and services will always change because of supply and demand fluctuations that have nothing to do with money. Recall what happened to the price of cell phones—the original one 30 years ago cost $3,995, and the price of handhelds has plunged since

their debut because of constant increases in productivity. If money were stable, in fact, such productivity increases would lead to a decline in the cost of living. Keynesians would scream, "deflation!" But, as in most things, they would be wrong.

7. **The central bank shouldn't manipulate interest rates except in a crisis.** Since World War II, monetary policy has been geared to setting short-term rates on the supposition that this helps guide activities of the economy and influences GDP. For example, interest rates have been used to "cool down" a "hot" economy. The idea that economies get cold or overheated is ridiculous.

   Because interest is the price of borrowing money, artificially setting interest rates is a form of price control, which means rationing and shortages. Price controls on interest are one reason for the misallocation of credit that has slowed the economic recovery in the past several years.

   Central banks should spur an economy by maintaining currency stability through open market operations. Domestically that means buying or selling bonds to increase or decrease the monetary base. Internationally, it means using foreign exchange reserves to buy or sell a currency. We don't need a central bank manipulating interest rates. If we had stable money, rates would naturally be lower.

8. **The euro would do fine if European policy makers maintained stable money.** The euro was launched in the early part of the 2000s, around the same time the Federal Reserve started to weaken the dollar. When the Fed misbehaves, it sucks in its wake most other central banks. The European Central Bank followed the lead of the United States and ended up creating too much money, although not on the scale of the Fed.

Even with today's problems, the euro has indeed succeeded in making intra-European trade easier. The euro also provided a refuge from the volatility of floating exchange rates.

Some Keynesian commentators trash the euro for the same reason they reject gold: they see its fixed exchange rate system as too rigid. One of their biggest delusions is that the euro has prevented nations of Southern Europe from recovering by keeping them from devaluing their monies. The truth is, had these countries continued with their own currencies, things would have been far worse. Many would have experienced a terrible inflation—in Greece, a hyper-inflation—and a lower standard of living than they have today. The euro, if anything, saved these countries from themselves. The real problem with Southern Europe and France is not the euro but domestic antigrowth restraints like rigid labor markets and high taxes.

9. **If there were stable money, the price of gold would not fluctuate.** The precious yellow metal is often misperceived as being too volatile to anchor the dollar effectively. Today's gold prices, however, are not driven by changes in supply. Remember, gold itself has a stable intrinsic value, which is why it's called the monetary Polaris. It is a refuge for investors during periods of weak or unstable money. The huge upsurges in the dollar price of gold in 1980 and 2011 reflected fears that the dollar's worth would rapidly decline. If there were a stable gold-based dollar, people would not seek to invest in gold to protect their money. Its price would fluctuate very little.

10. **In an ideal world the head of the Federal Reserve would be no more important than the director of the Office of Weights and Measures inside the Commerce Department.**

The Federal Reserve must stop trying to run the banking system and the economy.

It's Not Only the Money

We have said this before: getting the economy right starts with getting money right. But other things also have to be gotten right. Money is simply a facilitator of transactions. A return to prosperity that leads to a better future requires a thriving, entrepreneurial society that encourages transactions to take place. The only way to get there is with a system based on fiscally responsible government, reasonable regulation and taxation, and a political environment founded on rule of law.

Stable money fosters these conditions. But policy makers must also be committed to promoting, rather than discouraging, commerce. We need government. But the only way realistically to be able to pay for it is through a growing free economy that meets the needs of its people.

Unfortunately, too few policy makers today grasp the bigger picture. As a result too many nations, including the United States, have been mired in stagnation and instability.

The Global Outlook

The following are thoughts and recommendations concerning the broader challenges faced by nations and regions around the world, and what's needed to get their economies and money right.

The European Union. Along with being plagued by sovereign debt crises, most European nations have been punching below their weight economically because of major structural barriers: high taxes, bloated public sectors, and restrictive labor laws that make companies very reluctant to hire. The result has been that the continent has dramatically lagged in economic growth. To cite one example, despite its varied cultures and a population of nearly 500 million people, the region trails tiny Israel (with a population of barely 8 million) in high-tech innovation.

The European Union's highly bureaucratic officialdom persists in believing that the answers to its woes are monetary expansion, lower interest rates, and so-called austerity—their euphemism for piling still more taxes on the heavily burdened private sector. Germany, whose relatively robust economy has made it the effective paymaster of the European Union, helping bail out countries such as Greece, has demanded higher taxes. Spain raised its top income tax rate to 52%. Italy and Portugal boosted their value-added taxes and other levies. France effectively raised its top rate on salaries to 75%. Greece hiked every conceivable levy, sending its economy into a bone-crunching recession. Meanwhile, the public sectors in these countries have largely been spared.

The global lack of understanding about money can be seen in commentaries bemoaning the fact that, because of the euro, countries cannot devalue their currencies to spark recovery. Monetary policy cannot overcome the obstacles to wealth creation created by excessive taxation, government spending, and job-killing labor laws. The key to resurgence in the European Union is structural reforms like lowering tax rates. Privatization—spinning off parts of the massive government bureaucracies—is also an easy source of needed cash.

Since 2008 Poland has privatized over 1,000 companies, large and small, raising billions in euros. Unfortunately the government took a step backward when it confiscated, Argentina-style, a portion of Polish citizens' pension funds.

The real problem is the devotion of Europe's political culture to the care and feeding of the welfare state. Germany made some internal reforms under chancellor Gerhard Schröder, a Social Democrat, in the early part of the 2000s that involved reforming welfare payments and tightening unemployment rules. The changes cost Schroder his job, but they enabled Germany to weather the crisis of 2008–2009 better than the rest of Western Europe. Nonetheless, the German government under Schroder's successor, Angela Merkel, has been whittling away at those reforms.

Other countries, though, are seeing the light. Sweden has cut taxes, with good effect. During the Great Recession, Estonia resisted the temptation to engage in a Keynesian spending binge. Its spending cuts earned the government a rebuke from Keynesian scold Paul Krugman, but the country's economic success speaks for itself: Estonia has become a leading high-tech center (Skype was developed there). It is growing, whereas most of the rest of the European Union is barely breathing.

China. The country's economic success, like Japan's and Germany's before, has aroused charges in Congress of currency manipulation. Observers also point to the ghost cities built to keep the economy humming during the financial crisis—including one with full replicas of Paris's Eiffel Tower and the Champs-Elysées—as proof that China's rapid expansion has been built on the sands of misallocated credit and artificial stimulus. There are definitely white elephants. But the reason for China's economic miracle is that the Chinese make products that people want. Its success has also been based on the fact that, until recently, it's had a better record than many countries for maintaining a relatively stable currency.

In the mid-1990s, when the dollar was fairly sound, Beijing pegged the yuan to the dollar at a fixed rate, believing that currency stability would spur trade. It did. China's global trade has since expanded more than 15-fold. In its monetary policies, China has taken its cue from Hong Kong, which similarly tied its dollar to the U.S. dollar in the early 1980s. The commitment of both Hong Kong and China to monetary stability enabled both to successfully defend their economies against the fierce speculative attacks that took place during the Asian Contagion in 1997–1998.

The question is, what does China do now? One big problem is its capital markets. The major banks cater to state-owned companies, but the bulk of the Chinese economy is made up of approximately 43 million small private companies, many operating in a legal and financial twilight zone. They borrow, at stiff rates of interest, from so-called shadow banks.

Investment has also been hampered by the fact that China's state-owned banks pay interest rates less than the rate of inflation. This has turned off many Chinese investors, who have sought investments with higher yields. The state-owned banks responded by setting up so-called trust companies that would lend to private companies at high yields. But many of these loans went bad. China's government has had to bail out many of these firms.

If China is to continue leading the world in economic growth, it must encourage a system of capital creation that better meets the needs of both its entrepreneurs and investors. Beijing is taking some steps in this direction, such as moving toward market-set interest rates over the next couple of years. Unfortunately it has also adopted a bad habit from the West— let us hope temporarily—of weakening its currency and letting it gyrate against the dollar more than it has in the past.

Japan. This country has been stuck in a rut for over 20 years. Its economic mistakes are legion. Its national debt is approaching a breathtaking 250% of GDP. That's even higher than Greece, whose debt/GDP ratio is 170%, and the United States, whose ratio is a little over 100%.

Over the past two decades rampant government spending, including more than 20 big stimulus packages, has dissipated Japan's immense wealth. The misunderstanding of money on the part of the nation's policy makers is monumental. In the late 1980s, the country underwent a frenzied real estate boom. As in the United States, it was the result of loose money, as well as a response to a tax code that rewarded companies for buying and holding on to real estate. Building codes and regulations also added costs and encouraged inefficient use of precious land.

The government popped the bubble when it tightened and imposed fierce tax increases. The resulting deflation smacked the rest of the economy hard. The government then embarked on what became an unending spending binge to stimulate the economy and fix the mess it created.

Japanese monetary policy has zigzagged. The bias has traditionally been toward tight money. But ignoring history and the U.S. experience, Japan has recently been toying with its own version of quantitative easing to devalue the yen vis-à-vis the dollar to stimulate growth.

The move will fail not only because cheap money never does any lasting good but also because the government is continuing the tax increases that have become an obsession over the past 20 years. Prime minister Shinzō Abe has confirmed that the doubling of the national sales tax enacted by his predecessor will continue on schedule. Another drag: Japan's ferocious social security payroll taxes, which unlike those in the United States have no salary caps. These levies are scheduled to go from about 30% to over 37% by 2018. The top income tax rate is moving to 55%. Japan's corporate tax rate is the worst in the world, with the single exception of the United States.

Prime Minister Abe has lately begun attacking Japan's suffocating regulations, such as limits on the height of buildings and land-use laws that make it difficult to use urban real estate efficiently. These much-needed efforts will be for naught, however, if Japan doesn't learn the lessons of money: governments can't conjure up resources out of thin air. Stimulus packages take resources from people and businesses that would employ and invest them better than any public sector bureaucrat. High taxes kill incentives and destroy capital.

Emerging Markets. These countries have been the victims of their own malfeasance as well as of the Fed's fluctuating dollar policy. Many emerging nations, including Russia, Nigeria, and Brazil, are rich in natural resources and have the same problems as Spain did in the Middle Ages. They have fallen prey to the resource trap and have grown overly dependent on these assets. A number also have overbearing governments that prevent the emergence of entrepreneurial market economies.

Each year the World Bank conducts a survey of 189 economies and issues its findings in a publication called *Doing Business*. It ranks countries in 11 categories ranging from the difficulty of starting a business to dealing with construction permits to "getting electricity." Brazil routinely ranks in the bottom half. Until recently so did Russia, but it has announced that it is making a concerted effort to improve its standing.

Brazil, Russia, and other resource-rich nations experienced impressive growth in the earlier part of the last decade because of the commodities boom set off by the weak dollar. The same thing happened to resource-rich countries in the 1970s after the ending of the Bretton Woods gold standard system caused the dollar to decline. But the expansions of the past 10 years were no more durable than they were 40 years ago.

The travails of these beleaguered countries stand in stark contrast to the growth that has taken place in such nations as South Korea, Hong Kong, Taiwan, Poland, the Czech Republic, and Israel. All have generated wealth through saner monetary policies and more open markets.

The Baltic states of Estonia, Lithuania, and Latvia are making similar strides. Years ago, all three put in flat tax regimes and conducted very sound monetary policies. Estonia now uses the euro.

Abundant resources don't have to be a curse. Chile is rich in copper. Thirty years ago, it made a concerted effort to start diversifying its economy. One initiative that helped create a secure retirement system in addition to creating capital was privatizing social security. The reform has been a spectacular success. How the system will fare under the new socialist president, Michelle Bachelet, remains to be seen.

Malaysia also has enormous resources. Like Chile, it is working to broaden its economic base by welcoming foreign direct investment in manufacturing, technology, and services.

All these countries have largely eschewed Keynesian economics. They recognized that printing money does not create wealth—investment and work do.

The jury is still very much out, meanwhile, with Turkey, Brazil, South Africa, Thailand, and Indonesia. If they learn to keep their monies sound and adopt sensible tax regimes like the flat tax, they will make real breakthroughs.

The United States. Just as the wave of tax cuts that swept the world in the 1980s and 1990s originated with the Reagan reforms in the early 1980s, the impetus for major monetary reform must now come from the United States.

This is starting to happen. On the tax front, a consensus is emerging for major tax simplification. More than three years ago

President Obama appointed a commission, dubbed Simpson-Bowles, to study the country's fiscal challenges. Amazingly, both Democrats and Republicans signed on to the idea of simplifying the U.S. tax code and cutting tax rates across the board. The president ignored the commission. But the idea continues to gain momentum. Many congressional Democrats are putting together proposals for simplification. The president won't give a green light for a serious effort in this area, at least not until after the congressional elections in 2014. If the White House indicated a real interest, an agreement would be rapidly reached on removing certain business preferences and sharply reducing the corporate tax rate, which, as noted, stands as the highest in the developed world. After the presidential election of 2016, there should also be a mandate for radical tax simplification on the personal side. These reforms will provide the legitimacy for other countries to follow suit.

As for monetary policy, the United States is still far away from the intellectual understanding needed for implementing a new gold standard. Given the manifest failures of Keynesian monetary policies in the United States, Europe, and Japan, however, this is at last beginning to change.

The loss of patience with the Fed's failure to generate growth after the Panic of 2008–2009, along with concern about its expanding power, were among the factors that brought about the scaling back of QE. Fears that Janet Yellen, long known as dovish on the dollar, might change course and abandon the taper caused some 26 senators to vote against her nomination.

These sentiments are likely to grow and provide the impetus for major reform. This reexamination will come not so much from economists but from others who will examine the issues with fresh, unprejudiced eyes.

One of the things that will strike people is that the United States very successfully operated under a gold standard for 180 years. America's performance since then has been anything but impressive.

Events have a way of undermining reigning orthodoxies. The Keynesian experiment has failed, and the question will become: What will replace it? Remember that the disasters of the 1970s were also a repudiation of Keynes, but the continuing hostility among conservative economists to a gold standard prevented the restoration of a Bretton Woods–like system. The recent experience of the United States and the rest of the world since then, particularly in the last decade, makes the failures of Keynesianism and monetarism impossible to ignore.

Our hope is that this book, and others like it, will help provide the insights and impetus for much-needed change.

THE NUGGET

Instability and insufficient growth are not the new normal.
A new gold standard will come.

Notes

Preface: The Crisis of Modern Economics—and Money

x   *government spending, free trade, and sound money*   "The Wealth of Nations," Adam Smith Institute, accessed March 6, 2014, http://www
.adamsmith.org/wealth-of-nations.

x   *tools such as spending, taxes, interest rates, and regulations*   Peter Drucker,
"Schumpeter and Keynes," *Forbes*, May 23, 1983.

x   *to achieve smooth, perpetual growth*   "Monetarism," *Investopedia*, accessed
March 6, 2014, http://www.investopedia.com/terms/m/monetarism.asp.

xi   *how are economists so confident that they can predict the future?*   George
Gilder, *Knowledge and Power: The Information Theory of Capitalism and How
It Is*" (Washington, DC: Regnery, 2013), pp. 22, 270.

xi   *a ratio that held for more than 200 years*   Nathan Lewis, *Gold: The Once and
Future Money* (Hoboken, NJ: John Wiley & Sons, 2007), pp. 29–30.

xi   *Mathematical Principles of Natural Philosophy*   "Sir Isaac Newton," *En-
cyclopaedia Britannica*, March 1, 2014, http://www.britannica.com
/EBchecked/topic/413189/Sir-Isaac-Newton.

xi   *complicated clock governed by immutable laws*   Edward Dolnick, *The Clock-
work Universe: Isaac Newton, the Royal Society, and the Birth of the Modern
World* (New York: HarperCollins, 2011), p. xvii.

xii   *precious metal itself through the buying and selling of bonds*   Lewis, op. cit.,
p. 255.

xii   *rise at the expense of lower wages for workers*   Mark Skousen, *The Making of
Modern Economics: The Lives and Ideas of the Great Thinkers* (Armonk, NY:
M.E. Sharpe, 2001), p. 108.

xii *The General Theory of Employment, Interest, and Money* Library of Congress Online Catalog, http://catalog.loc.gov/.

xii *an equilibrium in which demand and supply were in balance* Drucker, op. cit.

xii–xiii *economy, upon which production was dependent* Drucker, op. cit.

xiv *His predictions of mass famine* Thomas Robert Malthus, *An Essay on the Principle of Population*, Library of Economics and Liberty, http://www .econlib.org/library/Malthus/malPop.html.

xv *government is 20%, and investment the rest* Mark Skousen, "Beyond GDP: Get Ready for a New Way to Measure the Economy," Forbes.com, December 16, 2013, http://www.forbes.com/sites/realspin/2013/11/29/beyond -gdp-get-ready-for-a-new-way-to-measure-the-economy/.

xv *a new statistic called gross output* Ibid.

xv *George Gilder's book* Knowledge and Power. Gilder, op. cit.

xvi *Answer: we know more* Jerry Bowyer, "George Gilder Is Optimistic That We're Due for a Surprising Leader," Forbes.com, August 28, 2013, http://www.forbes.com/sites/jerrybowyer/2013/08/28/george-gilder -is-optimistic-that-were-due-for-a-surprising-leader/#/sites/jerrybowyer /2013/08/21/george-gilder-explains-why-stock-markets-have-devolved -into-a-world-of-noise/?&_suid=13937952166100286389310989470 6.

xvi–xvii *and its industrial output fiftyfold* Gilder, op. cit., p. 477.

Chapter 1: How We Got Here

8 *more than 318 points, or 2%, in a single day* Anora Mahmudova, "U.S. Stocks Tumble; Dow Drops 318 Points," MarketWatch.com, January 24, 2014, http://www.marketwatch.com/story/us-stocks-sell-off-another -triple-digit-drop-for-dow-2014-01-24.

8 *a "1929 feeling" is back on Wall Street* John J. Xenakis, "World View: That '1929 Feeling' May Be Back on Wall Street," Breitbart.com, January 25, 2014, http://www.breitbart.com/Big-Peace/2014/01/24/25-Jan -14-World-View-That-1929-feeling-may-be-back-on-Wall-Street.

9 *purchasing power has declined by more than 80%* Lewis E. Lehrman, "The Nixon Shock Heard 'Round the World" (graph), *Wall Street Journal*, August 15, 2011, http://online.wsj.com/news/articles/SB100014240531119 04007304576494073418802358.

10 *has declined by about 26%* Bureau of Labor Statistics, U. S. Department of Labor, Consumer Price Index Inflation Calculator, available at http:// www.bls.gov/data/inflation_calculator.htm.

10 *more frequent crises and downturns* Michael Bordo et al., "Is the Crisis Problem Growing More Severe?" *Economic Policy* 16 (32), April 2001, pp. 53–82.

10 *during the period of quantitative easing (QE)* William L. Watts, "Treasurys Rally for Third Day as Taper Comfort Increases," MarketWatch .com, December 10, 2013, http://www.marketwatch.com/story/treasurys -gain-as-investors-factor-in-taper-prospects-2013-12-10.

10   *dramatically weakened on the global markets*   "'Fragile Five' Countries Face Taper Crunch," *Financial Times*, December 17, 2013, http://www.ft .com/intl/cms/s/2/407c42ac-6703-11e3-a5f9-00144feabdc0.html#axzz 2ukSLUaSi.

11   *money never made it into the economy*   Robert Auerbach, "Massive Misconceptions About Where the Bernanke Fed's Money Explosion Went," *Huffington Post*, June 25, 2013, http://www.huffingtonpost.com/robert -auerbach/massive-misconceptions-ab_b_3490373.html.

11   *Treasuries and mortgage-backed securities*   David Malpass, "The Fed 'Twist' That Won't Dance," *Wall Street Journal*, September 21, 2011, http://online.wsj .com/news/articles/SB10001424053111904060604576570980769992022.

12   *subprime mortgage market with cheap dollars*   Peter Ferrara, "How the Government Created a Financial Crisis," Forbes.com, May 5, 2011, http:// www.forbes.com/sites/peterferrara/2011/05/19/how-the-government -created-a-financial-crisis/.

13   *too low for too long*   Peter Wallison, "Don't Be Fooled About Low Rates and the Housing Bubble," RealClearMarkets.com, January 23, 2013, http://www.realclearmarkets.com/articles/2013/01/23/dont_be_fooled _about_low_rates_and_the_housing_bubble_100106.html.

13   *around $95 a barrel these days*   "United States Energy Information Administration, the United States Department of Energy, Petroleum & Other Liquids," available at http://www.eia.gov/dnav/pet/hist/LeafHandler .ashx?n=pet&s=f000000__3&f=a.

14   *from Haiti to Bangladesh to Egypt*   George Melloan, "The Federal Reserve Is Causing Turmoil Abroad," *Wall Street Journal*, February 23, 2011, http://online.wsj.com/news/articles/SB1000142405274870465 7704576150202567815380; and Javier Blas, "Global Food Prices Hit Record High," *Financial Times*, January 5, 2011, http://www.ft.com/intl /cms/s/0/51241bc0-18b4-11e0-b7ee-00144feab49a.html?siteedition =intl#axzz2usqHqaXs.

14   *in 1971 costs $5.78 in 2014*   Bureau of Labor Statistics, U.S. Department of Labor, Consumer Price Index Inflation Calculator, available at http:// www.bls.gov/data/inflation_calculator.htm.

14   *to buy the equivalent goods and services*   Ibid.

14   *a mere 17 cents*   Ibid.

14   *a 17% cut in pay*   Mark Gimein, "For U.S. Men, 40 Years of Falling Income," Bloomberg.com, December 31, 2013, http://go.bloomberg.com /market-now/2013/12/31/for-us-men-40-years-of-falling-income/.

14   *single-earner family has fallen behind*   Ibid.

16   *breathtakingly high rates of interest*   Ianthe Jeanne Dugan and Ruth Simon, "Alternative Lenders Peddle Pricey Commercial Loans," *Wall Street Journal*, January 7, 2014, http://online.wsj.com/news/articles/SB 10001424052702304477704579256123272658660.

16 *short-term loans can exceed 50%* Ibid.

16 *supervisory or enforcement action* Gillian Tan, "Pressed by Regulators, U.S. Banks Skip Deals," *Wall Street Journal*, January 22, 2014, http://online.wsj .com/news/articles/SB40001424052702304302704579334820201530010.

17 *has too much power* "74% Want to Audit the Federal Reserve," Rasmussen Reports, November 8, 2013, http://www.rasmussenreports.com /public_content/business/general_business/november_2013/74_want _to_audit_the_federal_reserve.

17 *annual rate of nearly 4%* Louis Woodhill, "What Is It About a Stable Dollar That Paul Krugman Doesn't Understand?" Forbes.com, August 29, 2012, http://www.forbes.com/sites/louiswoodhill/2012/08/29/what -is-it-about-a-stable-dollar-that-paul-krugman-doesnt-understand/.

17 *average rate of around 3%* Ibid.

17 *56% higher than it actually was* Ibid.

17 *$1.3 trillion deficit* Ibid.

17–18 *one-quarter of the size of China's* Ibid.

18 *unemployment averaged less than 5%* Charles Kadlec, "Nixon's Colossal Monetary Error: The Verdict 40 Years Later," Forbes.com, August 15, 2011, http://www.forbes.com/sites/charleskadlec/2011/08/15/nixons -colossal-monetary-error-the-verdict-40-years-later/.

18 *it never rose above 7%* Ibid.

18 *around 8% since 2008* Ibid.

18 *inflation, 1.5% higher* Charles Kadlec, "An International Gold Standard Beats the Rule of the Governing Elite," Forbes.com, December 19, 2011, http://www.forbes.com/sites/charleskadlec/2011/12/19/an-international -gold-standard-beats-the-rule-of-the-governing-elite/.

18 *federal debt stood at $436 billion* Rich Danker, "To Lower the Debt Ceiling, Fix the Monetary System," Forbes.com, March 30, 2011, http://www .forbes.com/sites/richdanker/2011/03/30/to-lower-the-debt-ceiling -fix-the-monetary-system/.

18 *more than $17 trillion* Stephen Dinan, "U.S. Debt Jumps a Record $328 Billion—Tops $17 Trillion for First Time," *Washington Times*, October 18, 2013, http://www.washingtontimes.com/news/2013/oct/18/us-debt -jumps-400-billion-tops-17-trillion-first-t/.

18 *same year that the Fed started implementing QE* Peter Ferrara, "Obama's Budget: The Decline and Fall of the American Economy," Forbes .com, February 16, 2012, http://www.forbes.com/sites/peterferrara /2012/02/16/obamas-budget-the-decline-and-fall-of-the-american -economy/.

18 *downgrades on their bonds* Matthias Sobolewski and Dina Kyriakidou, "S&P Downgrades Nine Euro Zone Countries," *Reuters*, January 14, 2012, http://www.reuters.com/article/2012/01/14/us-eurozone -sp-idUSTRE80C1BC20120114.

19 *final days under Ben Bernanke* Jonathan Spicer and Jason Lange, "Yellen Stays the Course, Says Fed to Keep Trimming Stimulus," *Reuters*, February 11, 2014, http://www.reuters.com/article/2014/02/11/us-usa-fed -idUSBREA1A06O20140211.

19 *"Too many people are unemployed."* Michael Lindenberger, "Janet Yellen Says She'll Pursue Full Employment," *Dallas Morning News*, February 11, 2014, http://bizbeatblog.dallasnews.com/2014/02/janet-yellen-says -shell-pursue-full-employment.html/.

20 *$85 billion in bonds a month* Greg Robb, "Fed Tapers Bond-Buying Program by $10 Billion," MarketWatch.com, December 18, 2013, http:// www.marketwatch.com/story/fed-tapers-bond-buying-program-by-10 -billion-2013-12-18.

21 *peaking at $1,896.50 in 2011* Data available from the London Bullion Market Association's daily gold price fixings, http://www.lbma.org.uk /pages/?page_id=53&title=gold_fixings.

21 *rate of growth from 1968 to 1982* Louis Woodhill, "The Mystery of Income Inequality Broken Down to One Simple Chart," Forbes .com, March 28, 2013, http://www.forbes.com/sites/louiswoodhill /2013/03/28/the-mystery-of-income-inequality-broken-down-to-one -simple-chart/.

22 *Secrets of the Temple* William Greider, *Secrets of the Temple: How the Federal Reserve Runs the Country* (New York: Simon & Schuster, 1987).

22 *misunderstood what I said* Binyamin Appelbaum, "A Fed Focused on the Value of Clarity," *New York Times*, December 13, 2012, http://www.nytimes .com/2012/12/14/business/economy/a-federal-reserve-that-is-focused -on-the-value-of-clarity.html.

22 *speak without ever saying anything* Mike Moskow, "Seven Lessons from Real Life," commencement address (December 2002), master's of business graduation ceremony, presented at the Kellogg School of Management of Northwestern University, Evanston, IL.

Chapter 2: What Is Money?

28 *used as money during colonial times* Federal Reserve Bank of Minneapolis, "The History of Money," http://www.minneapolisfed.org/community _education/teacher/history.cfm.

28 *cigarettes as money during World War II* Irene Finel-Honigman, *A Cultural History of Finance* (New York: Routledge, 2010), p. 164.

28 *giant coins to roll it around* Milton Friedman, *Money Mischief: Episodes in Monetary History* (New York: Harcourt Brace & Company, 1994), pp. 3–4.

29 *unless you were politically connected* Hedrick Smith, *The Russians* (Quadrangle /New York Times Book Company, 1976), pp. 26–27.

30 *neutral, impersonal arbiter* Forrest McDonald, *Alexander Hamilton: A Biography* (New York: W.W. Norton & Company, 1982), p. 4.

30 *society fluid and open to merit*   Ibid.

31 *rising interest rates in the United States*   Ian Talley, "Taper Shock Helped Emerging Markets Rebalance, Report Says," *Wall Street Journal*, December 4, 2013, http://blogs.wsj.com/economics/2013/12/04/taper-shock -helped-emerging-markets-rebalace-report-says/.

32 *holds the record for stability*   Nathan Lewis, *Gold: The Once and Future Money* (Hoboken, NJ: John Wiley & Sons, 2007), p. 30.

32 *ratio for the pound to gold in 1717*   Ibid.

33 *franc's value vis-à-vis the euro*   Graeme Wearden, "Swiss Bid to Peg 'Safe Haven' Franc to the Euro Stuns Currency Traders," *The Guardian*, September 6, 2011, http://www.theguardian.com/business/2011/sep/06 /switzerland-pegs-swiss-franc-euro.

34 *strengthening the greenback*   Jacob Schlesinger, "Bush Adviser Minimizes Fears over Dollar's Continued Slide," *Wall Street Journal*, May 31, 2002, http://online.wsj.com/news/articles/SB1022796033572248600.

34 *downgraded U.S. credit in 2011*   Zachary A. Goldfarb, "S&P Downgrades U.S. Credit Rating for First Time," *Washington Post*, August 5, 2011, http://www.washingtonpost.com/business/economy/sandp -considering-first-downgrade-of-us-credit-rating/2011/08/05/gIQA qKeIxI_story.html.

35 *cyclical stagnation in Washington*   Liu Chang, "U.S. Fiscal Failure Warrants a de-Americanized World," Xinhua News Agency, November 13, 2013, http://news.xinhuanet.com/english/indepth/2013-10/13 /c_132794246.htm.

35 *a "de-Americanized world" with a new reserve currency*   Ibid.

35 *currency in place of the dollar*   Blake Ellis, "States Seek Currencies Made of Silver and Gold," CNNMoney.com, February 3, 2012, http://money .cnn.com/2012/02/03/pf/states_currencies/.

35 *as late as the mid-1800s*   Ron Paul and Lewis Lehrman, *The Case for Gold: A Minority Report of the U.S. Gold Commission*, 2d ed. (Auburn, AL: Ludwig von Mises Institute, 2007), pp. 30–66.

36 *used in that state as money*   Ellis, op. cit.

36 *kingpin known as Dread Pirate Roberts*   "Manhattan U.S. Attorney Announces Seizure of Additional $28 Million Worth of Bitcoins Belonging to Ross William Ulbricht, Alleged Owner and Operator of 'Silk Road' Website," press release, U.S. Attorney's Office, Southern District of New York, October 25, 2013.

36 *largest bitcoin trading exchange*   Chris O'Brien and Andrew Tangel, "Bitcoin Virtual Currency Is on the Verge of Collapse," *Los Angeles Times*, February 25, 2014, http://articles.latimes.com/2014/feb/25/business /la-fi-bitcoin-collapse-20140226.

37 *bitcoins up to $142 each*   Kashmir Hill, "Living on Bitcoin for a Week: The Journey Begins," Forbes.com, May 1, 2013, http://www.forbes.com

/sites/kashmirhill/2013/05/01/living-on-bitcoin-for-a-week-the-journey
-begins/.

37   *as much as 61% in a single day*   David Seaman, "It's War Between Bitcoin's True Believers and Speculators," Businessinsider.com, April 11,
2013, http://www.businessinsider.com/why-bitcoin-is-falling-2013-4.

37   *pushing monetary values down further*   Paul and Lehrman, op. cit.

37   *through the mechanism of prices*   Friedrich Hayek, *Denationalisation of
Money: The Argument Refined: An Analysis of the Theory and Practice of Con-
current Currencies*, 3d ed. (London, U.K.: The Institute of Economic Affairs, 1990), pp. 85–86; found online at mises.org/books/denationalisation
.pdf.

38   *the economy of knowledge with which it operates*   Friedrich Hayek, "The
Uses of Knowledge in Society," *American Economic Review* 35, no. 4
(1945), http://www.econlib.org/library/Essays/hykKnw1.html.

38   *around $200 in 1979 dollars*   Martyn Williams, "Happy Birthday! The
Walkman Turns 30," Macworld, July 1, 2009, http://www.macworld
.com/article/1141475/walkman.html.

38   *big as a shoebox cost $3,995*   "Cost of a 1983 Motorola Cell Phone:
$3,995," SFGate.com, August 17, 2011, http://www.sfgate.com/business
/article/Cost-of-a-1983-Motorola-cell-phone-3-995-2334996.php.

39   *costs a mere $50*   Steve Forbes and Elizabeth Ames, *Freedom Manifesto:
Why Free Markets Are Moral and Big Government Isn't* (New York: Crown
Business, 2012), p. 103.

39   *instrument of commerce and a measure of value*   Adam Smith, *Wealth of Nations*, vol. 1, book 4, chap. 1, available at the Library of Economics and
Liberty, http://www.econlib.org/library/Smith/smWN12.html.

39   *there was no demand for them*   Ibid.

40   *maintains and employs the people*   Ibid.

40   *beyond what he himself has occasion for*   Adam Smith, *Wealth of Nations*,
vol. 1, book 1, chap. 1, available at the Library of Economics and Liberty,
http://www.econlib.org/library/Smith/smWN1.html.

40   *different ranks of the society*   Ibid.

40   *introducing order into our finances*   Michael McConnell, "What Would
Alexander Hamilton Do?" *Defining Ideas* (Hoover Institution journal),
July 22, 2011, http://www.hoover.org/publications/defining-ideas/article
/86451.

41   *menaces our independence*   Alexander Hamilton, *The Works of Alexander
Hamilton*, vol. 3, ed. Henry Cabot Lodge (New York: G.P. Putnam &
Sons, 1904), p. 362.

Chapter 3: Money and Trade

43   *combat in peace and war*   William R. Thompson, *The Emergence of the
Global Political Economy* (London: Routledge Press, 2000), p. 126.

44 *mines of Peru are to Spain* Frank Trentmann, ed., *The Oxford Handbook of the History of Consumption* (New York: Oxford University Press, 2012), p. 624.

44 *greatness and power of this State* Fordham University, "Jean Baptiste Colbert (1619–1683): Memorandum on Trade, 1664," *Modern History Sourcebook*, http://www.fordham.edu/halsall/mod/1664colbert.asp.

44 *equating wealth and strength* Thompson, op. cit., p. 127.

45 *annual income to the U.S. economy* Scott C. Bradford, Paul L. E. Grieco, and Gary Clyde Hufbauer, "The Payoff to America from Globalisation," *World Economy* 29(7), July 2006, pp. 893–916.

46 *that he was in favor of a strong dollar* Takashi Nakamichi, "Geithner Affirms Strong Dollar Policy," *Wall Street Journal*, November 11, 2009, http://online.wsj.com/news/articles/SB125792362908743307.

46 *weak dollar more desirable* Christina D. Romer, "Needed: Plain Talk About the Dollar," *New York Times*, May 21, 2011, http://www.nytimes.com/2011/05/22/business/economy/22view.html?pagewanted=all.

47 *what was known as the Triffin dilemma* Sandra Kollen Ghizoni, "Nixon Ends Convertibility of U.S. Dollars to Gold and Announces Wage/Price Controls," FederalReserveHistory.org, November 22, 2013, http://www.federalreservehistory.org/Events/DetailView/33.

47 *money shortage and less global growth* Sylvia Nasar, "Robert Triffin, 81, an Economist Who Backed Monetary Stability" (obituary), *New York Times*, February 27, 1993, http://www.nytimes.com/1993/02/27/nyregion/robert-triffin-81-an-economist-who-backed-monetary-stability.html.

47 *trade deficit by the early 1970s* U.S. Bureau of the Census, "U.S. Trade in Goods and Services—Balance of Payments (BOP) Basis Value in Millions of Dollars 1960 through 2012," February 8, 2013, http://www.census.gov/foreign-trade/statistics/historical/gands.txt.

48 *the dollar had to be devalued* Roger Lowenstein, "The Nixon Shock," Businessweek.com, August 4, 2011, http://www.businessweek.com/magazine/the-nixon-shock-08042011.html.

48 *closed the "gold window"* Lewis E. Lehrman, "The Nixon Shock Heard 'Round the World," *Wall Street Journal*, August 15, 2011, http://online.wsj.com/news/articles/SB10001424053111904007304576494073418802358.

48 *announced to control inflation* Daniel Griswold, "The Unhappy 40th Anniversary of Nixon's Wage and Price Controls," Cato Institute, August 15, 2011, http://www.cato.org/blog/unhappy-40th-anniversary-nixons-wage-price-controls.

49 *formally pronounced dead in early 1973* Federal Reserve Bank of Richmond, "FAQs: Gold & Silver," http://www.richmondfed.org/faqs/gold_silver/.

49 *no country on a gold standard* John Black, Nigar Hashimzade, and Gareth Myles, *A Dictionary of Economics* (New York: Oxford University Press, 2003), p. 141.

49 *lost 45% of its value* Trader Joe, "Stock Market Crash—1974," iStockAnalyst
.com, June 26, 2009, http://www.istockanalyst.com/article/viewarticle
/articleid/3314883.

49 *followed by the Arab oil embargo* Michael L. Ross, "How the 1973 Oil
Embargo Saved the Planet," *Foreign Affairs*, October 15, 2013, http://
www.foreignaffairs.com/articles/140173/michael-l-ross/how-the-1973
-oil-embargo-saved-the-planet.

49 *sharply raised interest rates* Board of Governors of the Federal Reserve
System, "Bank Prime Loan Rate Changes: Historical Dates of Changes
and Rates," http://research.stlouisfed.org/fred2/data/PRIME.txt.

49 *monetary base contracted* National Mining Association, "Historical
Gold Prices—1833 to Present," http://www.nma.org/pdf/gold/his_gold
_prices.pdf.

49 *unemployment shot up* "Unemployment Rate. President: Richard Mil-
hous Nixon." PortalSeven.com, accessed December 2, 2013, http://portals
even.com/employment/unemployment_rate_for_president_term.jsp
?president=Richard%20Milhous%20Nixon.

51 *intents and purposes did not exist* Callum Henderson, *Currency Strategy*
(Hoboken, NJ: John Wiley & Sons, 2006), p. 203.

51 *classical gold standard periods* Michael Bordo, Barry Eichengreen, Dan-
iela Klingebiel, and Maria Soledad Martinez-Peria, "Is the Crisis Problem Growing More Severe?" *Economic Policy* 16(32), April 2001, pp.
53–82, http://www.sfu.ca/~djacks/courses/ECON372/Papers/Bordo
%20et%20al,%20Is%20the%20Crisis%20Problem%20Growing%20
More%20Severe.pdf.

51 *with Asia and the European Union* Office of the Press Secretary, "Remarks by the President in the State of the Union Address," WhiteHouse
.gov, February 12, 2013, http://www.whitehouse.gov/the-press-office
/2013/02/12/remarks-president-state-union-address.

52 *to revive a stagnant U.S. economy* Helene Cooper, "Obama Sets Ambitious
Export Goal," *New York Times*, January 28, 2010, http://www.nytimes
.com/2010/01/29/business/29trade.html?_r=0.

52 *deficits with Germany, Japan, and other countries* Jeff Macke, "Black Monday: The 1987 Market Crash Revisited," Yahoo! Finance, October 19,
2012, http://finance.yahoo.com/blogs/breakout/black-monday-1987
-market-crash-revisited-113951060.html.

52 *more than 22% of its value, in a single day* Tim Metz, Alan Murray, Thomas
E. Ricks, and Beatrice E. Garcia, "Stocks Plummet 508 Amid Panicky
Selling," *Wall Street Journal*, October 20, 1987, http://online.wsj.com
/news/articles/SB10000872396390444734804578064571593598196.

52 *that set off the Great Depression* Jude Wanniski, *The Way the World Works*,
4th ed. paperback (Washington, DC: Regnery, 1998), p. 136.

53 *envisioned such a doomsday scenario* Eamonn Fingleton, "Apocalypse Soon: The U.S. Dollar's Grim Future—and How to Prepare for It," Forbes.com, July 15, 2013, http://www.forbes.com/sites/eamonn fingleton/2013/07/15/apocalypse-soon-the-u-s-dollars-grim-future-and -how-to-prepare-for-it/.

53 *scenario might unfold* James Rickards, *Currency Wars: The Making of the Next Global Crisis*, reprint edition (New York: Portfolio Trade, 2012), p. 4.

53 *his family to Singapore* David Yin, "Singapore Needs Immigrants, Says Jim Rogers," Forbes.com, June 6, 2013, http://www.forbes.com/sites /davidyin/2013/06/06/singapore-needs-immigrants-says-jim-rogers/.

54 *Treasuries to their reserves* Daniel Kruger, "China Treasury Holdings Drop to 6-Mo. Low as Yields Rise," *Bloomberg News*, October 22, 2013, http://www.bloomberg.com/news/2013-10-22/china-treasury-holdings -drop-to-6-mo-low-as-yields-rise.html.

54 *known informally as "paper gold"* Jamil Anderlini, "China Calls for New Reserve Currency," *Financial Times*, March 24, 2009, http://www.ft.com/cms /s/0/7851925a-17a2-11de-8c9d-0000779fd2ac.html#axzz2mXeDqFQH.

55 *imports are regarded as subtractions* Mark Skousen, *Economic Logic*, 4th ed. (Washington, DC: Regnery, 2013), p. 349.

55 *roughly 350 of the last 400 years* Daniel Griswold, "America's Maligned and Misunderstood Trade Deficit," Cato Institute, April 20, 1998, http://www.cato.org/publications/trade-policy-analysis/americas -maligned-misunderstood-trade-deficit.

56 *"oil country tubular goods"—for example, pipelines* Mark J. Perry, "Nations Don't Trade with Each Other; Individuals Do" (blog), January 5, 2010, http://mjperry.blogspot.com/2010/01/countries-dont-trade-with-each -other.html.

56 *need so much steel pipe* Mark Crawford, "Shale Exploration Drives the Demand for Steel," WellServicingMagazine.com, May/June 2012, http://www.wellservicingmagazine.com/cover-story/2012/05/shale -exploration-drives-the-demand-for-steel/.

56 *foreign divisions of American companies* U.S. Department of Commerce, "U.S. Goods Trade: Imports & Exports by Related Parties 2012," US Census Bureau Press Release CB13-66, May 2, 2013, http://www.census.gov /foreign-trade/Press-Release/2012pr/aip/related_party/rp12-text.pdf.

56 *content in China's exports is about 50%* Robert Koopman, Zhi Wang, and Shang-jin Wei, "How Much of Chinese Exports Is Really Made in China?" Office of Economics, U.S. International Trade Commission, March 2008, http://www.usitc.gov/publications/332/working_papers /ec200803b_revised.pdf.

56 *wholesales at about $180* Andrew Batson, "Not Really 'Made in China,'" *Wall Street Journal*, December 15, 2010, http://online.wsj.com/news /articles/SB10001424052748704828104576021142902413796.

56   *sells for around twice its cost*   Mark Rogowsky, "Apple's Addiction: It
     Can't Just Say No to Profit Margins," Forbes.com, September 11, 2013,
     http://www.forbes.com/sites/markrogowsky/2013/09/11/marginal
     -cost-and-benefit-apples-addiction-to-iphone-profits/.

57   *trade deficits do not cost jobs*   Griswold, "America's Maligned and Misun-
     derstood Trade Deficit," op. cit.

58   *balance of payments data released by the Department of Commerce*   Depart-
     ment of Commerce, Bureau of Economic Analysis website, www.bea
     .gov; see quarterly "US International Transactions" press releases.

58   *It doesn't show anything else*   Marc Chandler, *Making Sense of the Dollar:
     Exposing Dangerous Myths about Trade and Foreign Exchange* (Hoboken,
     NJ: Bloomberg Press, 2009), pp. 14, 21.

58   *the capital account and the financial account*   Ibid., pp. 488–492.

59   *income receipts, and asset sales*   Mark J. Perry, "Think of 'Trade Deficits' as
     'Job-Generating, Capital-Creating Foreign Investment Surpluses for a
     Better America,'" American Enterprise Institute, March 14, 2013, http://
     www.aei-ideas.org/2013/03/think-of-trade-deficits-as-offsetting-job
     -creating-foreign-investment-surpluses-for-a-better-america/.

59   *balanced by a foreign investment surplus*   Daniel Griswold, "The Truth
     About Trade Deficits," Cato Institute, June 14, 2011, http://www.cato.org
     /publications/commentary/truth-about-trade-deficits-jobs.

60   *a more market-oriented exchange rate*   "The Yuan Scapegoat," *Wall Street
     Journal* Review and Outlook (editorial), March 18, 2010, http://online.wsj
     .com/news/articles/SB10001424052748704743404575127511778280940.

60   *the yuan was pegged to the dollar*   Edward Lazear, "Chinese 'Currency
     Manipulation' Is Not the Problem," *Wall Street Journal*, January 7, 2013,
     http://online.wsj.com/news/articles/SB10001424127887323320404578
     213203581231448.

60   *has been pegged to a basket of currencies*   Yumi Kuramitsu and Jake Lee,
     "China Ends Yuan Dollar Peg, Shifts to Currency Basket," Bloomberg
     .com, July 21, 2005, http://www.bloomberg.com/apps/news?pid=news
     archive&sid=a04ESaRrTpcU.

60   *increased 21% between 2005 and 2008*   Lazear, op. cit.

60   *continued to grow vigorously*   U.S. Census Bureau, "Trade in Goods with
     China," http://www.census.gov/foreign-trade/balance/c5700.html.

61   *about 80 yen to the dollar in 2012*   FXTOP.COM historical exchange
     rates, http://fxtop.com/en/historical-exchange-rates.php.

61   *other Asian nations, such as Korea and Taiwan*   Takashi Nakamichi and Tat-
     suo Ito, "Japan's Call for Weaker Yen Spurs Talk of Copycat Moves," *Wall
     Street Journal*, December 27, 2012, http://online.wsj.com/news/articles
     /SB10001424127887323984704578205303116695058.

62   *second-most-traded reserve currency after the dollar*   Bill Conerly, "Fu-
     ture of the Dollar as World Reserve Currency," Forbes.com, October

25, 2013, http://www.forbes.com/sites/billconerly/2013/10/25/future-of
-the-dollar-as-world-reserve-currency/.

63 *teetered on the brink of insolvency*   CNN Library, "European Debt Crisis
Fast Facts," September 14, 2013, http://www.cnn.com/2013/07/27/world
/europe/european-debt-crisis-fast-facts/.

64 *such suggestions "insane"*   Louis Woodhill, "The ECB, Not Greece,
Threatens the Euro," RealClearMarkets, January 18, 2011, http://www
.realclearmarkets.com/articles/2011/01/18/the_ecb_not_greece_threatens
_the_euro_98831.html.

64 *would simply disintegrate*   Ibid.

64 *another roller-coaster fiat currency like the dollar*   Mark Hendrickson, "The
Euro Is a Frankenstein Currency," Forbes.com, June 21, 2012, http://
www.forbes.com/sites/markhendrickson/2012/06/21/the-euro-is-a
-frankenstein-currency/.

64 *have now adopted it*   "Euro Area Member States," Eurozone Portal, accessed March 5, 2014, http://www.eurozone.europa.eu/euro-area/euro
-area-member-states/.

64 *close-knit nations many times easier*   George Melloan, "The Euro Has Been
a Smashing Success," *Wall Street Journal*, March 8, 2010, http://online
.wsj.com/news/articles/SB1000142405274870386270457509981292072
41300.

66 *two-thirds of existing $100 bills reside outside the United States*   Jacob Gold-
stein, "Most $100 Bills Live Outside the U.S.," NPR.org, April 17, 2013,
http://www.npr.org/blogs/money/2013/04/12/177051690/most-100
-bills-live-outside-the-u-s.

66 *rose to around 66% in 2012*   John C. Williams, "Cash Is Dead! Long Live
Cash!" *Federal Reserve Bank of San Francisco 2012 Annual Report*, http://
www.frbsf.org/publications/federalreserve/annual/2012/2012_Annual
_Report_Essay.pdf.

68 *increasing short-term interest rates*   Ronald I. McKinnon, "Tapering
Without Tears—How to End QE3," *Wall Street Journal*, October 27,
2013, http://online.wsj.com/news/articles/SB1000142405270230479940
4579153693500945608.

69 *fallen sharply to 34% of GDP*   Kimberly Amadeo, "National Debt by
Year," About.com, accessed March 5, 2014, http://useconomy.about
.com/od/usdebtanddeficit/a/National-Debt-by-Year.htm.

Chapter 4: Money Versus Wealth

71 *about her views of the economy*   Annalyn Kurtz, "Smooth Sailing for
Yellen in Front of Senate," Money.CNN.com, November 14, 2013, http://
money.cnn.com/2013/11/14/news/economy/janet-yellen-confirmation
-hearing/.

72 *GDP growth of just under 2%* "Gross Domestic Product," Bureau of Economic Analysis, accessed February 27, 2014, http://www.bea.gov /national/xls/gdpchg.xls.

72 *balance sheet from $900 billion to $3.7 trillion in 2013* Board of Governors of the Federal Reserve System, "Credit and Liquidity Programs and the Balance Sheet: Recent Balance Sheet Trends," FederalReserve.gov, accessed December 19, 2013, http://www.federalreserve.gov/monetarypolicy /bst_recenttrends.htm.

72 *bank reserves had already reached $124 billion* Board of Governors of the Federal Reserve System, "Aggregate Reserves of Depository Institutions and the Monetary Base," FederalReserve.gov, accessed December 17, 2013, http://www.federalreserve.gov/releases/h3/current/.

72 *many times the normal level* Ibid.

72 *interest rates known as Operation Twist* Nick Nasad, "FOMC Does the 'Twist,' but Markets Respond with Risk-Off and USD Strength," *FX Times*, September 21, 2011, http://www.fxtimes.com/fundamental-updates/fomc -does-the-twist-but-markets-respond-with-risk-off-and-usd-strength/.

73 *the Zimbabwe dollar was worth more than the U.S. dollar* "A Worthless Currency," *The Economist*, July 17, 2008, http://www.economist.com /node/11751346.

73 *destruction of the country's agricultural economy* "Q&A: Zimbabwe's Economy," *BBC News*, July 31, 2007, http://news.bbc.co.uk/2/hi/6922441.stm.

73 *hyperinflation second only to that of Hungary after Wrold War II* Steve H. Hanke and Nicholas Krus, "Working Paper No. 8: World Hyperinflations," Cato Institute, August 15, 2012, http://www.cato.org/publications /working-paper/world-hyperinflations.

73 *a hot novelty item among collectors* Patrick McGroarty and Farai Mutsaka, "How to Turn 100 Trillion Dollars into Five and Feel Good about It," *Wall Street Journal*, May 11, 2011, http://online.wsj.com/news/articles /SB10001424052748703730804576314953091790360.

75 *accuses advocates of stable money of "inflation hysteria"* Paul Krugman, "Free-Floating Inflation Hysteria," NYTimes.com, November 5, 2013, http://krugman.blogs.nytimes.com/2013/11/05/free-floating-inflation -hysteria/?_r=0.000.

75 *I don't see risks to financial stability* Neil Irwin, "Janet Yellen Faced the Senate Today. Here's Everything You Need to Know," Washington post.com (Wonkblog), November 14, 2013, http://www.washingtonpost .com/blogs/wonkblog/wp/2013/11/14/janet-yellen-faces-the-senate -today-click-here-for-up-to-the-minute-updates/.

75 *got as low as 1.1%* Bureau of Labor Statistics, "Consumer Price Index, November 2013," U.S. Department of Labor Press Release USDL-13- 2390, accessed December 19, 2013, http://www.bls.gov/news.release /pdf/cpi.pdf.

75 *in about a decade* "Consumer Price Index—Average Price Data, Ground Beef, 100% Beef, per lb.," Bureau of Labor Statistics, accessed March 6, 2014, http://data.bls.gov/timeseries/APU0000703112.

75 *about double what it was less than 10 years ago* Bureau of Labor Statistics, http://data.bls.gov/cgi-bin/surveymost.

75 *increased by 25% in less than one year* Michael Sivy, "If There's No Inflation, Why Are Prices Up So Much?" Time.com, March 12, 2013, http://business.time.com/2013/03/12/if-theres-no-inflation-why-are-prices-up-so-much/#ixzz2o1plLDlJ.

76 *market basket increased more than 44%* Peter Schiff, "Inflation Propaganda Exposed," Euro Pacific Capital, January 10, 2013, http://www.europac.net/commentaries/inflation_propaganda_exposed.

76 *ranges from as low as 5% to as high as 10%* John Williams, "Alternate Inflation Charts," Shadow Government Statistics, accessed March 6, 2014, http://www.shadowstats.com/alternate_data/inflation-charts.

76 *gold was three times what it was in 2003* Goldprice.org, accessed March 6, 2014, http://goldprice.org/gold-price-history.html.

76 *370 to 506, an increase of nearly 37%* Reuters.com, accessed October 10, 2013.

77 *collapse of the German economy, and the rise of Hitler* Richard Finger, "The Federal Reserve Is Making a Big Mistake," Forbes.com, September 20, 2013, http://www.forbes.com/sites/richardfinger/2013/09/20/the-federal-reserve-is-making-a-big-mistake.

77 *when the economy is weak* Binyamin Appelbaum, "In Fed and Out, Many Now Think Inflation Helps," *New York Times*, October 26, 2013, http://www.nytimes.com/2013/10/27/business/economy/in-fed-and-out-many-now-think-inflation-helps.html?_r=0.

78 *not something to worry about* Ibid.

78 *comes out of nowhere and hits you* Amity Shlaes, "Watch Bernanke's 'Little' Inflation Capsize U.S.," Bloomberg.com, March 14, 2012, http://www.bloomberg.com/news/2012-03-14/watch-bernanke-s-little-inflation-capsize-u-s-amity-shlaes.html.

78–79 *weren't producing enough money* Ibid.

79 *already turned their money into wallpaper* Ibid.

79 *can come as fast as a gust* Ibid.

79 *a graph that became known as the Phillips curve* Kevin D. Hoover, "Phillips Curve," Library of Economics and Liberty, accessed March 24, 2014, http://www.econlib.org/library/Enc/PhillipsCurve.html.

80 *economists whose work disproved the Phillips curve* Brian Domitrovic, "The Economics Nobel Goes to Sargent & Sims: Attackers of the Phillips Curve," Forbes.com, October 10, 2011, http://www.forbes.com/sites/briandomitrovic/2011/10/10/the-economics-nobel-goes-to-sargent-sims-attackers-of-the-phillips-curve/.

80 *labor participation rates at a 35-year low*   "Labor Force Statistics from the Current Population Survey: Unemployment Rate—Civilian Labor Force—LNS14000000," Bureau of Labor Statistics, accessed March 6, 2014, http://data.bls.gov/cgi-bin/surveymost?ln.

80 *inflation and unemployment regularly move in tandem*   Brian Domitrovic, "The Fed Is Failing Its Unemployment Mandate," Forbes.com, September 20, 2011, http://www.forbes.com/sites/briandomitrovic/2011/09/20/the-fed-is-failing-its-unemployment-mandate/.

80 *higher levels than during the financial crisis*   "Unemployment Rates in the United States Since 1948," DaveManual.com, accessed March 24, 2014, http://www.davemanuel.com/historical-unemployment-rates-in-the-united-states.php.

80 *both rappelled down a cliff*   Domitrovic, "The Fed Is Failing Its Unemployment Mandate," op. cit.

80 *examples are most of the 1920s and 1960s*   For the 1920s: "The Measurement and Behavior of Unemployment," National Bureau of Economic Research, 1957, p. 215; for the 1960s: "Household Data Annual Averages: Employment Status of Civilian Noninstitutional Population, 1943 to date," National Bureau of Economic Research.

81 *Why does poverty exist anywhere on earth?*   Ron Paul, "The Coming Debt Limit Drama: Government Wins, We Lose," The-Free-Foundation.org, January 21, 2013, http://www.the-free-foundation.org/tst1-21-2013.html.

81 *would actually* welcome *inflation*   Appelbaum, op. cit.

81 *those who are the earliest recipients of the new money*   Murray N. Rothbard, "What Has Government Done to Our Money?" Ludwig von Mises Institute, accessed March 6, 2014, http://mises.org/money/3s2.asp.

82 *punish the virtuous, the millions of responsible savers*   Finger, op. cit.

82 *we can see the cash when we want*   Catherine Rampell, "As Low Rates Depress Savers, Governments Reap Benefits," NYTimes.com, September 10, 2012, http://www.nytimes.com/2012/09/11/business/as-low-rates-depress-savers-governments-reap-the-benefits.html?pagewanted=all.

82 *I shall leave to be considered*   John Locke, *The Works of John Locke*, vol. 5 (London: Thomas Davison, Whitefriars, 1823), p. 145.

83 *an additional $500 billion interest expense*   Finger, op. cit.

83 *which amounted to $536 billion in 2012*   Kaiser Family Foundation, "Medicare Spending and Financing Fact Sheet," KFF.org, November 14, 2012, http://kff.org/medicare/fact-sheet/medicare-spending-and-financing-fact-sheet/.

83 *now costs around $80 billion a year*   U.S. Department of Agriculture, Food and Nutrition Service, "Supplemental Nutrition Assistance Program Participation and Costs" (program data), fns.usda.gov, February 7, 2014, http://www.fns.usda.gov/pd/snapsummary.htm.

84 *from $3 a barrel to almost $40*   The source for $3 oil: Energy Information Administration, http://eia.gov/dnav/pet/hist; the almost $40: James L.

Williams, "Oil Price History and Analysis," WTRG Economics, http://wtrg.com/prices.htm, accessed March 24, 2012.

84 *employees in the oil and gas industry has increased by over 30%*   Bureau of Labor Statistics, "Oil and Gas Extraction," Series CES1021100001, http://data.bls.gov/pdq/SurveyOutputServlet.

84 *calls such ventures "noble flops"*   Rich Karlgaard, "Ahead of Their Time: Noble Flops," Forbes.com, August 14, 2013, http://www.forbes.com/sites/richkarlgaard/2013/08/14/ahead-of-their-time-noble-flops/.

84 *families bought pianos even if they didn't play them*   Adam Fergusson, *When Money Dies: The Nightmare of the Weimar Collapse* (London: William Kimber, 1975), p. 64; available online at ThirdParadigm.org, http://thirdparadigm.org/doc/45060880-When-Money-Dies.pdf.

85 *collapse of the savings and loans in the 1980s*   Jim Powell, "The Pleasures and Perils of Tax Loopholes," Forbes.com, March 7, 2012, http://www.forbes.com/sites/jimpowell/2012/03/07/the-pleasures-and-perils-of-tax-loopholes/.

86 *culprits were Fannie Mae and Freddie Mac*   Peter J. Wallison, "Fannie, Freddie Caused the Financial Crisis," *USA Today*, November 25, 2011, http://www.aei.org/article/economics/financial-services/housing-finance/fannie-freddie-caused-the-financial-crisis/.

87 *lowered the federal funds rate to 1%*   Federal Reserve Press Release, June 25, 2003, http://www.federalreserve.gov/boarddocs/press/monetary/2003/20030625/.

87 *grew at levels equivalent to the inflationary 1970s*   Robert P. Murphy, "Evidence that the Fed Caused the Housing Boom," Ludwig von Mises Institute, Mises Daily, December 15, 2008, http://mises.org/daily/3252.

87 *subprime mortgage market grew 200%*   Financial Crisis Inquiry Commission, *Financial Crisis Inquiry Report*, January 2011, p. 70, http://www.gpo.gov/fdsys/pkg/GPO-FCIC/pdf/GPO-FCIC.pdf.

87 *homeless man in Saint Petersburg, Florida, managed to buy five houses*   Steve Forbes and Elizabeth Ames, *Freedom Manifesto* (New York: Random House, 2012), p. 149.

87 *interest rates, which reached 5.25% in June 2006*   Robert P. Murphy, "Did the Fed Cause the Housing Bubble?" Ludwig von Mises Institute, Mises Daily, April 14, 2008, http://mises.org/daily/2936.

87 *write down the value of their capital*   Brian S. Wesbury and Robert Stein, "Bernanke Finally Fingers Mark-to-Market," National Review.com, March 8, 2010, http://www.nationalreview.com/articles/229276/bernanke-finally-fingers-mark-market/brian-s-wesbury.

88 *brought inflated prices back down to reality*   Alex J. Pollock, "Americans' Pre-Crisis Wealth Was an Illusion," American Enterprise Institute, June 21, 2012, http://www.aei-ideas.org/2012/06/americas-pre-crisis-wealth-was-an-illusion/.

88   *it increases income inequality*   Zoran Balac, "Monetary Inflation's Effect on Wealth Inequality," Ludwig von Mises Institute, August 6, 2008, http://mises.org/journals/qjae/pdf/qjae11_1_1.pdf.

89   *Wall Street was ecstatic*   Bernard Condon, "Dow Jones Climbs 206 Points on Fed Stimulus News," *Huffington Post*, September 13, 2012, http://www.huffingtonpost.com/2012/09/13/dow-jones-fed-stimulus_n_1882063.html.

89   *cheaper for the government to borrow*   Anthony Randazzo, "How Quantitative Easing Helps the Rich and Soaks the Rest of Us," Reason.com, September 13, 2012, http://reason.com/archives/2012/09/13/occupy-the-fed.

89   *gains in the hundreds of billions of dollars*   "Low Dollar Helps Fuel Record High Price for Crude Oil," *New York Times*, October 26, 2007, http://www.nytimes.com/2007/10/26/business/worldbusiness/26iht-oil.4.8070642.html.

89   *opened up new domestic energy sources*   Christine Harvey and Asjylyn Loder, "Fracking Boom Pushes U.S. Oil Output to 25-Year High," *Bloomberg News*, December 11, 2013, http://www.bloomberg.com/news/2013-12-11/fracking-boom-pushes-u-s-oil-output-to-25-year-high.html.

90   *a barrel of oil from $4.31 to $10.11*   David Hammes and Douglas Willis, "Black Gold: The End of Bretton Woods and the Oil-Price Shocks of the 1970s," *Independent Review*, March 22, 2005, http://www.thefreelibrary.com/Black+gold%3A+the+end+of+Bretton+Woods+and+the+oil-price+shocks+of+the...-a0131605501.

90   *gasoline would probably be around 30 cents a gallon*   Ralph Benko and Charles Kadlec, *The 21st Century Gold Standard* (Washington, DC: Webster's Press, 2011) and available online at AGoldenAge.com, http://agoldenage.com/downloads/goldbook_with_cover_final.pdf.

90   *whom inflationism has impoverished, not less than of the proletariat*   John Maynard Keynes, *Essays in Persuasion* (New York: W. W. Norton & Co., 2011), first published 1931.

90   *credit usually ends up being rationed*   Taner M. Yigit, "Effects of Inflation Uncertainty on Credit Markets: A Disequilibrium Approach," Bilkent University, Ankara, undated, http://economics.bilkent.edu.tr/papers/02-09%20DP_T.Yigit.pdf.

91   *not a lot of financing right now*   Lynn Tilton, "Financing for Small Business" WSJ Startup of the Year, undated, http://projects.wsj.com/soty/mentor/lynn-tilton.

91   *tepid for so long*   Cathy McMorris Rodgers, "Reverse the Fed's Monetary Practices," Forbes.com, September 21, 2010, http://www.forbes.com/2010/09/21/federal-reserve-spending-barack-obama-opinions-contributors-cathy-mcmorris-rodgers.html.

91 *skewed credit markets* Steve Forbes, "Finally! The Fed May Stop Poison-ing the Economy," Forbes.com, July 15, 2013, http://www.forbes.com/sites/steveforbes/2013/06/26/finally-the-fed-may-stop-poisoning-the-economy/.

92 *worth just 17 cents in 1971 dollars* U.S. Department of Labor, Bureau of Labor Statistics, CPI Inflation Calculator, http://www.bls.gov/data/inflation_calculator.htm.

92 *an astonishing 68% decline in wealth* National Journal staff, "Pew Re-search: Older Americans' Net Worth Up; Younger Americans' Net Worth Down," NationalJournal.com, November 7, 2011, http://www.nationaljournal.com/economy/pew-research-older-americans-net-worth-up-younger-americans-net-worth-down-20111107.

93 *working people—not just rich people—prospered* Benko and Kadlec, op. cit.

94 *hyperinflation that has reached as high as 5,000%* Gary Marx, "For Poor Argentines, 'There Is No Work,'" *Chicago Tribune*, May 20, 1990, http://articles.chicagotribune.com/1990-05-20/news/9002110268_1_buenos aires-poor-argentines-argentina.

94 *more than double the government's numbers* Ken Parks, "New Program Sets Stage for Annual Wage Talks," *Wall Street Journal*, January 3, 2014, http://online.wsj.com/news/articles/SB1000142405270230387070457929849150428503838, quoted at http://argentinasalvajizada.wordpress.com/2014/01/07/argentine-update-jan-6-2014/.

94 *from 35 to 50% lower than the official exchange rate* Graciela Ibáñez, "Travel Alert: Dollars Fetch a Premium in Black Markets of Argen-tina, Venezuela," Forbes.com, January 15, 2014, http://www.forbes.com/sites/janetnovack/2014/01/15/travel-alert-dollars-fetch-a-premium-in-black-markets-of-argentina-venezuela/.

95 *the bolívar was devalued 992%* Moisés Naim, "Venezuela's Move to De-value Is Desperate," FT.com, February 13, 2013, http://www.ft.com/intl/cms/s/0/8fd30252-75d5-11e2-9891-00144feabdc0.html#axzz2qfdm IUdo.

95 *currency is woefully misaligned* Ibid.

95 *achieve a 7.5% growth rate in 2010* "Brazil GDP—Real Growth Rate," In-dex Mundi, accessed March 6, 2014, http://www.indexmundi.com/brazil/gdp_real_growth_rate.html.

96 *that have too many foreign employees* Sara Hamdan, "Saudi Arabia to Fine Firms with Too Many Foreign Workers," *New York Times*, November 21, 2012, http://www.nytimes.com/2012/11/22/world/middleeast/saudi-arabia-to-fine-firms-with-too-many-foreign-workers.html?_r=0.

96 *and barred new Internet taxes* Mark Bautz, "How a Capital-Gains Cut Will Change the Way You Invest," CNNMoney.com, August 1, 1997, http://money.cnn.com/magazines/moneymag/moneymag_archive/1997/08/01/229754/index.htm; Matthew L. Wald, "Attention Internet

Shoppers: No New Taxes," *New York Times*, October 9, 1998, http://
www.nytimes.com/1998/10/09/business/attention-internet-shoppers
-no-new-taxes.html.

97 *gold price fell* "Historical Gold Prices—1833 to Present," National Mining Association, accessed March 6, 2014, http://www.nma.org/pdf/gold
/his_gold_prices.pdf.

97 *under $2 a bushel in 1999* "Agricultural Prices," U.S. Department of Ag-
riculture, National Agricultural Statistics Service, December 30, 1999,
http://usda01.library.cornell.edu/usda/nass/AgriPric//1990s/1999
/AgriPric-12-30-1999.pdf.

97 *as low as $10 a barrel* "The Next Shock?" *The Economist*, March 4, 1999,
http://www.economist.com/node/188181.

97 *a level it has not yet touched since* Declan McCullagh, "Nasdaq 5,000: Ten
Years After the Dot-Com Peak," CNET.com, March 10, 2010, http://
news.cnet.com/8301-10784_3-10466637-7.html.

97 *went above $400 an ounce in late 2003–2004* Goldprice.org, http://goldprice
.org/gold-price-history.html.

Chapter 5: Money and Morality

99 *not one man in a million can diagnose* John Maynard Keynes, *The Economic
Consequences of the Peace* (New York: Harcourt, Brace, and Howe, 1920),
chap. 5; available online from the Library of Economics and Liberty
at http://www.econlib.org/library/YPDBooks/Keynes/kynsCP6.html
#VI.13.

100 *undermined by currency debasements* Dylan Grice, "The Loss of Trust and
the Great Disorder," *Edelweiss Journal*, no. 9, October 2012, p. 1, http://
www.edelweissjournal.com/pdfs/EdelweissJournal-009.pdf.

100 *the situation becomes unbearable* Paul Hein, "The Root of All Evil," Lew
Rockwell.com, March 4, 2009, http://www.lewrockwell.com/2009/03
/paul-hein/the-root-of-all-evil/.

102 *followed by Argentina, South Africa, Egypt, India, and Turkey* Ciaran Ryan,
"Riot Alert: Look Out Argentina, South Africa, Turkey, and India," *Economic Policy Journal*, February 27, 2013, http://www.economicpolicy
journal.com/2013/02/riot-alert-look-out-argentina-south.html.

102 *the ultimate flare-up of unrest and violence* Chris Becker, "A Response
to a Criticism of My Inflation-Social Unrest Research," ChrisLBecker
.com (blog), February 13, 2013, http://chrislbecker.com/2013/02/13
/response-to-a-criticism-of-my-inflation-social-unrest-research/.

102 *during the presidencies of George W. Bush and Barack Obama* "Parti-
san Polarization Surges in Bush, Obama Years," Pew Research Center for the People & the Press, June 4, 2012, http://www.people-press
.org/2012/06/04/partisan-polarization-surges-in-bush-obama-years/.

102 *few question the ideas behind government or central banks* Grice, op. cit., p. 5.

102 *money printing exercise is to turn society against itself* Michael Skocpol, "Dylan Grice: Witch Hunts, Inflation Fears, and Why I'm Bearish in 2013," Advisor Perspectives, January 22, 2013, http://advisorperspectives .com/newsletters13/pdfs/Dylan_Grice-Witch_Hunts_Inflation_Fears _and_Why_Im_Bearish_in_2013.pdf.

103 *the marketplace is infused with trust* Bruce Yandle, "Lost Trust: The Real Cause of the Financial Meltdown," *Independent Review*, Winter 2010, pp. 343–344, http://www.independent.org/pdf/tir/tir_14_03_02_yandle.pdf.

103 *shared norms, on the part of other members of that community* Francis Fukuyama, *Trust: Human Nature and the Reconstitution of Social Order*, Kindle Ed. (New York: Free Press, 2008), p. 26.

104 *have relied more heavily on smaller family businesses* Ibid., p. 30.

104 *such as Norway (1.5%) and Australia (2.5%)* Trading Economics, Interest Rate, Country List, www.tradingeconomics.com/country-list/interest -rate.

104 *that prevailed in the nineteenth century* Nathan Lewis, "The 1870–1914 Gold Standard: The Most Perfect One Ever Created," Forbes.com, January 3, 2013, http://www.forbes.com/sites/nathanlewis/2013/01/03/the -1870-1914-gold-standard-the-most-perfect-one-ever-created/.

104 *decline of faith in the system since the early to mid-1960s* "Public Trust in Government: 1958–2013," Pew Research Center for the People & the Press, October 18, 2013, http://www.people-press.org/2013/10/18/trust -in-government-interactive/; "Lack of Trust—Caused by Institutional Corruption—Is Killing the Economy," *Washington's Blog*, May 4, 2012 (citing the Chicago Booth/Kellogg School Financial Trust Index), http:// www.washingtonsblog.com/2012/05/trust.html; Ron Fournier and Sophie Quinton, "In Nothing We Trust," *National Journal*, April 19, 2012, http://www.nationaljournal.com/features/restoration-calls/in-nothing -we-trust-20120419.

104 *sharp dives during the double-digit inflation* Public Trust in Government (Pew), op. cit.

105 *the market's "trust technology"* Yandle, op. cit., pp. 345–346.

105 *setting off a wave of foreclosures* Ibid., p. 358.

106 *people lose confidence in you* Mark Landler, "The U.S. Financial Crisis Is Spreading to Europe," *New York Times*, October 1, 2008, p. C1, http:// www.nytimes.com/2008/10/01/business/worldbusiness/01global.html ?pagewanted=print.

107 *nearly 49% at the height of the crisis in March 2012* "Greece Government Bond 10Y," Trading Economics, accessed March 6, 2014, http://www .tradingeconomics.com/greece/government-bond-yield.

107 *stiffing its bondholders for 50% of their loans* "Greece's Default: The Wait Is Over," *The Economist*, March 17, 2012, http://www.economist.com/node /21550271.

107 *was feared by everybody* "Most Popular Scapegoats for Europe's Crisis," CNBC.com, May 24, 2011, http://www.cnbc.com/id/43106681.

108 *Food Price Index reported a 25% surge in prices* "FAO Food Price Index," Food and Agriculture Organization of the United Nations, http://www .fao.org/worldfoodsituation/foodpricesindex/en/; "World Food Prices Reach New Historic Peak," Food and Agriculture Organization of the United Nations, February 3, 2011, http://www.fao.org/news/story/en /item/50519/icode/.

108 *Arab Spring protests were largely over food prices* Alaa Shahine, "Tunisia Revolt Threatens Rulers Sharing Ben Ali's Regime Model," *Bloomberg News*, January 17, 2011, http://www.bloomberg.com/news/2011-01-16 /tunisian-uprising-may-threaten-arab-rulers-sharing-ben-ali-s-regime -model.html.

108 *jumped 18% in 2009, compared with 5% in 2006* George Melloan, "The Federal Reserve Is Causing Turmoil Abroad," *Wall Street Journal*, February 23, 2011, http://online.wsj.com/news/articles/SB100014240527487 04657704576150202567815380.

108 *U.S.-driven global inflation was threatening global stability* Ibid.

109 *Those to whom the system brings windfalls* Keynes, op. cit.

109 *during its hyperinflation, Germany blamed the Jews* Grice, op. cit., pp. 2–3.

109 *driving down the value of his country's bonds* Sewell Chan and Jack Ewing, "Greek Leader Wants to Restrict Speculative Trades," *New York Times*, March 8, 2010, http://www.nytimes.com/2010/03/09/business/global /09drachma.html?_r=0.

109 *a symbol of banker incompetence and greed* Rod Mills and Martin Brown, "Sir Fred's £3m Mansion Hit by Bank Protesters," *Daily Express*, March 26, 2009, http://www.express.co.uk/news/uk/91106/Sir-Fred-s-3m -mansion-hit-by-bank-protesters.

109 *while ordinary people are made unemployed, destitute, and homeless* Aislinn Simpson, "Sir Fred Goodwin Attack: Bank Bosses Are Criminals Group Claims Responsibility," *Telegraph*, March 25, 2009, http://www.telegraph .co.uk/finance/newsbysector/banksandfinance/5048091/Sir-Fred-Goodwin -attack-Bank-Bosses-Are-Criminals-group-claims-responsbility.html.

110 *as the unit of money did during the inflation* Grice, op. cit., p. 4.

110 *this system is rigged for a very few* Shannon Jones, "Detroit: 'This System Is Rigged for a Very Few,'" World Socialist Website, October 19, 2011, http://www.wsws.org/en/articles/2011/10/occd-o19.html.

111 *lend the same money back to the government at two or three percent* Matt Taibbi, "Wall Street Isn't Winning—It's Cheating," *Rolling Stone*, October 25, 2011, http://www.rollingstone.com/politics/blogs/taibblog /owss-beef-wall-street-isnt-winning-its-cheating-20111025.

112 *the great majority of Americans are still living in a depressed economy* Paul Krugman, "Rich Man's Recovery," *New York Times*, September 12,

2013, p. A25, http://www.nytimes.com/2013/09/13/opinion/krugman
-rich-mans-recovery.html.

112 *those super-high incomes come from the financial industry* Ibid.

112 *and he received taunts and threats* Landon Thomas Jr., "What's Broken in
Greece? Ask an Entrepreneur," *New York Times*, January 29, 2011, http://
www.nytimes.com/2011/01/30/business/30greek.html?pagewanted=all.

112 *unemployment in Greece is nearly 28%* Ian Silvera, "Greek Unemployment Rate Climbs to Record High as Eurozone Jobless Holds," *International Business Times*, January 9, 2014, http://www.ibtimes.co.uk
/greek-unemployment-rate-climbs-record-high-eurozone-jobless-holds
-1431636.

112 empresario, *the word for businessman, has come to mean* criminal Max
Chafkin, "A Constant Feeling of Crisis," *Inc.*, June 2011, http://www.inc
.com/magazine/201106/doing-business-in-argentina.html.

113 *"macroprudential" strategies in monetary and financial regulation* International Monetary Fund, "New Policies to Fend Off Financial Crises,"
IMF Survey Magazine, September 16, 2013, http://www.imf.org/external
/pubs/ft/survey/so/2013/POL091613A.htm; Bianca De Paoli and Matthias Paustian, "Coordinating Monetary and Macroprudential Policies,"
Federal Reserve Bank of New York Staff Reports, no. 653, November
2013, http://www.newyorkfed.org/research/staff_reports/sr653.pdf.

113 *decrees their actions a "systemic" threat* John H. Cochrane, "The Danger of an All-Powerful Federal Reserve," *Wall Street Journal*, August 26,
2013, http://online.wsj.com/news/articles/SB10001424127887323906800
04579036571835323800.

114 *avert a lawsuit over its sale of mortgage securities* Ben Protess and Jessica Silver-Greenberg, "In Extracting Deal from JPMorgan, U.S. Aimed
for Bottom Line," *New York Times*, DealBook (blog), November 13,
2013, http://dealbook.nytimes.com/2013/11/19/13-billion-settlement
-with-jpmorgan-is-announced/.

114 *doubling its risk and compliance team* "Robbery at J.P. Morgan," *Wall
Street Journal*, September 29, 2013, http://online.wsj.com/news/articles
/SB10001424127887324619504579026860113942236.

115 *has fallen below that of all other people in the Western world* Jimmy Carter,
"Crisis of Confidence," The Carter Center, July 15, 1979, http://www
.cartercenter.org/news/editorials_speeches/crisis_of_confidence.html.

115 *the rupee, which reached a record low in 2013* Mike Obel, "Why India's
Currency, the Rupee, Has Plummeted to a Record Low Against the Dollar," *International Business Times*, August 28, 2013, http://www.ibtimes
.com/why-indias-currency-rupee-has-plummeted-record-low-against
-dollar-1401400.

115 *ban the import of duty-free flat screens by airline passengers* "Government
Targets TV Imports by Passengers as Rupee Plummets," Reuters, Au-

gust 19, 2013, http://in.reuters.com/article/2013/08/19/india-economy
-imports-idINDEE97I09Z20130819.

115 *was now "focused on simply surviving"*   Annie Gowen, "In India, Economic
Slowdown and Inflation Cause Middle Class to Defer Dreams," *Washington Post*,
November 5, 2013, http://www.washingtonpost.com/world/economic-slow
down-inflation-cause-indias-middle-class-to-defer-dreams/2013/11/05/
ace864ba-4189-11e3-b028-de922d7a3f47_story.html.

116 *their kids won't be better off than they were*   "Remarks by the President
on Economic Mobility," The White House, Office of the Press Secretary, December 4, 2013, http://www.whitehouse.gov/the-press-office
/2013/12/04/remarks-president-economic-mobility.

117 *force almost everyone to join in the dance*   Theodore Dalrymple, "Inflation's
Moral Hazard," *City Journal* 19 (3), Summer 2009, http://www.city-journal
.org/2009/19_3_otbie-inflation.html.

117 *other standards will fade away as well*   Hein, op. cit.

117 *annual Corruption Perceptions Index*   "Corruption Perceptions Index 2013,"
Transparency International, http://cpi.transparency.org/cpi2013/results/.

117 *increased a lot over the last two years*   Deborah Hardoon and Finn Hein-
rich, "Global Corruption Barometer 2013," Transparency International,
July 19, 2013, p. 6, http://www.transparency.org/whatwedo/pub/global
_corruption_barometer_2013.

117 *to replace 10 ministers in his cabinet*   The *Times of Israel* staff and the Associated Press, "Erdogan Replaces 10 Ministers Amid Corruption scandal," *Times of Israel*, December 26, 2013, http://www.timesofisrael.com
/erdogan-replaces-10-government-ministers-amid-corruption-scandal/.

117 *degrees in fields such as law and medicine*   Olga Yatskevich, "Corruption in
Education in Belarus," 10th International Anti-Corruption Conference,
October 2001, http://www.10iacc.org/content-ns.phtml?documents
=300&art=20.

118 *cost of a bribe in that country "more than tripled"*   "Bribery Affected by Inflation Too," RT.com, January 27, 2012, http://rt.com/business/corruption
-russia-849/.

118 *had to pay fines totaling more than $6 billion*   Christopher Alessi and Mo-
hammed Aly Sergie, "Understanding the Libor Scandal," Council on
Foreign Relations Backgrounder, December 5, 2013, http://www.cfr
.org/united-kingdom/understanding-libor-scandal/p28729.

118 *100,000 euros of customers at the Bank of Cyprus*   Andrew Higgins, "Cyprus
Bank's Bailout Hands Ownership to Russian Plutocrats," *New York Times*,
August 21, 2013, http://www.nytimes.com/2013/08/22/world/europe
/russians-still-ride-high-in-cyprus-after-bailout.html/.

119 *What more do you need to know?*   Paul Toscano, "'Run for the Hills' Now,
I'm Doing It: Jim Rogers," CNBC, March 28, 2013, http://www.cnbc.com
/id/100600824.

119 *abandon their mortgages in the wake of the financial crisis* Tess Vigeland, "They Walked Away, and They're Glad They Did," *New York Times*, November 8, 2011, http://www.nytimes.com/2011/11/09/your-money /life-goes-on-some-find-after-leaving-an-underwater-mortgage.html ?pagewanted=all.

119 *charges clients an enrollment fee of $199 to $395* Ibid.

120 *financially rational to walk away, that's what you do* Ibid.

120 *default rates are at their highest levels since 1995* Shahien Nasiripour and Chris Kirkham, "Student Loan Defaults Surge to Highest Level in Nearly Two Decades," *Huffington Post*, September 30, 2013, http://www .huffingtonpost.com/2013/09/30/student-loans-default_n_4019806 .html.

121 *loan payments that were double his rent* Kelsey Sheehy, "Undergrads Blow It with Student Loan Refunds," *U.S. News & World Report*, July 24, 2013, http://www.usnews.com/education/best-colleges/paying-for-college /articles/2013/07/24/undergrads-blow-it-with-student-loan- refunds.

121 *from 12% to around 17.5% in 2013* "Consumer Credit Outstanding as a Percent of GPD," Economagic.com, http://www.economagic.com /gif/g69025002520941408636468145648 24.gif; Neal Irwin, "Consumer Debt Is Soaring: That's Good News (for Now)," *Washington Post Wonk- blog*, July 8, 2013, http://www.washingtonpost.com/blogs/wonkblog /wp/2013/07/08/consumer-debt-is-soaring-thats-good-news-for-now/.

121 *from 13% to under 5% today* "Personal Saving Rate (PSAVERT)," FRED Economic Data, Federal Reserve Bank of St. Louis, updated December 23, 2013, http://research.stlouisfed.org/fred2/series /PSAVERT/.

121 *to depend less and less on effort and production* Henry Hazlitt, "Inflation vs. Immorality," *Freeman*, January 1, 1977, http://www.fee.org/the_freeman /detail/inflation-vs-immorality#axzz2r24trZUK.

122 *resulting in a rash of home invasion robberies* Ryan Villarreal, "Protests Mount Against Argentina's President over Currency, Crime and Cor- ruption," *International Business Times*, November 9, 2012, http://www .ibtimes.com/protests-mount-against-argentinas-president-over -currency-crime-corruption-868860.

122 *first rise in violent and property crime in two decades* Terry Frieden, "U.S. Violent Crime up for First Time in Years," CNN.com, October 17, 2012, http://www.cnn.com/2012/10/17/us/violent-crime/.

122 *U.S. crime rate and the Misery Index* Chor Foon Tang and Hooi Hooi Lean, "New Evidence from the Misery in the Index in the Crime Func- tion," *Economics Letters* 102 (2), 2009.

122 *falls on the inflation rate* John M. Nunley, Richard Alan Seals Jr., and Joachim Zietz, "The Impact of Macroeconomic Conditions on Property

Crime," Auburn Economics Working Paper (Auburn University, 2011), p. 18, http://johnnunley.org/prop_crime_4_3_2013_final.pdf.

122 *the first serious deflation in 50 years* Miguel Llanos, "Crime in Decline, but Why? Low Inflation Among Theories," MSNBC.com, September 20, 2011, http://www.nbcnews.com/id/44578241/ns/us_news-crime _and_courts/t/crime-decline-why-low-inflation-among-theories/# .Ut57GGQo7wc.

122 *doubled from 1.6% to 3.2%* "Consumer Price Index, 1913–," The Federal Reserve Bank of Minneapolis, accessed March 6, 2013, http://www .minneapolisfed.org/community_education/teacher/calc/hist1913.cfm.

123 *increase in crime categories* Bureau of Justice Statistics Press Release, op. cit.

123 *quickly followed by an increase in crime rates* Chor Foon Tang and Hooi Hooi Lean, "Will Inflation Increase Crime Rate? New Evidence from Bounds and Modified Wald Tests," *Global Crime* 8 (4), November 2007, pp. 311–323, https://www.ncjrs.gov/App/publications/abstract.aspx? ID=243186.

123 *no longer pays income taxes* David B. Muhlhausen and Patrick Tyrrell, "The 2013 Index of Dependence on Government," The Heritage Foundation, Special Report 142, Chart 1, November 21, 2013, http://www .heritage.org/research/reports/2013/11/the-2013-index-of-dependence -on-government.

123 *from $37.6 billion to $78.4 billion in fiscal year 2012* Ibid.; "Supplemental Nutrition Assistance Program Participation and Costs," U.S. Department of Agriculture, accessed March 6, 2014, http://www.fns.usda.gov /pd/snapsummary.htm.

124 *a withering of civil society* Muhlhausen and Tyrell, op. cit.

124 *relentlessly consuming the life of the nation* J. P. Cooper, *The New Cambridge Modern History*, vol. 4: *The Decline of Spain and the Thirty Years War, 1609-48/59* (Cambridge University Press, 1970), p. 477; available online at http://bit.ly/KKa9gn.

125 *little more than a piece of junk* Lawrence W. Reed, *Are We Rome?*, Foundation for Economic Education (2013), pp. 5–8, http://www.fee.org /files/doclib/20130620_FEEAreWeRomeCover1V5.pdf.

125 *ultimately their civilization* Ibid., p. 9.

Chapter 6: The Gold Standard

127 *making the results public* "74% Want to Audit the Federal Reserve," *Rasmussen Reports*, November 8, 2013, http://www.rasmussenreports.com /public_content/business/general_business/november_2013/74_want _to_audit_the_federal_reserve.

128 *accepted legal tender in the state of Utah* Charles Riley, "Utah: Forget Dollars. How About Gold?" CNNMoney.com, March 29. 2011, http://

money.cnn.com/2011/03/29/news/economy/utah_gold_currency/index
.htm?iid=EL.

128 *allow the use of gold as payment* "Utah House Passes Bill Recognizing
Gold, Silver as Legal Tender," FoxNews.com, March 4, 2011, http://
www.foxnews.com/politics/2011/03/04/utah-house-passes-recognizing
-gold-silver-legal-tender/.

128 *with a proposal for a new gold standard* Louis Woodhill, "Gold Isn't
Money, But It Should Be Used to Define the Value of the Dollar,"
Forbes.com, April 18, 2013, http://www.forbes.com/sites/louiswoodhill
/2013/04/18/gold-isnt-money-but-it-should-be-used-to-define-the
-value-of-the-dollar/2/.

128 *seen as the gold standard's Woodstock* Ralph Benko, "Gold Defined
Money and Monetary History at the Cato Institute: A Velvet Underground Event?" Forbes.com, July 29, 2013, http://www.forbes.com
/sites/ralphbenko/2013/07/29/gold-defined-money-and-monetary
-history-at-the-cato-institute-a-velvet-underground-event/.

129 *remained unmatched for the next 100 years* Nathan Lewis, "The 1870–
1914 Gold Standard: The Most Perfect One Ever Created," Forbes.com,
January 3, 2013, http://www.forbes.com/sites/nathanlewis/2013/01/03
/the-1870-1914-gold-standard-the-most-perfect-one-ever-created/.

131 *cast aside the wisdom of sound money* Theodore Phalan, Thomas Rus-
tici, and Deema Yazigi, "The Smoot-Hawley Tariff and the Great Depression," *Freeman*, February 29, 2012, http://www.fee.org/the_freeman
/detail/the-smoot-hawley-tariff-and-the-great-depression#axzz2
uf2wQ89w.

132 *all the gold that has been mined is still in existence* Ed Prior, "How Much
Gold Is There in the World?" BBC.com, March 31, 2013, http://www
.bbc.com/news/magazine-21969100.

133 *particles mined in the time of the Pharaohs* Roy Jastram, *The Golden Constant: The English and American Experience, 1560–1976* (New York: John
Wiley & Sons, 1977), p. 189.

133 *price increases averaging only 1.7% a year* Nathan Lewis, *Gold: The Once
and Future Money* (Hoboken, NJ: John Wiley & Sons, 2007) p. 119.

133 *growth rate quickly returned to normal* Ibid.

133 *were equivalent to an ounce of gold* Nathan Lewis, "To Achieve a Successful
Gold Standard, You Don't Need Gold Coins," Forbes.com, August 2, 2012,
http://www.forbes.com/sites/nathanlewis/2012/08/02/to-achieve-a
-successful-gold-standard-you-dont-need-gold-coins/.

133 *in excess of 60 to 1* Historic figures of the gold/silver ratio until 2012
are available at MeasuringWorth.com. Daily gold/silver ratios are available from Kitco Metals Inc., http://www.kitco.com/gold.londonfix
.html.

134 *missing from British coins by the end of the seventeenth century*   Charles Larkin, "The Great Re-coinage of 1696," Department of Economics & Institute for International Integration Studies, Trinity College Dublin, September 25, 2006; available at the Federal Reserve Bank of Atlanta, http://www .atl-res.com/finance/LARKIN2.pdf.

134 *a moral transgression no different from counterfeiting*   Murray Rothbard, *Economic Thought Before Adam Smith: An Austrian Perspective on the History of Economic Thought*, vol. 1 (Auburn, AL: Ludwig von Mises Institute, 2006), pp. 317–323, http://mises.org/document/3985/Economic -Thought-Before-Adam-Smith-An-Austrian-Perspective-on-the -History-of-Economic-Thought-Volume-I.

134 *a ratio that stood unchanged until 1931*   Lewis, *Gold: The Once and Future Money*, op. cit.

135 *slightly devalued to $20.67*   Alan Reynolds, *Economic Education Bulletin* 23(10), October 1983, American Institute for Economic Research, p. 1.

135 *all adopted gold-based money*   Lewis, "The 1870–1914 Gold Standard," op. cit.

136 *throughout the world, including India, Argentina, China, Malaya, and Africa*   Nathan Lewis, *Gold: The Monetary Polaris* (New Berlin, NY: Canyon Maple Publishing, 2013), pp. 105–118.

136 *capital flows, not until 1999*   Ibid., p. 113.

137 *surged a jaw-dropping 682%*   Ibid., p. 74.

137 *after adopting a gold standard in 1897*   Richard Pipes, *The Russian Revolution* (New York: Random House, 1990), pp. 78–80.

137 *highest economic growth rate in Europe on the eve of World War I*   Ibid.

137 *from its archenemy Germany*   John Mosier, *Verdun: The Lost History of the Most Important Battle of World War 1, 1914–1918* (New York: NAL Caliber, 2013) p. 123.

138 *trade and finance are built upon credit*   Sir Norman Angell, *The Great Illusion: A Study of the Relation of Military Power to National Advantage* (New York: Cosimo, 2010, original 1909), pp. 71–72.

138 *insuring their ships with British companies in London*   Niall Ferguson, *The Ascent of Money: A Financial History of the World* (New York: Penguin Books, 2008), p. 188.

139 *1.2 million pounds at 8%*   Lewis, *The Monetary Polaris*, op. cit., p. 87.

139 *far higher than the 4% rates the Dutch were paying*   Ibid.

139 *with no maturity at a rate as low as 3%*   Lewis, *The Once and Future Money*, op. cit., pp. 30–31.

139 *that rate went down to 2½%*   Ibid.

139 *Consols—that had no maturity, was 3.15%*   Lewis, "The 1870–1914 Gold Standard," op. cit.

140 *traded with a small risk premium*   Lewis, *Gold: The Monetary Polaris*, op. cit., p. 113.

140 *slid to 3% by 1902* Ibid.

140 *reliable foundation for all financial and economic activity* Ibid., p. 72.

140 *150-year bond at an interest rate of 3%!* Gene Laber, "Bond Covenants and Forgone Opportunities: The Case of Burlington Northern Railroad Company," *Financial Management*, June 6, 1992, http://www.thefree library.com/Bond+covenants+and+forgone+opportunities%3A+the+ case+of+Burlington...-a013632928.

140 *an average of 4.8% a year* Nathan Lewis, "The Correlation Between the Gold Standard and Stupendous Growth Is Clear," Forbes.com, April 11, 2013, http://www.forbes.com/sites/nathanlewis/2013/04/11/the -correlation-between-the-gold-standard-and-stupendous-growth-is -clear/.

140 *2000 to 2012, it rose a total of 7%* Ibid.

141 *never gotten out of hand like it has* Daniel Ryan, "The Gold Standard: Power to the People," TheGoldStandardNow.org, April 16, 2011, Lehrman Institute, http://www.thegoldstandardnow.org/key-blogs-6/217 -gold-standard-power-to-people.

142 *spent by nations like France (3 to 4%)* Jasen Castillo et al., "Military Expenditures and Economic Growth," The Rand Corporation, Monograph Report, 2001, pp. 11–48.

142 *my re-election hinges on the Federal Reserve and a bunch of f****** bond traders* David J. Lynch and Cordell Eddings, "Obama Says Real Boss in Default Showdown Means Bond Call Shots," Bloomberg.com, October 11, 2013, http://www.bloomberg.com/news/2013-10-11/obama-says-real -boss-in-default-showdown-means-bonds-call-shots.html/.

142 *you can intimidate everybody* Bob Woodward, *The Agenda* (New York: Simon & Schuster, 1995), p. 139.

143 *cost of living in Great Britain went up 0.1% a year* Nathan Lewis lecture at Cato Institute on February 12, 2014, Washington, DC.

144 *above 3%, based on the highly imperfect CPI calculations* Steve Forbes calculation using numbers from Inflationdata.com/CPI.

144 *around $3.50 and has been far higher* "Retail Motor Gasoline and On-Highway Diesel Fuel Prices, 1949–2011," 2012 Annual Energy Review, Table 5.24, U.S. Energy Information Administration.

145 *height of around 21% to 5%* Effective Federal Funds Rate, Board of Governors of the Federal Reserve System, 2014, Fedprimerate.com.

145 *a high of 15.75% in 1981 to a little over 6% in the 1990s* Sidney Homer and Richard Sylla, *A History of Interest Rates* (Hoboken, NJ: John Wiley & Sons, 2005), pp. 644–645.

145 *than in all of Europe and Japan put together* George Gilder conversation with Steve Forbes, May 16, 2012.

146 *channel their energies elsewhere* John Tamny, "August 15, 1971: President Nixon's Golden Error," RealClearMarkets.com, August 15, 2011,

http://www.realclearmarkets.com/articles/2011/08/15/august_15_1971
_president_nixons_golden_error_99193.html.

146 *make today's cars look positively pedestrian*   John Tamny, "David Stock-
man Brings New Meaning to 'Flawed Economic Analysis,'" Forbes.com,
April 1, 2013, http://www.forbes.com/sites/johntamny/2013/04/01
/david-stockman-brings-new-meaning-to-flawed-economic-analysis/2/.

151 *legislation introduced by U.S. Representative Ted Poe*   Louis Woodhill,
"Gold Isn't Money, but It Should Be Used to Define the Value of the
Dollar," Forbes.com, April 18, 2013.

151 *attack the system by buying up supplies of gold*   Ibid.

155 *was a believer in sound money*   Nathan Lewis, "Though It Nearly Strangled Reagan's Revolution, Soft Money Conservatives Revive Friedman's
Monetarism," Forbes.com, August 12, 2012, http://www.forbes.com
/sites/nathanlewis/2012/08/12/though-it-nearly-strangled-reagans
-revolution-soft-money-conservatives-revive-friedmans-monetarism/;
and Seth Lipsky, "A Commission for the Fed's Next 100 Years," *Wall
Street Journal*, March 25, 2013, http://online.wsj.com/news/articles/SB
10001424127887324103504578379020635729326.

156 *exchange rate has to be adjusted*   Christopher Beam, "Gold Rush," Slate
.com, November 9, 2010, http://www.slate.com/articles/business/money
box/2010/11/gold_rush.html.

157 *high of $1,900 an ounce in 2011*   Hibah Yousuf, "Gold Tops $1,900,
Looking 'a Bit Bubbly,'" CNNMoney.com, August 23, 2011, http://
money.cnn.com/2011/08/22/markets/gold_prices/.

157 *most liquid part of the money supply, is $2.6 trillion*   Figures available from
the Federal Reserve Bank of St. Louis's Federal Reserve Economic Data
system, http://research.stlouisfed.org/fred2/.

158 *U.S. population grew from 4 million to 76 million*   "Fast Facts," United States'
Census Bureau, U.S. Department of Commerce, http://www.census
.gov/history/www/through_the_decades/fast_facts/.

159 *stable money has never caused a financial crisis*   Nathan Lewis, "Let It Be
Known That No Financial Crisis Was Ever Caused by Stable Money,"
Forbes.com, October 14, 2012, http://www.forbes.com/sites/nathanlewis
/2012/10/14/let-it-be-known-that-no-financial-crisis-was-ever-caused
-by-stable-money/.

160 *with the top rate going from 25% to 63%*   Lewis, *Gold: The Once and Future
Money*, op. cit., p. 228.

160 *devalued the franc in 1936*   Christian Saint-Etienne, *The Great Depression,
1929–1938: Lessons for the 1980s* (Stanford, CA: Hoover Institution Press,
1984), p. 25.

161 *borrowing pounds and then selling them to buy marks*   Sebastian Mallaby,
More Money Than God: Hedge Funds and the Making of the New Elite (New
York: Penguin Group, 2010), pp. 147–171.

161 *the humiliated government caved and it floated the pound* Ibid.

161 *attack on the ruble failed* Emma O'Brien, "Russia Fueling Ruble Tumble with Loans, Banks Say," Bloomberg.com, February 5, 2009, http://www .bloomberg.com/apps/news?pid=newsarchive&sid=alZcF5bve18o; Eric McCarthy, "Russian Ruble Leads Emerging-Market Currency Rally," *Wall Street Journal*, April 25, 2013, http://online.wsj.com/news/articles /SB10001424127887323789704578444761251628342.

Chapter 7: Surviving in the Meantime

163 *around $74,000 in 2013* "CPI Inflation Calculator," Bureau of Labor Statistics, http://data.bls.gov/cgi-bin/cpicalc.pl?cost1=100%2C000 .00&year1=2000&year2=2013.

164 *beat the Dow or the Standard & Poor's 500 Index (S&P 500)* "How to Start Investing," The Motley Fool, accessed March 6, 2014, http://www.fool .com/seminars/sharebuilder/index.htm?sid=0008&lid=400&pid=0.

164 *hold on to your pocketbook if anyone tells you otherwise* "Inflation: How to Protect Your Capital," *Forbes*, April 1, 1974, p. 28.

165 *no one can accurately forecast a whim* Louis Woodhill, "It's Very Good That Gold Was a Bad Investment This Year," Forbes.com, December 25, 2013, http://www.forbes.com/sites/louiswoodhill/2013/12/25/its-very -good-that-gold-was-a-bad-investment-this-year/.

166 *hundreds of individual stocks lost a lot more* Alexandra Twin, "For Dow, Another 12-Year Low," CNNMoney, March 9, 2009, http://money.cnn .com/2009/03/09/markets/markets_newyork/; Dealbook, "Slump Humbles Blue-Chip Stocks," *New York Times*, March 6, 2009, http://dealbook .nytimes.com/2009/03/06/slump-humbling-blue-chip-stocks-once -dows-pride/?_php=true&_type=blogs&_r=0.

166 *plunged 75% as many appeared headed for collapse* Peter Slatin, "Recharged REITs," Forbes.com, June 5, 2009, http://www.forbes.com /forbes/2009/0622/finance-reits-commercial-real-estate.html.

166 *shareholders in many such institutions were wiped out altogether* "KBW Bank Index (KBX), 1/3/07–4/3/09," Yahoo! Finance, accessed March 6, 2014, http://yhoo.it/1hY2B9z.

168 *gold's price remained around $350 an ounce* "Daily Gold Price History," USAGOLD, accessed March 6, 2014, http://www.usagold.com/reference /prices/history.html.

168 *5% from price appreciation of shares and 4½% from dividends* Jeremy J. Siegel, *Stocks for the Long Run: The Definitive Guide to Financial Market Returns and Long-Term Investment Strategies*, 4th ed. (New York: McGraw-Hill, 2008), pp. 12–13.

168 *the Dow appreciated 15-fold* Dow Jones Industrial Average (DJIA) History Chart, October 1, 1929 thru December 26, 2013," FedPrimeRate .com, http://www.fedprimerate.com/djia-chart-history.htm.

169 *3% a year, you come out ahead*   You can confirm this calculation using Bankrate's IRA calculator, entering a single $10,000 contribution at age 23, and a 9% return, http://www.bankrate.com/calculators/retirement /traditional-ira-plan-calculator.aspx.

169 *saw the Dow Jones Industrial Average go down almost 90%*   "Bear Markets: Wall Street's Worst," BBC News, November 1, 2004, http://news.bbc .co.uk/2/hi/business/3746044.stm.

170 *but also in Poland, Hungary, and Argentina*   "Government Has Contemplated Seizing Pension Money for over a Decade," *Washington's Blog*, October 20, 2013, http://www.washingtonsblog.com/2013/10/govern ment-has-contemplated-seizing-pension-money-for-over-a-decade .html.

170 *social security accounts that were privatized 30 years ago*   "Piñera vs. Piñera in the Battle of Chilean pensions," *Santiago Times*, June 27, 2013, http:// santiagotimes.cl/pinera-vs-pinera-in-the-battle-of-chilean-pensions/.

171 *index funds today are immensely popular*   John C. Bogle, "The First Index Mutual Fund: A History of Vanguard Index Trust and the Vanguard Index Strategy," speech on April 2007 [quoting Rex Sinquefield of American Nation Bank], http://www.vanguard.com/bogle_site/lib /sp19970401.html; Morgan Korn, "Have Index Funds Become Too Popular?," The Daily Ticker, December 13, 2013, http://finance.yahoo.com /blogs/daily-ticker/have-index-funds-become-too-popular-164329264 .html.

172 *at least 1.5% for the typical mutual fund*   "Vanguard Total Stock Market Index Fund Shares," Vanguard, accessed March 6, 2014, https://personal .vanguard.com/us/funds/snapshot?FundId=0085&FundIntExt=INT.

174 *people approach investing the way they should play tennis*   Rick Ferri, "Indexing Hero Charles Ellis," Forbes.com, June 18, 20012, http://www.forbes .com/sites/rickferri/2012/06/18/indexing-hero-charles-ellis/.

175 *inflation got as high as 4% in the past decade*   "Current U.S. Inflation Rates: 2004–1014," U.S. Inflation Calculator, accessed March 6, 2014, http://www.usinflationcalculator.com/inflation/current-inflation-rates/.

176 *the worst February for stocks since 1933*   Peter A. McKay, "Brutal February for Blue Chips," *Wall Street Journal*, March 1, 2009, http://online.wsj .com/news/articles/SB123573389322793621.

176 *40 times higher*   "Dow Jones Industrial Average (1900–Present Monthly)," StockCharts.com, accessed April 6, 2014, http://stockcharts .com/freecharts/historical/djia1900.html.

177 *continued to pull money out of equity funds until late 2012*   Andrew Ross Sorkin, "Why Are Investors Fleeing Equities? Hint: It's Not the Computers," *New York Times*, August 6, 2012, http://dealbook.nytimes .com/2012/08/06/why-are-investors-fleeing-equities-hint-its-not-the -computers/?_php=true&_type=blogs&_r=0.

177 *Fed's quantitative easing programs had created a bubble*   Peter Schiff, "After Bernanke, More Turbulence: Opposing View," *The Peter Schiff Show*, January 31, 2013, https://www.schiffradio.com/blog?action=blog Archive&blogTag=quantitative%20easing.

177 *mature on optimism, and die on euphoria*   John Christy, "Believe in the Market's Healthy Skepticism," Forbes.com, February 5, 2010, http://www.forbes.com/2010/02/05/templeton-canon-msci-personal-finance -investing-ideas-novo-nordisk.html.

177 *when everyone is saying the sky is falling, you take your money out*   Steve Forbes interview with Daniel Kahneman, Forbes.com, January 24, 2013, http://www.forbes.com/sites/steveforbes/2013/01/24/nobel-prize -winner-daniel-kahneman-lessons-from-hitlers-ss-and-the-danger-in -trusting-your-gut/.

178 *in which he warned about market "irrational exuberance"*   "Remarks by Chairman Alan Greenspan," The Federal Reserve Board, December 5, 1996, http://www.federalreserve.gov/boarddocs/speeches/1996/19961205.htm.

178 *peaked in 1997, not 2000*   Charles P. Himmelberg, James M. Mahoney, April Bang, and Brian Chernoff, "Recent Revisions to Corporate Profits: What We Know and When We Knew it," Current Issues in Economics and Finance, Federal Reserve Bank of New York, March 2004, vol. 10, no. 3, esp. Chart 1, http://www.newyorkfed.org/research/current_issues /ci10-3/ci10-3.html.

179 *the banks went away and the coffeehouses returned*   Conversation between Peter Drucker and Steve Forbes, 1983.

181 *the Nikkei is at 15,000*   "Nikkei 225," 1984-Present, Yahoo! Finance, accessed March 6, 2014, http://yhoo.it/1fsyEqd.

182 *junk bonds have done far better than higher-rated debt issues*   Thomas Kenny, "High-Yield Bonds: The Historical Performance Numbers, Year-by-Year Total Returns 1980–2013," About.com Bonds, http://bonds.about.com /od/corporatebonds/fl/High-Yield-Bonds-The-Historical-Performance -Numbers.htm.

183 *equities have been slaughtered, down more than 50%*   Myra P. Saefong, "Can Gold Miners Dig Out of Bottomless Pit?" MSN Money, December 17, 2013, http://money.msn.com/investment-advice/can-gold-miners -dig-out-of-bottomless-pit.

187 *help keep you on your program*   Northwestern MutualVoice Team, "Why a Financial Advisor Is Like a Personal Trainer," Forbes.com, June 11, 2013, http://www.forbes.com/sites/northwesternmutual/2013/06/11/why-a -financial-advisor-is-like-a-personal-trainer/.

Chapter 8: Looking Ahead

190 *no longer be poor nations*   Bill Gates and Melinda Gates, "3 Myths that Block Progress for the Poor," 2014 Gates Annual Letter, p. 7, http://

annualletter.gatesfoundation.org/~/media/Annual%20Letter%202014
/PDFs/2014_GatesAnnualLetter_ENGLISH_1.pdf.

192 *move that slowed its domestic economy*   "Turkish Central Bank Makes Massive Rate Hikes to Stem Lira Fall," Reuters. *World News Digest*. Infobase Learning, January 28, 2014, http://wnd.infobaselearning.com/recordurl .aspx? wid=96208&nid=137818&umbtype=1.

192 *flooded the country to buy the Swiss franc*   "Stock Markets: European, U.S. Markets Plunge over Economic Fears," *Facts On File. World News Digest*. Infobase Learning, August 4, 2011, http://wnd.infobaselearning.com /recordurl.aspx?wid=96208&nid=456203&umbtype=0.

192 *increase in value against the euro*   "Swiss National Bank Sets Minimum Exchange Rate at CHF 1.20 per euro," Swiss National Bank press release, September 6, 2011, http://www.snb.ch/en/mmr/reference/pre_20110906 /source/pre_20110906.en.pdf.

193 *to borrow vast amounts of money*   "Greece," *The World Factbook*, Central Intelligence Agency, accessed March 6, 2014, https://www.cia.gov /library/publications/the-world-factbook/geos/gr.html; Jack Ewing and Landon Thomas Jr., "Turkey's Central Bank Aggressively Raises Rates," *New York Times*, January 28, 2014, http://www.nytimes.com/2014/01/29 /business/international/stress-on-turkish-currency-eases-before-central -banks-emergency-session.html.

193 *The original one 30 years ago cost $3,995*   Steven F. Hayward, *The Age of Reagan: The Conservative Counterrevolution, 1980–1989* (New York: Crown Forum, 2009), p. 31.

194 *although not on the scale of the Fed*   "Statistical Data Warehouse," European Central Bank, accessed March 6, 2014, http://sdw.ecb.europa.eu /browse.do?node=bbn129.

197 *has demanded higher taxes*   Erik Kirschbaum, "Germany's SPD Demands Tax on Rich Despite Merkel Veto," Reuters, November 9, 2013, http:// www.reuters.com/article/2013/11/09/germany-coalition-idUSL5N0IU 06V20131109.

197 *raised its top income tax rate to 52%*   "Spain," 2014 Index of Economic Freedom, Heritage Foundation, accessed March 6, 2014, http://www .heritage.org/index/country/spain.

197 *raised its top rate on salaries to 75%*   Rudy Ruitenberg, "France's Hollande Gets Court Approval for 75% Millionaire Tax," *Bloomberg*, December 29, 2013, http://www.bloomberg.com/news/2013-12-29/france-s-hollande -gets-court-approval-for-75-millionaire-tax.html.

197 *sending its economy into a bone-crunching recession*   "Greece: Voters Reject Austerity in Legislative Elections," *Facts On File. World News Digest*. Infobase Learning, May 8, 2012, http://wnd.infobaselearning.com/record url.aspx?wid=96208&nid=483642&umbtype=0.

197 *public sectors in these countries have largely been spared* David Malpass, "And the Crisis Winner Is? Government," *Wall Street Journal*, December 16, 2011.

197 *raising billions in euros* "Billion Counter," Poland Ministry of Treasury, http://msp.gov.pl/en/privatisation-plan/portfolio-of-companies/3952,dok.html.

197 *a portion of Polish citizens' pension funds* Norma Cohen and Jan Cienski, "Poland Pension Reform Reversal Highlights Public Disillusion," *Financial Times*, February 5, 2014, http://www.ft.com/intl/cms/s/0/8ddeb5bc-6293-11e3-bba5-00144feabdc0.html#axzz2wdcS2D7S.

198 *tightening unemployment rules* "Wunderreform," *Economist*, March 16, 2013, http://www.economist.com/news/europe/21573583-ten-years-how-does-germanys-agenda-2010-package-rate-wunderreform.

198 *Sweden has cut taxes, with good effect* James Pethokoukis, "Sweden's Amazing Supply-Side, Tax-Cut Experiment," *AEIdeas* (public policy blog of the American Enterprise Institute), May 9, 2012, http://www.aei-ideas.org/2012/05/swedens-amazing-supply-side-tax-cut-experiment/.

198 *a rebuke from Keynesian scold Paul Krugman* Paul Krugman, "Estonian Rhapsody," *The Conscience of a Liberal* (Paul Krugman blog at NYTimes.com), June 6, 2012, http://krugman.blogs.nytimes.com/2012/06/06/estonian-rhapsdoy/.

198 *leading high-tech center (Skype was developed there)* "How Did Estonia Become a Leader in Technology?," *Economist*, July 30, 2013, http://www.economist.com/blogs/economist-explains/2013/07/economist-explains-21.

198 *misallocated credit and artificial stimulus* Harry Wilson, "The $15 Trillion Shadow over Chinese Banks," *Telegraph*, February 1, 2014, http://www.telegraph.co.uk/finance/newsbysector/banksandfinance/10611931/The-15-trillion-shadow-over-Chinese-banks.html.

199 *has since expanded more than 15-fold* Euromonitor International, subscription database, http://www.euromonitor.com/usa, accessed February 27, 2014.

199 *from so-called shadow banks* Lingling Wei and Bob Davis, "China's 'Shadow Banks' Fan Debt-Bubble Fears," *Wall Street Journal*, June 25, 2013, http://online.wsj.com/news/articles/SB10001424127887324637504578563570021019506.

199 *has had to bail out many of these firms* Ibid.

200 *and the United States, whose ratio is a little over 100%* International Monetary Fund, "Taxing Times," *Fiscal Monitor*, October 2013, http://www.imf.org/external/pubs/ft/fm/2013/02/pdf/fm1302.pdf.

200 *the country underwent a frenzied real estate boom* Martin Fackler, "Take It from Japan: Bubbles Hurt," *New York Times*, December 25, 2005, http://

www.nytimes.com/2005/12/25/business/yourmoney/25japan.html?page
wanted=all.

200 *devalue the yen vis-à-vis the dollar to stimulate growth*   Hiroko Tabuchi,
"Japan Keeps Monetary Policy Steady Amid Deflation Fight," *New York Times*, May 22, 2013, http://www.nytimes.com/2013/05/23/business
/global/japan-keeps-monetary-policy-steady.html.

200 *enacted by his predecessor will continue on schedule*   Hiroko Tabuchi, "Japan Sales Tax to Increase Next Year, Abe Says," *New York Times*, October 1, 2013, http://www.nytimes.com/2013/10/02/business/international
/japan-sales-tax-to-increase-next-year-abe-says.html.

200 *top income tax rate is moving to 55%*   Nathan Lewis, "Japan's Long Slide into Overtaxation," Forbes.com, December 6, 2013, http://www.forbes
.com/sites/nathanlewis/2013/12/06/japans-long-slide-into-overtaxation
/print/.

201 *Brazil routinely ranks in the bottom half*   Doing Business, Measuring Business Regulations (website of The Doing Business Project), The World Bank, http://www.doingbusiness.org.

202 *a concerted effort to start diversifying its economy*   T. Eliot Gaiser, "Chile's Strong Economy: A Case of Positive Policy and Freedom," *The Foundry* (Heritage Foundation blog), January 23, 2013, http://blog.heritage
.org/2013/01/23/chile-strong-economy-a-case-of-positive-policy-and
-freedom/.

202 *investment in manufacturing, technology, and services*   "2013 Investment Climate Statement—Malaysia," U.S. Department of State, Bureau of Economic and Business Affairs, March 2013, http://www.state.gov/e/eb
/rls/othr/ics/2013/204686.htm.

203 *cutting tax rates across the board*   "The Moment of Truth," The National Commission on Fiscal Responsibility and Reform, December 2010, http://www.fiscalcommission.gov/sites/fiscalcommission.gov/files
/documents/TheMomentofTruth12_1_2010.pdf.

Recommended Reading

The following titles are good reads for any investor:

Bogle, John C., *The Little Book of Commonsense Investing: The Only Way to Guarantee Your Fair Share of Stock Market Returns* (Hoboken, NJ: John Wiley & Sons, 2007).

Dreman, David, *Contrarian Investment Strategies: The Psychological Edge* (New York: Free Press, 2012).

Ellis, Charles D., *Winning the Loser's Game: Timeless Strategies for Successful Investing*, 6th ed. (New York: McGraw-Hill Education, 2013).

Fisher, Ken, with Lara Hoffmans, *The Little Book of Market Myths: How to Profit by Avoiding the Investment Mistakes Everyone Else Makes* (Hoboken, NJ: John Wiley & Sons, 2013).

Fisher, Ken, with Lara Hoffmans and Jennifer Chou, *The Only Three Questions That Still Count: Investing by Knowing What Others Don't* (Hoboken, NJ: John Wiley & Sons, 2012).

Malkiel, Burton G., *A Random Walk Down Wall Street: The Time-Tested Strategy for Successful Investing*, 10th ed. (New York: W.W. Norton & Co., 2012).

Malkiel, Burton G., and Charles D. Ellis, *The Elements of Investing: Easy Lessons for Every Investor* (Hoboken, NJ: John Wiley & Sons, 2013).

Schifrin, Matthew, *The Warren Buffetts Next Door: The World's Greatest Investors You've Never Heard of and What You Can Learn from Them* (Hoboken, NJ: John Wiley & Sons, 2010).

Siegel, Jeremy J., *Stocks for the Long Run: The Definitive Guide to Financial Market Returns and Long-Term Investment Strategies*, 5th ed. (New York: McGraw-Hill Education, 2014).

Skousen, Mark, *Investing in One Lesson* (Washington, DC: Regnery Publishing, 2007).

Index

About the Authors

Steve Forbes is coauthor of the *New York Times* bestseller *Power Ambition Glory* and the *Wall Street Journal* bestseller *How Capitalism Will Save Us*. Forbes is chairman and editor-in-chief of Forbes Media, which publishes *Forbes* magazine, with a circulation of nearly 1 million readers. Combined with *Forbes Asia*, *Forbes Europe*, and the company's licensee editions, the magazine reaches close to 6 million global readers. Forbes.com reaches 65 million unique monthly visitors; Forbes websites include Forbes.com, RealClearPolitics.com, RealClearMarkets.com, RealClearSports.com, and RealClearWorld.com.

Elizabeth Ames has written two previous books with Steve Forbes, *How Capitalism Will Save Us* and *Freedom Manifesto*. She is founder of BOLDE Communications, which has provided media relations and strategic consulting to a wide range of corporate and individual clients. She speaks to business groups, and her journalism and commentary have appeared in a wide range of print and online outlets.